AN
ABSOLUTE
SORT OF
CERTAINTY

AN
ABSOLUTE
SORT OF
CERTAINTY

*The Holy Spirit and
the Apologetics of*
JONATHAN EDWARDS

STEPHEN J. NICHOLS

P U B L I S H I N G
P.O. BOX 817 • PHILLIPSBURG • NEW JERSEY 08865-0817

© 2003 by Stephen J. Nichols

Page design and typesetting by Lakeside Design Plus

Printed in the United States of America

Library of Congress Cataloging-in-Publication Data

Nichols, Stephen J., 1970–
    An absolute sort of certainty : the Holy Spirit and the apologetics of Jonathan Edwards / Stephen J. Nichols.
        p.   cm.
    Revision of the author's thesis—Westminster Theological Seminary
    Includes bibliographical references (p.) and index.
    ISBN 0-87552-791-4
    1. Edwards, Jonathan, 1703–1758. 2. Holy Spirit—History of doctrines—18th century. I. Title.

BX7260.E3N525 2003
230'.58'092—dc21

                                                        2003047120

For my parents,
George and Diane Nichols,
with love and gratitude

CONTENTS

ACKNOWLEDGMENTS

This book is a revision of my dissertation completed at Westminster Theological Seminary. I owe a large debt to my advisor, Scott Oliphint, and my second reader, Sam Logan. Scott's attention to detail and rigorous scholarship were a model; Sam's enthusiasm for the subject was inspiring. George Marsden graciously served as an external reader, offering his keen insight and most welcome approval.

During my study of Edwards, my life and thought have been enriched by a wonderful cadre of scholars. It is my pleasure to offer my public thanks to these friends: Richard Bailey, Charles Hambrick-Stowe, Sean Lucas, Jerry McDermott, Ken Minkema, Sam Storms, Doug Sweeney, and Peter Thuesen.

I also owe a debt of gratitude to George and Shirley Claghorn, friends of Edwards and Edwards students everywhere. Those who know them, know they are gracious, kind, and giving. I could not be more grateful that our paths have crossed.

Allan Fisher and Thom Notaro of P&R Publishing continue to make the task of writing a joy. I am also grateful to the administration at Lancaster Bible College and for the faculty development grant program for enabling me to write.

My wife, Heidi, has been a constant companion, providing support, encouragement, and love. I could not be more blessed.

The earlier form of this book, the dissertation, marked a culmination of many years of schooling. Supporting me all along the way have been my parents, George and Diane Nichols. They sacrificed much, taught me a great deal, and, most importantly, displayed the love of Christ. As a small token, this book is for you.

Manuscript page from sermon on 2 Peter 1:16. The doctrine appears in the bottom right: "Doc[trine:] That Seeing the Glory of [Christ] is what tends to assure the heart of the truth of the Gosp[el]." Courtesy of Beinecke Rare Book and Manuscript Library, Yale University.

INTRODUCTION

Finding the center in any field of inquiry presents a rather diffi-cult challenge. Given the postmodern ethos, some might be inclined to claim that such centers do not even exist. Postmodern sensibili-ties aside, however, the task remains difficult because it requires one to account not only for the presence of various elements within a system, but also to explain how these divergent aspects coalesce, in-form each other, and contribute to a systematic whole. When one is treating a complex thinker such as Jonathan Edwards, the task grows even more difficult.

Recently, interpreters of Jonathan Edwards have turned to apolo-getics in the hope of finding the center of Edwards's thought and the interpretive key to understanding this formidable Colonial fig-ure. Studies by Michael McClymond and Gerald McDermott, as well as those of others, have explored the potential reward of this approach. Others, such as Leon Chai, while not addressing apolo-getics explicitly, do so implicitly by reexamining Edwards's rela-tionship to the Enlightenment.

This approach to Edwards as an apologist may seem somewhat out of place. He never wrote an apologetics text *per se*. He is a theo-logian to some, a philosopher to others, and a pastor to still others, but rarely is he anyone's apologist. Yet approaching Edwards as an apologist has much to commend it, and may be more useful than other interpretive grids. Apologetics finds itself in the dialectic be-

1

tween theology and philosophy. Consequently, it makes sense of the disparate or, according to some, competing sides of Edwards. Apologetics relieves the tension between Edwards as a churchman and Edwards as a philosopher. In short, apologetics not only accounts for the different aspects of Edwards's writings, but brings them together into a cohesive whole.

If Edwards may be understood through the paradigm of apologetics, then the task remains to determine the nature of his apologetics. This work intends to reveal the contours of his apologetics by focusing on his treatment of particular doctrines pertaining to the Holy Spirit, such as inspiration, regeneration, illumination, and especially assurance. Edwards places each of these doctrines in the context of the philosophical debates of his day. The Enlightenment's preoccupation with the problem of knowledge interested Edwards from the time he first read John Locke as a student at Yale until he made the final entries in his notebooks shortly before his untimely death. He wrestled with epistemology as he worked out his theology of the Holy Spirit; he developed his theology, as it were, in full view of philosophy and vice versa.

Edwards's doctrines of inspiration, regeneration, illumination, and assurance show that he anchors his apologetic theocentrically, or perhaps pneumatocentrically, as these various aspects of the work of the Holy Spirit combine to produce an "absolute sort of certainty." These words come from his notebook "The Mind," and pertain to the Spirit's work of inspiration. The best evidence of inspiration, Edwards argues, is the sense of absolute certainty that attaches to Scripture. This sense of certainty is produced by the Holy Spirit and reflects Scripture's divine beauty and excellence.

Edwards closely connects the Spirit's work in the giving of revelation to his work in illuminating revelation in the individual. However, he does not equate or confuse them. He follows Paul's logic in 1 Corinthians 2, arguing that in order to see divine revelation, which is authored by the Spirit, one must be illumined by the Spirit. Nonetheless, in keeping with Edwards's Calvinism, one is prejudiced against such testimony by the noetic effects of sin. Consequently, the internal witness of the Holy Spirit (*internum testimonium Spiritus Sancti*) is necessary for the individual to see this testimony and be assured of its truthfulness.

These doctrines also relate to such epistemological issues as knowledge, perception, and verification. This work seeks to explore the interplay between these doctrines and issues. To put the matter differently, this work unfolds Edwards's apologetics by examining his epistemology and his theology in relation to each other. Before such an undertaking, however, further investigation of the interpretation of Edwards is in order. Accordingly, the first chapter offers a brief survey of various interpreters of Edwards and sets the stage for understanding him as an apologist. Beginning with Perry Miller, the chapter summarizes numerous studies from the last few decades and evaluates their contributions to understanding the Edwardsean corpus. This chapter ends by arguing, as mentioned above, that apologetics proves quite promising in interpreting Edwards and grasping his thought.

Next follows Edwards's treatment of the problem of knowledge, as the second chapter explores his perspective on revelation. The doctrine of inspiration serves well in grounding both his theory of knowledge and his apologetical construct, as revelation functions as the epistemic base from which he proceeds. The particular work of the Holy Spirit within the Trinity receives special attention here, as well. Chapter 3 covers familiar terrain in unfolding Edwards's understanding of perception through a study of "the new sense." First, attention is given to the Enlightenment, including an examination of the work of Newton, Locke, Berkeley, and the Cambridge Platonists. Next follows an examination of Edwards's theological milieu, as his understanding of regeneration and illumination take shape against the backdrop of his Reformed and Puritan heritage. This chapter ends by addressing the role that the new sense plays in his apologetic.

Chapters 4 and 5 move into less charted waters, as Edwards's use of assurance is set forth in terms of the internal witness of the Holy

Spirit. Chapter 4 begins by placing Edwards in the larger context of Reformed thinking on assurance. It also addresses his more immediate context by exploring the controversies surrounding the revivals of his day in the Great Awakening. This chapter further explores Edwards's attention to the problem of self-deception. Chapter 5 then brings his thought on assurance into conversation with contemporary epistemological discussions of belief, testimony, and knowledge. His apologetic methodology, modeled in his treatises and sermons, also receives attention. This chapter ends with a summary of his apologetic.

Edwards's use of the sermon as a tool for apologetics is explored in the last chapter. Before specific sermons are examined, his sermon style is set within the context of Puritan preaching, or, in the words of William Perkins, "the art of prophesying." Edwards, located squarely within this tradition, utilizes the sermon as the primary occasion for his practice of apologetics. This chapter offers a close reading of two unpublished sermons in order to bring the ideas from the previous chapter into systematic expression.

I

EDWARDS AS AN APOLOGIST

Applying one of Jonathan Edwards's own favorite analogies, one may liken the sum of his thought to a great ocean into which flows "a large and long river, having innumerable branches beginning in different regions, and at a great distance one from another." All of these branches, he observes, unite to reach their common destination.[1] Edwards uses this illustration to exhibit the doctrine of providence, yet it also fittingly illustrates the task of understanding Edwards. Since Perry Miller's revitalization of studies in Colonial Puritanism and Edwards, many interpreters have sought to identify the single river of influence that resulted in such a great ocean of pastoral, theological, and philosophical production.

TOWARD AN UNDERSTANDING OF EDWARDS

Miller himself identifies the fount as John Locke's *An Essay Concerning Human Understanding.* In his classic biography of Edwards, Miller observes, "The reading of it had been the central and decisive event in his life"—at a mere fourteen years of age. Miller ac-

---

1. *The Works of Jonathan Edwards,* vol. 9, *A History of the Work of Redemption,* ed. John F. Wilson (New Haven: Yale University Press, 1989), 520.

knowledges Edwards's debt to the Reformed and Puritan tradition, but argues that Edwards transcended his environment. In Miller's estimation, the "antiquated metaphysic" of that tradition held New England captive. God was absolute and arbitrary, and reality was deterministic. Locke, argues Miller, offered Edwards an escape through experience and sensation. Edwards skillfully molded these concepts into a new way of perceiving God and his activity in this world. The God of Edwards "does not rend the fabric of nature or break the connection between experience and behavior." According to Stephen Stein, Miller relegates Calvinism to a secondary role in the thought of Edwards, distances Edwards from his Puritan forbears in terms of the doctrine of the covenant, and downplays the influence of his biblical studies on his thought. Edwards was, in Miller's estimation, "holding himself by brute will power within the forms of ancient Calvinism." He adds, "We know that Edwards failed to revitalize Calvinism. He tried to fill old bottles with new wine, yet none but himself could savor the vintage."[2] Edwards was unable to free himself entirely from his theological moorings, so Miller in the final analysis regards his life as a tragedy.

Norman Fiering critiques Miller while nevertheless following Miller's paradigm. Rather than finding the source of Edwards's thought in Locke, Fiering opts for Malebranche. He views Edwards primarily as a moral philosopher, standing in a tradition that is largely misunderstood today. Thus, this portrait of Edwards is often obscured. Edwards, according to Fiering, is not so much a tragic hero—he is just misunderstood.[3] Clyde Holbrook also differs slightly from Miller in viewing Edwards as ultimately victorious over his Calvinistic theology. Holbrook pits Edwards's own modified view of God against the Calvinist view. Holbrook describes Edwards's view as theological objectivism, and interprets his notion of God as Being

---

2. Perry Miller, *Jonathan Edwards* (New York: William Sloane Associates, 1949), 52, 55, 195–96. For Stein's interpretation of Miller, see his foreword to Conrad Cherry, *The Theology of Jonathan Edwards: A Reappraisal* (Bloomington: Indiana University Press, 1990), ix–xi.

3. Norman Fiering, *Jonathan Edwards's Moral Thought and Its British Context* (Chapel Hill: University of North Carolina Press, 1981), 3–12.

itself, so that God is the "supreme authority and excellence and is the source of all value," against the Calvinistic concept.[4] Holbrook argues that Edwards's triumph consists in releasing this form of theological objectivism—which is theological only to the extent that his ontology is defined by deity—from Calvinism. In the end, Holbrook's interpretive key to understanding Edwards may just as well be defined as philosophical objectivism, a distant relative to the Calvinism that Edwards advocated.

Many follow Miller's line of interpreting Edwards—what Iain Murray refers to as "the anti-supernatural animus"[5]—as a tragic figure whose theology arrested his philosophical development. Such interpreters include nineteenth-century intellectuals like George Bancroft, Harriet Beecher Stowe, and Oliver Wendell Holmes, twentieth-century biographers of Edwards like Ola Winslow, and historians of philosophy like Peter Gay, Paul Anderson and Max Fisch, Elizabeth Flower and Murray Murphey, and Bruce Kuklick.[6]

For instance, Ola Winslow identifies Edwards's flaw as defending "an outworn dogmatic system instead of letting the new truth find more appropriate forms of its own."[7] Kuklick's appraisal is also representative of this viewpoint. Edwards's early forays into philosophy, which, argues Kuklick, overshadowed his theological pursuits, were eclipsed by the pressing theological and pastoral concerns generated by the revivals. His early career as a philosopher gave way to

---

4. Clyde Holbrook, *The Ethics of Jonathan Edwards: Morality and Aesthetics* (Ann Arbor: University of Michigan Press, 1973), 5.

5. Iain Murray, *Jonathan Edwards: A New Biography* (Edinburgh: Banner of Truth, 1987), xxix. Murray, in fact, argues that with Miller's biography "the anti-supernatural animus comes to its fullest expression."

6. Oliver Wendell Holmes, "Jonathan Edwards," in *The Works of Oliver Wendell Holmes*, vol. 8, *Pages from an Old Volume of Life: A Collection of Essays, 1857–1881* (Boston: Houghton, Mifflin, 1892), 366–70; Ola Elizabeth Winslow, *Jonathan Edwards, 1703–1758* (New York: Collier Books, 1961); Peter Gay, *A Loss of Mastery: Historians in Colonial America* (Berkeley: University of California Press, 1966), 88–117; Paul Russell Anderson and Max Harold Fisch, *Philosophy in America: From the Puritans to James* (New York: Octagon Books, 1969), 74–81; Elizabeth Flower and Murray G. Murphey, *A History of Philosophy in America*, 2 vols. (New York: Capricorn Books, 1977), 1:137–99; Bruce Kuklick, *Churchmen and Philosophers: From Jonathan Edwards to John Dewey* (New Haven: Yale University Press, 1985).

7. Winslow, *Jonathan Edwards, 1703–1758*, 326.

that of a theologian, and so Edwards "took refuge in systematic divinity."[8] Such interpretations view Edwards as a tragic figure, facing a tragic choice and choosing the lesser good.

Samuel Eliot Morison sees Edwards facing the same choice, yet his judgment differs. Morison observes that "in another environment he might have acquired the fame of George Berkeley." He "might have been a naturalist or a great literary figure, but he chose theology because he believed that an exploration of the relation between man and God was infinitely more important." Morison's Edwards faced a choice, but his life was not tragic. In fact, Morison concludes his discussion of Edwards by drawing attention to his perennial value:

> Whatever one's beliefs, one owes a respectful glance to that faith which made God everything and man nothing, which plunged some men into despair but to many gave fortitude to face life bravely; and to a chosen few, the supreme joy that comes from union with the Eternal Spirit, and supreme beauty that is the beauty of holiness.[9]

Conrad Cherry's *The Theology of Jonathan Edwards: A Reappraisal*, as Stephen Stein remarks, opens a "new chapter in the study of this influential New England Minister."[10] It is actually Miller's interpretation of Edwards that gets reappraised by Cherry. The new model challenges Miller's conclusions regarding the theology of Edwards, disputes his pejorative view of theology in the schema of Edwards's thought, and questions his identification of Edwards's source of influence. Terrence Erdt likewise questions Miller with respect to the concept of the "new sense," which figures prominently in Edwards's writings. "Miller," according to Erdt, "gave the impression that the term derived solely from Edwards' reading of Locke and that it constituted a new explanation of spiritual knowledge."[11] Erdt follows

8. Kuklick, *Churchmen and Philosophers*, 28.
9. Samuel Eliot Morison, *The Oxford History of the American People* (Oxford: Oxford University Press, 1965), 151, 153.
10. Stein's foreword to Cherry, *Theology of Jonathan Edwards*, ix.
11. Terrence Erdt, *Jonathan Edwards, Art and the Sense of the Heart* (Amherst: University of Massachusetts Press, 1980), 2.

Cherry's lead and looks for the background of the phrase not in Locke's *Essay,* but in Calvin and the seventeenth-century Puritans. Other interpreters in this line include Harold Simonson, Carl Bogue, Iain Murray, David Brand, and John Gerstner.[12] They locate the influence on Edwards squarely in Calvin and Puritan thought. Edwards's choice of theology over philosophy, far from squelching his potential, facilitated his insight and impact. Murray argues, "The plain fact is that Edwards' excursions into philosophy were only occasional and peripheral to his main thought; it was theology or 'divinity,' which belonged to the warp and woof of his life."[13]

Gerstner also disputes Miller's reading of the influences on Edwards. He concludes that Edwards's master was the Bible. David Brand and Carl Bogue argue for the pervasiveness of Calvinism and covenant theology, respectively, in his thought, making them the keys to unlocking the Edwardsean corpus. Harold Simonson, focusing on Edwards's sense of the heart, argues for a pietistic understanding of his thought. He observes that "[Edwards's] profound conviction that Calvinistic theology was experientially true . . . was Edwards' life-long theme."[14]

In a combined review of works on Edwards by Holbrook, Murray, and Lee, Robert Jenson offers insight into these two lines of interpreting Edwards. He speaks of "the ineradicable tendency of writing about Edwards: to construct some polarity—almost alien to Edwards—and then stretch him against it."[15] Edwards is viewed as either a philosopher or a theologian. Typically, these interpreters

12. Harold P. Simonson, *Jonathan Edwards: Theologian of the Heart* (Grand Rapids: Eerdmans, 1974); Carl Bogue, *Jonathan Edwards and the Covenant of Grace* (Cherry Hill, N.J.: Mack Publishing, 1975); Murray, *Jonathan Edwards: A New Biography;* John H. Gerstner, *The Rational Biblical Theology of Jonathan Edwards,* 3 vols. (Powhatan, Va.: Berea Publications, 1991–93); David C. Brand, *Profile of the Last Puritan: Jonathan Edwards, Self-Love, and the Dawn of the Beatific* (Atlanta: Scholars Press, 1991).

13. Murray, *Jonathan Edwards: A New Biography,* xx.

14. Simonson, *Jonathan Edwards: Theologian of the Heart,* 13.

15. Robert Jenson, review of *Jonathan Edwards, The Valley and Nature: An Interpretive Essay,* by Clyde Holbrook; *Jonathan Edwards: A New Biography,* by Iain Murray; and *The Philosophical Theology of Jonathan Edwards,* by Sang Hyun Lee, in *Christian Century* 106 (1989): 662.

view Edwards as conflicted by these contrary aims and methodologies. The next line of interpretations, however, ameliorates any such conflict.

H. Richard Niebuhr stands at the nexus of this group of interpreters, who read Edwards's theology and philosophy symbiotically, not antagonistically.[16] For example, Edwards's emphasis on experience strikes a consonant cord with Miller and Niebuhr. Niebuhr, however, syncopates that cord with the rhythm of theology. Donald Weber, referring to Niebuhr, comments, "Moreover, the Awakening worked toward a reconciliation between biblical doctrine and the testament of personal experience, rejoining components of Christian life that had been in dialectic opposition since the Reformation."[17] Edwards is presented as a theologian, albeit a neo-orthodox one. Niebuhr's understanding of Edwards can be illuminated by examining the works of those he inspired. Paul Ramsey, for example, in his introduction to a volume in *The Works of Jonathan Edwards,*[18] states, "It is a grave error, now or ever, to separate Edwards' philosophy from his theology, or his moral philosophy from his theological ethics."[19] This line of interpretation portrays Edwards not as a theologian or a philosopher, but as both in tension.

Other representatives of this group include James Carse, Douglas Elwood, Roland Delattre, and R. C. DeProspo. If Ramsey's comment above articulates the presupposition of this group, Carse in-

16. H. Richard Niebuhr, *The Kingdom of God in America* (New York: Harper and Row, 1937), 106–19.

17. Donald Weber, "The Recovery of Jonathan Edwards," in *Jonathan Edwards and the American Experience,* ed. Nathan O. Hatch and Harry S. Stout (Oxford: Oxford University Press, 1988), 63. Weber cites Niebuhr, *Kingdom of God in America.*

18. Begun in 1957 under the editorship of Perry Miller, *The Works of Jonathan Edwards,* published by Yale University Press, is the authoritative edition of Edwards's writings. Currently under the general editorship of Harry S. Stout, the edition has published twenty of a projected twenty-six volumes covering the major treatises and essays, and many previously published and unpublished sermons, letters, and personal writings, along with material from the notebooks of Jonathan Edwards. While not exhaustive, this collection of Edwards's writings will be the most complete and authoritative edition available.

19. Editor's introduction to *The Works of Jonathan Edwards,* vol. 8, *Ethical Writings,* ed. Paul Ramsey (New Haven: Yale University Press, 1989), 11.

dicates their main intention in the prologue to his discussion of Edwards: "My design in these pages is to bring Edwards as far forward as I can."[20] Edwards presents for Carse's reader, as he entitles a chapter of his book, "the urgent *Now!* for the languid will." On the one hand, Carse takes Edwards's message seriously, and not simply as a subject for historical study. Yet, making any historical figure a living interlocutor runs the risk of being anachronistic.

That risk may be most apparent in Douglas Elwood's interpretation of Edwards. He observes that Edwards the theologian and Edwards the philosopher may be reunited "by locating the principle of correlation in his doctrine of immediacy." Edwards's God, Elwood argues, reveals himself existentially and is apprehended in the moment of "religious experience." Thus, Elwood posits for Edwards "spiritual knowledge as a unique kind of intuition." However, Elwood reveals his anachronistic reading of Edwards when he writes that Edwards's argument for God "is an argument from revelation, though not revelation as authority but as living encounter."[21] Scott Oliphint observes that by arguing in such a way, Elwood "seems to want to make of Edwards a neo-orthodox theologian, as one untimely born."[22] Similarly, Elwood fits Edwards's view of knowledge into post-Kantian categories. Consequently, spiritual knowledge is, at best, differentiated from knowledge *per se*. But, as will be argued in the next chapter, this position is foreign to Edwards. The Edwards of this interpretation looks more like the modern interpreter.

Delattre also tries to understand Edwards both philosophically and theologically. Two categories receive primary attention: beauty and being. Beauty is fundamental to being, both divine and human, and is joined with sensibility—the twin principles of Edwards's aes-

20. James P. Carse, *Jonathan Edwards and the Visibility of God* (New York: Charles Scribner's Sons, 1967), 12.

21. Douglas J. Elwood, *The Philosophical Theology of Jonathan Edwards* (New York: Columbia University Press, 1960), 3, 17, 16.

22. Scott Oliphint, "Jonathan Edwards: Reformed Apologist," *Westminster Theological Journal* 57 (1995): 165.

11

thetics and ethics.[23] Beauty and sensibility, argues Delattre, are both philosophical and theological, and they bring together Edwards's endeavors in ontology, ethics, aesthetics, and theology. His theology informs his philosophy and vice versa. Along the same line is De Prospo's caricature of Edwards. Is Edwards "the scion of Puritanism or of the enlightenment or of Lockean idealism"? De Prospo rejects such "dialectically conflicting parts"—an inheritance, he argues, from Perry Miller. Instead, he presents a "unitary model" of Edwards's Puritanism, or theology, and his philosophical precocity.[24]

In this model, Edwards's philosophy and theology contribute to each other. That is, Edwards relieves the dialectic tension between theology and philosophy, between the Christian heritage and the post-Enlightenment, post-Kantian notions of the present age. Again, the question of anachronism looms over this group's understanding of Edwards. Is his theology, in fact, best read against twentieth-century views of knowledge, revelation, and the nature of one's relationship to God? Such readings of Edwards may make him seem relevant to the modern world, but they risk misrepresenting him as a contemporary thinker.

Other recent interpreters of Edwards who follow a similar line include Sang Hyun Lee, Leon Chai, and Robert Jenson. Lee portrays Edwards as a philosophical theologian whose thought "contributes to the discussions of contemporary philosophical theology [by its] dispositional reconception of the nature of divine being." According to Lee, Edwards posits an entirely new metaphysic from which he constructs his theology. God is dynamic, "everlastingly disposed to an everlasting process of self-enlargement or self-repetition in time and space."[25] Edwards shares the suppositions of process philosophy, argues Lee, though all the while he is controlled by Enlightenment discussions.

23. Roland Andre Delattre, *Beauty and Sensibility in the Thought of Jonathan Edwards* (New Haven: Yale University Press, 1968), 1–4.

24. R. C. De Prospo, *Theism in the Discourse of Jonathan Edwards* (Newark: University of Delaware Press, 1985), 9–10, 47, 53.

25. Sang Hyun Lee, *The Philosophical Theology of Jonathan Edwards* (Princeton: Princeton University Press, 1988), 4, 241.

12

Chai also places Edwards's thought squarely within the Enlightenment context. He observes that "the very nature of both his method and his objectives appears to be dictated by his Enlightenment predecessors." Edwards employs Enlightenment rationality in his arguments against Arminianism, for example. Yet Edwards, unrestrained by the Enlightenment's inability to transcend rationality and thus contain subjectivity, surpasses the Enlightenment by appealing to the transcendent, objective nature of religious affections. "Edwards," Chai argues, "thus attempts to overcome the limitations of ordinary perception so as to endow genuine religious experiences with indubitable certainty."[26] In the end, however, Chai does not see Edwards escaping his Enlightenment trappings, and thus Edwards fails in his efforts.

Robert Jenson also reads Edwards against the backdrop of the Enlightenment with a view toward bringing him into the present day. He notes that what people heard about Edwards "was often wrong," accounting for the less than complete, if not inaccurate, assessment of Edwards's thought. Jenson portrays Edwards first and foremost as a theologian—America's greatest and paradigmatic theologian, besides. The Enlightenment provides the backdrop for Edwards to expound his theology, both a *"critique in the service of the gospel* and the adumbration of universal *harmony* as encompassed in *triune* harmony."[27] Edwards's writings are a jeremiad with a philosophical twist. Like the others mentioned above, however, Jenson's interpretation results in an anachronistic reading that reflects more of Jenson than Edwards.

The readings of Lee, Chai, and Jenson differ from that of Miller because they do not present Edwards's philosophy in opposition to or hampered by his theology, but rather in a symbiotic relationship.

George Marsden's recent biography follows suit as Marsden is finely tuned to Edwards's seamless move from theology to philoso-

26. Leon Chai, *Jonathan Edwards and the Limits of Enlightenment Philosophy* (Oxford: Oxford University Press, 1998), v, 24–25, 114–16.

27. Robert Jenson, *America's Theologian: A Recommendation of Jonathan Edwards* (New York: Oxford University Press, 1988), vii, 196 (emphasis original).

phy and back again. Marsden's detailed analysis of his life and writings pays close attention to the theological and philosophical currents that shape the context of Edwards's thought. In fact, Marsden hopes for his book to "bridge the gap between the Edwards of the students of American culture and the Edwards of the theologians."[28]

The task for any current interpreter is to correlate the interpretations of Edwards with his actual writings and his actual context. Clyde Holbrook's comments after his own survey of interpretations still apply: "So the list [of interpretations] runs, always with the danger present that the interpretive motif will distort or eliminate some aspect of Edwards's total perspective which was for him of importance." He quickly adds a caveat: "At the same time, the richness of Edwards's thought cannot be explored without the aid of some interpretive tool."[29]

The present survey, though not exhaustive, reveals three schools of thought concerning Edwards.[30] The first, championed by Perry Miller, perceives Edwards as a philosopher, first and foremost. His theological concerns or heritage did little other than hamper his intellectual endeavors. This group views Edwards either as a great philosopher in spite of his theology (Miller), or as a potentially better philosopher, held back by his theology (Kuklick, Flower and Murphey, and Anderson and Fisch), or as a philosopher who was impoverished by his theology (Gay). The second school, led by Murray, portrays Edwards as a theologian and pastor. The third school sees Edwards as mediating theology and philosophy. For the most part, the representatives of this school tend to recast Edwards's theology. Edwards ends up as a neo-orthodox theologian (Niebuhr, Ram-

28. George M. Marsden, *Jonathan Edwards: A Life* (New Haven: Yale University Press, 2003), 502.

29. Holbrook, *Ethics of Jonathan Edwards,* 1–2.

30. For a recent, comprehensive bibliography of Edwards, see Sean Michael Lucas, "Jonathan Edwards between Church and Academy: A Bibliographic Essay," in *The Legacy of Jonathan Edwards: American Religion and the Evangelical Tradition,* ed. D. G. Hart, Sean Michael Lucas, and Stephen J. Nichols (Grand Rapids: Baker, 2003), 228–47.

sey, Carse, Elwood, Delattre, De Prospo), a process theologian (Lee), or a Lutheran (Jenson). Which approach best understands Edwards?

The best tool for understanding Edwards may be found in his own analogy of providence, mentioned at the beginning of this chapter. Pressing the analogy, we find that there were diverse influences from different areas. This is indeed literally true; Edwards was influenced by current thought on the Continent and by that in England and New England. It is also true metaphorically; Edwards was influenced from the different areas of learning—from logic to geography, from mathematics to natural science, and from rhetoric to divinity. And he managed to bring them together. This may account for the diversity of interpretations.

Of course, some of the interpretations mentioned above may be overstated, and the present study will take issue with some of them. Nevertheless, perhaps the accurate picture of Edwards that emerges is that of a mind captivated by *everything* with which it comes into contact. As Marsden argues, "The key to Edwards' thought is that everything is related because everything is related to God."[31] If so, Perry Miller overstates his thesis when he obscures Edwards's theological impulses. So also does Murray. The differences among the interpreters of Edwards, according to Murray, are existential or spiritual. "The division," he observes, "runs right back to the Bible, and, depending on where we stand in relation to Christ, we shall join ourselves to one side or the other in interpreting this man who was, first of all, a Christian." To be sure, one's own presuppositions affect one's interpretation. Murray's statement goes beyond this axiom, however, by presenting a false dilemma. His perspective also leads to problematic conclusions, as when he intones, "The plain fact is that Edwards' excursions into philosophy were only occasional and peripheral to his main thought."[32] It is one thing to argue that Edwards is Lockean. It is quite another to say that he engaged Locke,

31. Marsden, *Jonathan Edwards: A Life*, 460.
32. Murray, *Jonathan Edwards: A New Biography*, xxvii, xx.

or the Cambridge Platonists, or Malebranche, or the Enlightenment in crucial and substantive ways.

At this juncture, the work of Wallace Anderson and Wilson Kimnach is informative. Anderson challenges the data employed by Miller and thus greatly modifies Miller's thesis regarding Locke and Edwards. He does not picture Edwards as a fourteen-year-old enraptured with Locke's *Essay*. Rather, he observes, "There is nothing in this [Edwards's *Catalogue*] to indicate that he seriously studied the work during any part of the period of his undergraduate and graduate study." He quickly adds, however, "There is nevertheless some significant evidence that Edwards was exposed to the *Essay* during his student years." Anderson then goes directly to Miller's thesis by arguing against perceiving Locke's influence as "the intellectual ravishment of a schoolboy." But Edwards does engage Locke, Berkeley, and Newton, and not just during his years as a tutor at Yale. Indeed, Edwards's cryptic manuscript leaf, "Notes on Knowledge and Existence," from his Stockbridge years, reveals the elder Edwards wrestling with the nature of substance, existence, objects, and perception. Anderson's view of Edwards as a scientist applies equally to his view of him as a philosopher: "Edwards found no conflict between his scientific interests and his religious convictions and vocation, and his interest in science did not flag after his conversion."[33] Science served his understanding of God and his (and, for that matter, humanity's) relationship to the world.

Philosophy also served in this capacity for Edwards. The manuscript evidence does not reveal a man torn between pursuing philosophy and pursuing theology. His manuscript "The Mind" demonstrates this well. Edwards entered comments in this notebook from the 1720s until the early 1730s. He then set the work aside until he returned to add a few final entries in the 1750s. In these final en-

33. Thomas Schafer's careful work in dating Edwards provides Anderson with the necessary information to challenge Miller, as Anderson himself acknowledges in the editor's introduction to *The Works of Jonathan Edwards*, vol. 6, *Scientific and Philosophical Writings*, ed. Wallace E. Anderson (New Haven: Yale University Press, 1980), 9, 24–25, 33, 37.

tries, Edwards engages John Locke and, Anderson argues, first writes out one of the ideas he pursues in his argument against Arminianism in *Original Sin*.[34]

Wilson Kimnach's work poses another problem for a compartmentalized Edwards. He says, "Although the reputation of Jonathan Edwards is appropriately multi-faceted and he is deservedly recognized as theologian, philosopher, and pioneering psychologist, the popular conception of him as a preacher is essentially correct." This is not to pit Edwards as a preacher against him in his other roles. Rather, Kimnach draws attention to the sermon, "the one literary genre he mastered." Edwards's writings, including his notebooks (from the philosophically oriented "Miscellanies" to the exegetical "Notes on Scripture") and his published treatises (many of which were originally sermons), comprise, according to Kimnach, his "sermon mill." Kimnach's work shows three things: (1) the necessity of using the sermons in interpreting Edwards, (2) his concern to communicate his ideas, and (3) the interrelated nature of his writings and thought. Kimnach also points in the direction of an apologetic perspective on Edwards. For example, he observes that "Edwards took intellectual building materials from various authors as he needed them and reacted to particular ideas or theories from a wide variety of sources in developing his own concepts." He further speaks of Edwards's "creative receptivity" and "artistic interdependence" in handling his sources, "which resulted from his trust in the adequacy of Scripture to all human reflection."[35] Thus, the work of Anderson and Kimnach poses a problem for interpretations that compartmentalize Edwards.

APOLOGETICS AND UNDERSTANDING EDWARDS

The fact that these schools of interpretation conflict with each other does not mean that no interpretive tool for understanding Ed-

34. For Anderson's careful reckoning of these dates, see *Scientific and Philosophical Writings*, 326–29.

35. Editor's introduction to *The Works of Jonathan Edwards*, vol. 10, *Sermons and Discourses, 1720–1723*, ed. Wilson Kimnach (New Haven: Yale University Press, 1992), 3, xiii, 42, 9.

wards exists. Indeed, there is an identifiable center to the thought of Jonathan Edwards. The elusive interpretive tool does exist. Recently, Michael McClymond has argued that the interpretive tool consists of grasping the centrality of apologetics to the thought of America's most able theologian.[36] The picture that emerges in McClymond's study is that of an "artful theologian," craftily navigating both a rich theological heritage bequeathed by Augustine, Calvin, and the Puritan and Reformed tradition, and also the philosophical Enlightenment swirling about him. This engagement results in what McClymond refers to as Edwards's explicit apologetic, where he addresses apologetics directly, and his implicit apologetic, where, at various points in his writings—and, perhaps, underlying the entire corpus—Edwards erupts with proof of the truth of Christianity. The argument presented here follows McClymond broadly; the key to understanding Edwards is to understand him as an apologist.

By its nature, apologetics brings together philosophy and theology, theory and practice. For Edwards, this amounts to bringing together Lockean epistemology or the idealism of Cambridge Platonism with the Westminster Confession or the systematic theologies of Calvin, Wollebius, and Ames. This reading also accounts for the literary output of Edwards, from his highly theoretical treatises, such as *The Nature of True Virtue,* to his preferred genre of the sermon, from his exegetical notebooks to the "Miscellanies." His concern for apologetics explains his various roles as theologian, philosopher, and pastor. To view Edwards as an apologist also enhances his theology and philosophy. As Warfield observes, "The peculiarity of Edwards' theological work is due to the union in it of the richest religious sentiment with the highest intellectual powers."[37] Edwards's theology is philosophically informed, and his philosophy is theologically informed; both enrich each other.

36. Michael J. McClymond, *Encounters with God: An Approach to the Theology of Jonathan Edwards* (Oxford: Oxford University Press, 1998).

37. Benjamin B. Warfield, "Edwards and the New England Theology," in *Encyclopaedia of Religion and Ethics,* 13 vols., ed. James Hastings (New York: Charles Scribner's Sons, 1955), 5:225.

Edwards, however, never wrote a treatise on apologetics as such. To be sure, he engaged in apologetics in his writings on Arminianism, the Great Awakening, and events in his Northampton congregation. So he certainly modeled an apologetic. And from his writings one can cull out the contours of his apologetic.

The work of John H. Gerstner surfaces in discussions of Edwards's apologetic. Gerstner pays close attention to its theocentric nature, and he even goes so far as to structure his magnum opus around theological themes, according to the basic encyclopedia of a systematic theology.[38] There is much to be commended in Gerstner's work, as demonstrated in the pages below. His original assignment to edit one of the volumes in the Yale edition of Edwards's *Works,* an assignment that never came to fruition, provided Gerstner with ready access to the unpublished Edwardsean corpus. However, his work suffers from the same flaw that plagues many interpreters of Edwards, and that is that he imposes an interpretive grid on Edwards. Essentially, Gerstner enlists Edwards as a proponent of so-called classical apologetics in his critique of presuppositional apologetics.[39] Oliphint challenges such a reading of Edwards. He observes that the misunderstandings of Edwards by Gerstner and the coauthors of *Classical Apologetics* are "due more to their 'rationalism with a vengeance' than to their oftentimes insightful analyses."[40]

Other recent studies of Edwards's apologetics, such as those by Allyn Ricketts and Louis Mitchell, are also more attuned to the theocentric nature of his apologetics. Ricketts argues that its epistemological foundation is revelation, and "that Edwards holds reason to be thoroughly dependent upon revelation."[41] Mitchell relates Edwards's concept of beauty to the structure of religious experience,

38. Gerstner, *Rational Biblical Theology of Jonathan Edwards.*

39. See R. C. Sproul, John H. Gerstner, and Arthur Lindsley, *Classical Apologetics: A Rational Defense of the Christian Faith and a Critique of Presuppositional Apologetics* (Grand Rapids: Zondervan, 1984).

40. Oliphint, "Jonathan Edwards: Reformed Apologist," 166.

41. Allyn Lee Ricketts, "The Primacy of Revelation in the Philosophical Theology of Jonathan Edwards" (Ph.D. diss., Westminster Theological Seminary, 1995), 1.

which, when applied in his philosophical theology (viewed here as apologetics), provides him with a "range of metaphysical and theological usages." For Mitchell, beauty must be related to God's Trinitarian being: "In Edwards' doctrine of the Trinity his ontology, theology and understanding of beauty have their origin and integration."[42] The present study builds on the findings of both Ricketts and Mitchell, while applying their insight to new areas of consideration, namely, the intersection of Edwards's apologetics with his understanding of doctrines related to the Holy Spirit. Even more recently, Gerald McDermott has drawn attention to Edwards's apologetics by examining his thought regarding those who have never heard the gospel, as set forth within the context of his rebuttal of deism.[43]

Two points are evident from this quick survey. First, some interpreters of Edwards have focused on apologetics or, at least, on the intersection of theology and philosophy, rather than pitting one against the other. Second, there is still room for more work on Edwards's apologetics. If apologetics is indeed central to Edwards's thought, then more work in this area is certainly appropriate.

---

42. Louis Joseph Mitchell, "The Experience of Beauty in the Thought of Jonathan Edwards" (Ph.D. diss., Harvard University, 1995), 8, 27.

43. Gerald R. McDermott, *Jonathan Edwards Confronts the Gods: Christian Theology, Enlightenment Religion, and Non-Christian Faiths* (Oxford: Oxford University Press, 2000).

2

REVELATION: EDWARDS ON KNOWING

It is not he that has heard a long description of the sweetness of honey
that can be said to have the greatest understanding of it, but he that has tasted.

Jonathan Edwards, "A Spiritual Understanding of Divine Things"

According to Edwards, knowledge that matters is *spiritual* knowledge, or knowledge of the Spirit. Exploiting the ambiguous genitive "of the Spirit," he can say that this knowledge cuts two ways: it belongs to the Spirit, and it pertains to the things of the Spirit. And to know these things, Edwards argues, one must experience or taste them. Such an experience depends entirely upon the Spirit because spiritual knowledge is not naturally apprehended. "The natural man," as Paul writes, "receiveth not the things of the Spirit of God" (1 Cor. 2:14). In fact, Edwards defines spiritual knowledge as "the experiential knowledge of the saving operations of the Holy Spirit."[1]

---

1. "A Spiritual Understanding of Divine Things," in *The Works of Jonathan Edwards*, vol. 14, *Sermons and Discourses, 1723–1729*, ed. Kenneth P. Minkema (New Haven: Yale University Press, 1997), 80.

It would be a mistake, however, to infer that Edwards had a subjective or existential view of knowledge. His view of illumination is misunderstood if it is interpreted mystically, for it is safeguarded by the connection he makes between illumination and inspiration. Following Calvin, Edwards held that the Spirit works in dependence upon the Word. Consequently, the spiritual knowledge granted by illumination is the spiritual content of revelation. Inspiration and illumination are the province solely of the Holy Spirit.

All of this derives from Edwards's sermon "A Spiritual Understanding of Divine Things Denied to the Unregenerate," which he preached sometime between November 1723 and May 1724, when he was supplying the pulpit in Bolton, Connecticut. Much of his thought was summarized in this exposition of 1 Corinthians 2:14. Commenting on this sermon and three others from this period, Kenneth Minkema observes, "Though few in number, they were seminal in Edwards' evolution as a pastor." He adds, "In these sermons we see the themes that will occupy him intellectually and pastorally throughout his career."[2]

A few years later, Edwards preached another seminal sermon, "The Threefold Work of the Holy Ghost," probably in April 1729, at Northampton. This sermon contains parallels to his most famous sermon, "Sinners in the Hands of an Angry God," anticipates much of his thought in *Religious Affections*, and, according to Minkema, "anticipates his *Essay on the Trinity,* begun in early 1730." "Sinners," warns Edwards, "are in exceeding great danger. Awakened sinners see it, see God's anger flaming, they themselves hanging over the pit, God's sword drawn, his bow bent"—intense imagery that reappears later in "Sinners in the Hands of an Angry God." Edwards poses the question, "How may it be known whether the concerns that persons are under about the state of their souls are from the Spirit of God?"[3] Or,

2. Ibid. Minkema refers to this sermon as formative for Edwards's thinking on conversion and "anticipates in nearly every aspect *A Divine and Supernatural Light,* published in 1734" (p. 67).

3. Ibid., 371, 388.

as he asks later in *Religious Affections*, how does one recognize genuine religious affections? These two sermons are indeed formative.

They also set forth the Holy Spirit's crucial role in Edwards's view of knowledge, which includes the nature of knowledge, the connection between regeneration and perception, and the conviction of the Spirit as the source of assurance and certainty. The present chapter considers the first two of these ideas as we address the foundation of Edwards's apologetic: the basis and nature of knowledge.

In "A Spiritual Understanding of Divine Things," Edwards observes that Paul teaches that the Spirit of God "is the fountain and author of [spiritual knowledge], either by inspiration of the Scripture or by saving illumination." God's Word is the ground of truth, Edwards argues in "The Threefold Work of the Holy Ghost." Genuine convictions are "according to truth, etc., they are according to the Word of God."[4] The unshakable basis of knowledge is revelation.

In Edwards's apologetics, then, the Holy Spirit is the source of knowledge, as set forth in revelation. While this encompasses general revelation, the divinely inspired Scriptures are at the center of his attention and form the basis of his epistemology. In fact, when he speaks of "revelation," he typically is referring exclusively to Scripture, preferring the expression "light of nature" for the category of general revelation. He acknowledges, "There are many truths concerning God, and our duty to him, which are evident by the light of nature." But, he proceeds to argue, "Christian divinity, properly so called, is not evident by the light of nature; it depends on revelation. . . . Therefore it cannot be said, that we come to the knowledge of any part of Christian divinity by the light of nature." He then clarifies his understanding of revelation, concluding, "It is only the word of God, contained in the Old and New Testament, which teaches us Christian divinity."[5]

---

4. Ibid., 71, 390.
5. See "Christian Knowledge: or, The Importance and Advantage of a Thorough Knowledge of Divine Truth," in *The Works of Jonathan Edwards*, 2 vols., ed. Edward Hickman (1834; reprint, Edinburgh: Banner of Truth, 1974), 2:158.

Edwards by no means dismisses general revelation, as is especially evident in his typological writings, such as his *Images of Divine Things*. Nonetheless, he gives priority to special revelation and from there constructs his epistemology. As Scott Oliphint observes, revelation is foundational and presuppositional in Edwards's scheme: "We could say, then, that reasoning for Edwards presupposes the truth of revelation."[6] And, as demonstrated below, Edwards binds special revelation to the Holy Spirit, who functions instrumentally in the self-disclosure of the triune God. Following the Reformed tradition, while incorporating his own penetrating reflection, he argues for the unique role of the Holy Spirit in the extra-Trinitarian activity of revelation, which mirrors the Spirit's intra-Trinitarian function of communication and communion within the divine being.

Sounding a Theological Note: Edwards, Augustine, and Calvin

At first glance, Edwards's view of the Trinity, as unfolded in his unpublished essay on the Trinity, appears convoluted and perplexing. He begins by noting that "God is infinitely happy in the enjoyment of himself, in infinitely loving, and rejoicing in, His own essence and perfection, and accordingly it must be supposed that God perpetually and eternally has a most perfect idea of Himself, as it were an exact image and representation of Himself ever before him and in actual view." Edwards reasons that the image, or perfect idea, is actually God himself. Indeed, "the eternal, necessary, perfect, substantial, and personal idea which God hath of Himself" is his Son, the second person in the Trinity. "Nothing can more agree with the account of Scripture," declares Edwards, citing 2 Corinthians 4:4, Philippians 2:6, Colossians 1:15, and Hebrews 1:3. Paul teaches that the Son is the express image of God.

The Holy Spirit then emerges, in Edwards's thinking, as the bond of love between God and his express image. The Godhead "does

6. Scott Oliphint, "Jonathan Edwards: Reformed Apologist," *Westminster Theological Journal* 57 (1995): 177.

subsist in love," for John identifies the Holy Spirit as love indwelling the Christian in 1 John 4:12, which is to say that God indwells the Christian as stated in 1 John 4:13. Also, Paul equates the love of God with the indwelling Spirit in a variety of places, including Philippians 2:1, 2 Corinthians 6:6, Romans 15:30 and 5:5, Colossians 1:8, and Galatians 5:13–15. Further, Edwards fills the biblical images of the Holy Spirit with such meaning. He links the dove imagery with love by appealing to the Song of Solomon (notably, "His eyes are as the eyes of doves" in 5:12 and "my love, my dove" in 5:2). He interprets the river of life in Revelation 22:1 as the Holy Spirit, based on "the same apostle's own interpretation (John 7:38, 39)." Thus, the dove, "which is the emblem of love," and the river of life, which signifies God's love and delight, typify the Holy Spirit's intra-Trinitarian function as the bond of union and communion.

In his full statement on the Trinity in this essay, Edwards summarizes both the unity of the Trinity and the unique functions of each member:

And this I suppose to be that blessed Trinity that we read of in the Holy Scriptures. The Father is the Deity subsisting in the prime, unoriginated and most absolute manner, or the Deity in its direct existence. The Son is the Deity generated by God's understanding, or having an idea of Himself and subsisting in that idea. The Holy Ghost is the Deity subsisting in act, or the Divine essence flowing out and breathed forth in God's infinite love to and delight in himself. And I believe the whole Divine essence does truly and distinctly subsist both in the Divine idea and Divine love, and that of each of them are properly distinct persons.

He further observes that "all the Persons should be Co-eternal. Hereby we may more clearly understand the equality of the Persons among themselves, and that they are in every way equal in the society or family of the three."[7] Amy Plantinga Pauw refers to this as

7. Jonathan Edwards, "Essay on the Trinity," in *Treatise on Grace and Other Posthumously Published Writings*, ed. Paul Helm (Cambridge: James Clarke, 1971), 116, 118, 122.

one of two Trinitarian conceptions that are unique to Edwards, namely, "a social conception of the Godhead, according to which the Father, Son, and Holy Spirit form a 'family of three,' a divine society marked by love, consent, and unity of will." She then argues, "The second [concept] has been called the psychological conception of the Trinity, according to which the human mind knowing itself and loving itself provides a most fitting image of the Godhead." These two concepts not only are a unique contribution of Edwards to the development of the doctrine of the Trinity, but also "are interwoven in a variety of patterns throughout Edwards' theology."[8] She applies the social and psychological concepts of the Trinity to Edwards's eschatology and understanding of heaven. Her twin concepts, however, also apply to Edwards's epistemology, for both concepts of the Trinity reflect the intra-Trinitarian and extra-Trinitarian functions of each of the members.

The social conception of the Trinity accentuates the Spirit's role in the union of love between the members of the Trinity. The Spirit has a similar role in uniting believers to the Godhead. As Edwards observes, "The Holy Ghost being the love and joy of God is His beauty and happiness, and it is in our partaking of the same Holy Spirit that our communion with God consists." He further notes that, by drinking of the one Spirit (1 Cor. 12:13), "we enjoy the love and grace of the Father and of the Son, for the Holy Ghost is that love and grace."[9] Participation in the Spirit means participation in the benefits of Christ, and, hence, participation with the Father. Even as Edwards proceeds in the essay to emphasize the unique function of each member of the Trinity in the work of redemption, he continues to stress the Holy Spirit's role in enabling one to participate in the divine nature. Consequently, spiritual knowledge, or knowing the Trinity, depends entirely upon the work of the Spirit.

8. Amy Plantinga Pauw, " 'Heaven Is a World of Love': Edwards on Heaven and the Trinity," *Calvin Theological Journal* 30 (1995): 394. See also her full argument in *The Supreme Harmony of All: The Trinitarian Theology of Jonathan Edwards* (Grand Rapids: Eerdmans, 2002).

9. Edwards, "Essay on the Trinity," 117.

The psychological conception of the Trinity pertains to communication within and without the Trinity. Following Augustine's argument in *The City of God*, Edwards uses the human soul as a type of the Trinity. The human soul serves as a remarkable image of the Trinity in that it consists of "the mind, and the understanding or idea, and the spirit of the mind as it is called in Scripture, i.e., the disposition, the will or affection."[10] "Understanding" and "will" are crucial categories in Edwards's thought. He notes at the beginning of *A Treatise Concerning Religious Affections* that the understanding entails "perception and speculation, or [that] by which it [the soul] discerns and views and judges of things." Understanding then entails the elements of intellectual activity, or the basis of knowing. This is only part of the story, however. To argue that Edwards links knowledge solely to the understanding would truncate his view of knowledge. The will is also involved. He defines the will as "that by which the soul does not merely perceive and view things, but is some way inclined with respect to the things it views or considers; either is inclined to 'em, or is disinclined, and averse from 'em."[11] Given the full picture, knowledge involves both intellectual activity (the understanding) and participation (the will).

The faculty of the will goes by many names. "It is sometimes called the *inclination;* and, as it has respect to the actions that are governed by it, it is called the *will:* and the *mind,* with regard to the exercises of this faculty, is often called the *heart*."[12] At this point, Edwards has contributed nothing new to the discussion of human psychology. Allen Guelzo, in fact, places Edwards's view, especially as adumbrated in *Freedom of the Will,* within the history of theology from Augustine to Edwards's father's master's thesis at Harvard.[13] Edwards

---

10. Ibid., 126.

11. *The Works of Jonathan Edwards,* vol. 2, *Religious Affections,* ed. John E. Smith (New Haven: Yale University Press, 1957), 96.

12. Ibid., 96 (emphasis original).

13. Allen C. Guelzo, *Edwards on the Will: A Century of American Theological Debate* (Middletown, Conn.: Wesleyan University Press, 1989), 3, 17. See also Stephen J. Nichols, *Jonathan Edwards: A Guided Tour of His Life and Thought* (Phillipsburg, N.J.: P&R Publishing, 2001), 173–87.

enjoyed broad exposure to the matter not only at his East Windsor home, but also during his days at Yale, in dialogue with his fellow ministers, and in polemical engagements with, in the words of Paul Ramsey, "his antagonists"—Thomas Chubb, Daniel Whitby, and Isaac Watts.[14]

Edwards's focus on the will was not original, either. Guelzo places Edwards firmly in the voluntarist tradition, stretching back to Augustine and including, among others, Turretin, Ames, Timothy Edwards, and John Cotton. Nevertheless, Edwards's name "towers above them all" because of his discussion of the affections. In Edwards's terminology, the "vigorous and sensible exercises of this faculty [of the will] . . . are called the *affections*."[15] He goes on to argue that the affections should not then be considered a faculty separate from the will. In fact, as John E. Smith argues, "the essential point is that the affections manifest the center and unity of the self; they express the whole man and give insight into the basic orientation of his life."[16] Edwards's next moves are crucial. First, he observes "that true religion, in great part, consists in the affections." Then he argues that "the Scriptures do represent true religion, as being summarily comprehended in *love*, the chief of the affections, and fountain of all other affections."[17]

Edwards makes his contribution precisely at this point, as he unites his understanding of human psychology to the psychological conception of the Trinity. In his view, the understanding and the will, and the affections, reflect the self's desire for knowledge and love, both of which reflect the *imago Dei* in humanity. God's disposition

14. Editor's introduction to *The Works of Jonathan Edwards,* vol. 1, *Freedom of the Will,* ed. Paul Ramsey (New Haven: Yale University Press, 1957), 65.

15. Guelzo, *Edwards on the Will,* 3–5, 14, 97 (emphasis original).

16. Smith, editor's introduction to *Religious Affections,* 14. Edwards's insight here stretches back to his master's thesis or *quaestio,* in which he argues, "Per fidem hac thesi volumus totius Animae Receptionem Christi suorumque beneficiorum," a whole-souled response, not merely intellectual assent, or volitional choice, or display of affection; "sed totius Animae horum omnium implicantis" ("Quaestio: Peccator Non Iustificatur Coram Deo Nisi Per Iustitiam Christi Fide Apprehensam," in *Sermons and Discourses, 1723–1729,* 55).

17. *Religious Affections,* 99, 106. Some of the texts that Edwards cites as substantiating his claim are 1 Cor. 13, Gal. 5:14, and Matt. 22:37–40.

to self-knowledge and self-love also typifies human nature, in both the regenerate and the unregenerate state.

In his treatise on ethics, *The Nature of True Virtue,* Edwards illustrates this in terms of self-love. In the first chapter, he defines true virtue theoretically as "benevolence to Being in general." He proceeds to argue that benevolence is essentially love, echoing the first part of *Two Dissertations, Concerning the End for Which God Created the World* and his published sermon series *Charity and Its Fruits.* In *Charity and Its Fruits,* Edwards begins by making the case that "love [is] the sum of all virtue."[18] He also defines the cryptic "Being in general" as "God" in chapter 2 of *The Nature of True Virtue.* In other words, true virtue is love toward God.

Edwards also argues that this mirrors the Trinity: "From hence also it is evident that the *divine virtue,* or the virtue of the divine mind, must consist primarily in *love to himself,* or in the mutual love and friendship which subsists eternally and necessarily between the several persons in the Godhead." That which is not true virtue, which Edwards designates as "common morality," falls short of love directed to God; in short, it is self-love. This love fails to see the union, harmony, and propensity of individual beings with respect to God and is consumed with private interest over against the ultimate end of God's glory. It is, however, "as God constituted our nature"; it is a God-given disposition.[19] Regeneration enables one to turn love from the direction of the self outward, first toward God and then toward others. "True gratitude or thankfulness to God for his kindness to us," Edwards argues, "arises from a foundation laid before, of love to God for what he is in himself."[20]

However, Edwards does not entirely deprecate self-love, for he adds, "Self-love is not excluded from a gracious gratitude. . . . But something else is included; and another love prepares the way, and

---

18. *The Works of Jonathan Edwards,* vol. 8, *Ethical Writings,* ed. Paul Ramsey (New Haven: Yale University Press, 1989), 540, 129. See also the editor's introduction, 116–19.

19. Ibid., 557, 555, 578.

20. *Religious Affections,* 247.

lays the foundation, for these grateful affections."[21] In his scheme, the regenerate person's love of self is predicated upon, and governed by, love toward God; the unregenerate person's self-love has no such basis. And the essential difference, according to Edwards, revolves around one's relationship to the Holy Spirit, the source of our communion with, and participation in, God. Love, as reflected in humanity via the *imago Dei*, is not absent from the non-Christian, but present in the Christian. Rather, the difference lies in the direction of one's love.

The same is true of human knowledge. In his sermon entitled "A Divine and Supernatural Light," Edwards declares, "There is a twofold understanding or knowledge of good, that God has made the mind capable of."[22] First, there is notional or speculative knowledge, which is possessed by the unregenerate. Second, there is spiritual knowledge, or the new sense of the heart, which is possessed only by the regenerate. Both the unregenerate and the regenerate possess knowledge. But the object of their knowledge differs.

Before we proceed with our examination of Edwards's thought, it would be helpful to glance back at John Calvin. Calvin begins his *Institutes* by discussing the relationship between our knowledge of ourselves and our knowledge of God. "Man," according to Calvin, "never achieves a clear knowledge of himself unless he has first looked upon God's face, and then descends from contemplating him to scrutinize himself." Hence, all knowledge flows from the knowledge of God. What Calvin affirms about this knowledge is crucial. First he notes its relational aspect: "Now the knowledge of God, as I understand it, is that by which we not only conceive that there is a God but also grasp what befits us and is proper to his glory, in fine, what is to our advantage to know of him." Due to the Fall, human-

---

21. Ibid., 248. Edwards's views sparked a debate on disinterested benevolence among his followers. For a full discussion of the issues, see Joseph A. Conforti, *Jonathan Edwards, Religious Tradition, and American Culture* (Chapel Hill: University of North Carolina Press, 1995), 62–86.

22. John E. Smith, Harry S. Stout, and Kenneth P. Minkema, eds., *A Jonathan Edwards Reader* (New Haven: Yale University Press, 1995), 111.

ity is in rebellion against God and reconciliation is possible only through Christ's mediatorial role. To know God, argues Calvin, is to know him in fear and reverence, and that issues in worship. He writes, "Here indeed is pure religion: faith so joined with an earnest fear of God that this fear also embraces willing reverence, and carries with it such legitimate worship as is prescribed in the law."[23]

Calvin not only states that the knowledge of God is relational, but also makes the point that it is universal. Now these two ideas appear to contradict each other. Nevertheless, Calvin himself affirms that "there is within the human mind, and indeed by natural instinct, an awareness of divinity"—*Divinitatis sensum*.[24] This internal knowledge, however, is "smothered or corrupted." The knowledge of God is also known through the creation and the moral government of the universe. But such knowledge is also obscured by humanity's dullness and obstinacy. Ronald Wallace writes, "Until this perversity is cured . . . the natural man is forced to turn even the faint glimmer of truth he possesses into a vicious idol that is a mockery of the true God and whose possession can only the more confirm man in his alienation from the truth."[25] So, Calvin concludes, special revelation, or the Word of God, is absolutely necessary for man to have knowledge of God.

But even here Calvin raises the issue of one's relation to God. In a tantalizing statement, Calvin observes, "My readers therefore should remember that I am not yet going to discuss that covenant by which God adopted to himself the sons of Abraham, or that part of doctrine which has always separated believers from unbelieving folk, for it was founded in Christ."[26] Knowledge, in other words, is covenantal as it reflects the subject's relationship to it. Yet, knowledge is also objective and universal, through general and special rev-

23. John Calvin, *Institutes of the Christian Religion*, 2 vols., trans. Ford Lewis Battles, ed. John T. McNeill (Philadelphia: Westminster Press, 1960), 1.1.2, 1.2.1, 1.2.2.

24. Ibid., 1.3.1.

25. Ronald S. Wallace, *Calvin's Doctrine of the Word and Sacrament* (Edinburgh: Oliver and Boyd, 1953), 69.

26. *Institutes*, 1.6.1.

elation. Calvin is not positing two types of knowledge, but high-
lighting one's relationship to knowledge.

Returning to Edwards may clarify this point. In *Religious Affections*, he declares, "I say that the supremely excellent nature of divine things, is the first, or primary and original objective foundation
of the spiritual affections of true saints." He also distinguishes between the divine things in themselves and "any conceived relation
they bear to self, or self-interest."[27] In the context, Edwards draws
upon this distinction to highlight the disinterested nature of true religious affections. The distinction he makes between object and subject, however, helps us to understand his view of knowledge. Like
Calvin, Edwards wants to stress both the relationship that one has
to knowledge and the objective nature of knowledge. There are not
two worlds or two types of knowledge.

Again, Edwards appears to be contradicting his own distinction
between notional (or speculative) knowledge and spiritual knowledge. However, this distinction pertains more to the subject's relationship to knowledge than to knowledge in and of itself. At this
point, it may be helpful to clarify the concept of knowledge, especially the notion of objective knowledge. If knowledge consists of a
transaction between subject and object, then one can never separate the subject from knowledge. In saying that, however, one is not
embracing subjectivism. Take for instance the proposition that Jesus
Christ is Lord, a crucial piece of Christian knowledge. In Edwards's
scheme, this proposition can be known to some extent by anyone
who hears or reads Scripture. The words are there on the page, con-
stituting an objective item of knowledge. But while the subject is involved in this transaction, he adds nothing to the proposition itself.
Rather, the proposition adds to the subject this new information or
knowledge. Edwards would likely qualify this idea by pointing out
a few things. First, this knowledge lacks something. The quick answer that one might give is that this knowledge lacks an affective dimension; this knowledge should bring about within the subject a de-

27. *Religious Affections*, 240.

light in it. Thus, the affective dimension serves as the *sine qua non* of true knowledge. That, however, may miss Edwards's point entirely. What is lacking is more than an affective dimension; in Edwards's words, spiritual knowledge is lacking.

Returning again to Calvin, this is a matter of connecting belief and knowledge. Calvin observes, "When we call faith 'knowledge' we do not mean comprehension of the sort that is commonly concerned with those things which fall under human sense perception."[28] Paul Helm explains Calvin's point: "What is believed is . . . a case of knowledge by description rather than knowledge by acquaintance, and Calvin calls it knowledge because of its certainty, not because it is something that the believer can get to know for himself, by perception, for example."[29] There is a great deal to this observation that will have to wait until later, but relevant to the present discussion is Calvin's distinction between sense perception and faith or belief. Faith leads to a type of knowledge that participates in the truth of the proposition. Both Calvin and Edwards would argue that faith is given to the subject by God, specifically through the Spirit's work of regeneration. There is, then, a difference between believing the proposition that Jesus Christ is Lord and merely reading or hearing it. Even so, belief in the proposition, or, as Edwards would say, a spiritual knowledge of the proposition, adds nothing to the proposition itself. Edwards would also point out, as we will see below, that one can reject the proposition and claim that it is false. Doing so, however, does not make the proposition false.

To be sure, Edwards's understanding of regeneration as a transformation of the whole person (*totius animae*) means that a person prior to conversion is not capable of perceiving spiritual knowledge. In this Edwards adheres closely to Paul's teaching in Romans 1 that humanity knows God. Due to sinful rebellion, however, humanity attempts to suppress and pervert that knowledge (Rom. 1:18–23). Following Paul, and, for that matter, Calvin, Edwards observes, "The

---

28. *Institutes*, 3.2.14.
29. Paul Helm, *Varieties of Belief* (London: George Allen & Unwin, 1973), 102.

mind of man is naturally full of prejudices against the truth of divine things; it is full of enmity against the doctrines of the Gospel."[30] He explores this notion at length in his sermon "Man's Natural Blindness in the Things of Religion." This blindness is not due to a lack of capacity in human nature, nor is it due to ignorance; rather, it is due to sinful rebellion. Edwards observes, "There is a principle in [man's] heart, of such a blinding and besotting nature, that it hinders the exercise of his faculties about the things of religion." He proceeds to speak of the brutish blindness that manifests itself in suppressing the true knowledge of God. Referring to Romans 1, he writes, "Instead of acknowledging and worshipping the *true* God, they have fallen off to the worship of idols."[31]

This changes, however, when the divine and supernatural light is imparted at conversion. As Edwards notes elsewhere, "When a person has discovered to him the divine excellency of Christian doctrines, this destroys the enmity, removes those prejudices, and sanctifies the reason, and causes it to lie open to the force of arguments for their truth."[32] The arguments were true before the discovery of the divine excellence, but that discovery was required before the subject could see the truth of the arguments. Again, the intellectual faculty is not absent or present in the Christian or the non-Christian. All people possess such a faculty because of the *imago Dei,* not because of the autonomy of human reasoning or the infallibility of the natural faculty—two concepts that Edwards rejects.

To explain Edwards's understanding of the *imago Dei,* it will be helpful to relate his epistemology to his ontology. His concept of human psychology reflects his psychological concept of the Trinity. He argues that the "whole Divine office is supposed truly and properly to subsist in each of these three, viz., God and his understanding and love." He adds that "they have communion in One Another

30. "A Divine and Supernatural Light," in *Jonathan Edwards Reader,* ed. Smith, 112.
31. "Man's Natural Blindness in the Things of Religion," in *Works of Jonathan Edwards,* ed. Hickman, 2:247 (emphasis original). Toward the end of the sermon he notes, "There is not a mere absence of light, but a malignant opposition to the light" (p. 255).
32. "A Divine and Supernatural Light," 112.

and are as it were predicable of One Another." There are three elements of each member of the Trinity: being, which he designates as
God; understanding or intellect, which he designates as *understanding;* and will, which he designates as *love.* The members are affirmed
in their distinct personhood as possessing all three elements. Edwards concludes, "All the Three are Persons for they all have understanding and will."

However, the members are also uniquely related to these elements.
Edwards refers to the Father, as quoted above, as subsisting in "the
prime, unoriginated, and most absolute manner." The Son, then, is
the express image of God, God's perfect understanding of himself.
That is, the "second person in the Trinity . . . is the eternal, necessary, perfect, substantial, and personal idea which God hath of Himself." The Son is the essence of the self-knowledge of God. He functions uniquely, in an *opera ad intra* manner, as *understanding.* Edwards
argues that the third member of the Trinity also functions uniquely,
in an *opera ad intra* manner, as *love.* And it is the love of God "that
flows forth *ad extra.*"[33] That is, the love of God extends the Trinitarian union to include God's creation, and it is the Holy Spirit's
unique function to do so.

One could argue, based on this, that Edwards's understanding of
revelation is radically Christocentric. Indeed, John argues that Christ
was exegeting the Father (John 1:18), and the author of Hebrews
makes the case that God is now revealing himself through the Son—
a far superior revelation than before (Heb. 1:1–3). Stephen Stein argues that Edwards's Christocentrism reveals one of the most remarkable aspects of his biblical interpretation, and that this serves
as an interpretive key to understanding Edwards's writings. He notes,
"Edwards' typological hermeneutic provided a means to connect
virtually any text with Christ and his work of redemption. In that
respect Edwards' scholarly and pastoral activities were closely linked
with each other through his christocentric emphasis."[34]

33. "Essay on the Trinity," 120–21, 103, 131.
34. Editor's introduction to *The Works of Jonathan Edwards,* vol. 15, *Notes on Scripture,* ed.
Stephen J. Stein (New Haven: Yale University Press, 1998), 26.

This is true, however, only in terms of the subject of revelation. The activity of revelation is, for Edwards, radically pneumatocentric, for the Holy Spirit functions uniquely in the giving of revelation and in the illuminating of revelation. The Spirit's task is to reveal the Trinity *ad extra*. "The Holy Ghost," argues Edwards, "is the Deity subsisting in act, or the Divine essence *flowing out* and *breathed forth* in God's infinite love to and delight in Himself."[35] Both the "flowing out" and the "breathed forth" are the work of the Holy Spirit *ad extra*. The latter activity is the Spirit's giving of revelation by way of inspiration.

This brief exploration of Edwards's ontology is necessary for understanding his epistemology because his view of God structures his view of humanity and establishes that man is a rational being who is capable of knowing and a volitional being who is capable of willing. In the Augustinian-Calvinistic tradition, he also asserts that true knowledge derives only from the operation of the Holy Spirit, as the human activities of understanding and willing are directed toward God. And the difference between the regenerate, who use the understanding properly in a state of reconciliation, and the unregenerate, who distort the understanding in a state of rebellion, hinges upon one's relationship to the Holy Spirit. Spiritual knowledge is of the Spirit. And the objective locus of this knowledge is the Word of God, breathed forth by the Holy Spirit.

SOUNDING A PHILOSOPHICAL NOTE: EDWARDS AND LOCKE

Before this can be developed, however, it is necessary to explore Locke's influence on Edwards with respect to idealism and empiricism. Edwards follows Locke in asserting that "knowledge is . . . the perception of the union or disunion of ideas, or the perceiving whether two or more ideas belong to one another."[36] Locke begins book 4 of

---

35. "Essay on the Trinity," 118 (emphasis added).

36. "The Mind," in *The Works of Jonathan Edwards*, vol. 6, *Scientific and Philosophical Writings*, ed. Wallace E. Anderson (New Haven: Yale University Press, 1980), 385. Anderson points out that this is one of the later entries in "The Mind," probably written around 1748.

his *Essay Concerning Human Understanding* by reasoning that since the mind has only its own ideas as its object, "it is evident, that our Knowledge is only conversant about them."[37] Edwards similarly emphasizes perception. In a rough outline for a possible treatise on knowledge and existence, sketched out near the end of his life,[38] he notes that "real existence depends on knowledge and perception." He then raises the objection of the existence of material substance in order to answer it. In his refutation, he writes, "What we call body is nothing but a particular mode of perception; and what we call spirit is nothing but a composition and series of perceptions, or an universe of coexisting and successive perceptions connected by such wonderful methods and laws."[39]

Anderson, however, makes the case that Edwards employed idealism basically as an apologetic aimed at the deists. Consequently, Anderson argues that the chief influence on Edwards came from the Cambridge Platonists. Edwards set out "to develop a metaphysics that would be a conclusive answer to materialism." Anderson notes further how the mechanistic principles of Cartesian dualism, or occasionalism, limit the role of God. Thus, they proved unsatisfactory to Edwards. Instead, Edwards followed Henry More's Neoplatonic or Augustinian metaphysic. For Edwards, "reality consists in knowing and being perceived." In this sense, his idealism is "a logical consequence of the much more general metaphysical principle that nothing whatever can be without being known."[40] In Edwards's idealism, existence and knowledge depend entirely and immediately on God.

This observation has important implications. In "The Mind," Edwards defines truth as "the consistency and agreement of our ideas with the ideas of God."[41] This stresses the unity of God and his cre-

---

37. John Locke, *An Essay Concerning Human Understanding*, ed. Peter H. Nidditch (Oxford: Oxford University Press, 1975), 525.

38. Based on the watermark of the paper, the ink, and the handwriting, Anderson, following Thomas Schafer, dates this manuscript between 1755 and 1757 in *Scientific and Philosophical Writings*, 394–95.

39. Ibid., 398.

40. Anderson, editor's introduction to *Scientific and Philosophical Writings*, 54, 75, 77.

41. *Scientific and Philosophical Writings*, 341–42.

ation and the contingency of all knowledge upon God, thus making revelation essential. This also leads to Edwards's empiricism, reflected in his emphasis on perception and sensation. Further, as quoted at the beginning of this chapter, Edwards argues that the greatest understanding of honey comes from tasting it. It is important to remember, however, that while Locke offers a systematic discussion of experience as a source of knowledge, his position is not original. In fact, William Bouwsma relates Calvin's view of knowledge to the "Renaissance esteem for learning from experience," arguing that Calvin "allowed experience a large part in religious life."[42] Bouwsma adds that throughout the *Institutes* Calvin reveals his belief that knowledge is experience.

This is especially the case in Calvin's discussion of revelation. The guarantee of Scripture's veracity is its self-authentication. And the individual mind may rest "securely and constantly" in this argument. He goes on to write, "I speak of nothing other than what each believer experiences within himself."[43] Further, it is through faith that one comes to know God as Redeemer. This is not to suggest that Calvin is an empiricist. Rather, it is to suggest that, for Calvin, experience is essential to knowledge. And this is precisely Edwards's point, that one participates in knowledge. As McClymond suggests, for Edwards, "spiritual perception is the knowledge of a participant, and not that of a spectator."[44] Or, as stated above, knowledge is covenantal. Like his idealism, Edwards's empiricism also reflects the notion that knowledge depends entirely and immediately upon God, for he draws attention to the necessity of one's encounter with revelation.

Therefore, in both his idealism and his empiricism, Edwards does not merely adopt and modify Locke. Rather, drawing from many sources, he shapes idealism and empiricism according to his apologetic aims and posits a metaphysic and an epistemology similar to

42. William J. Bouwsma, *John Calvin: A Sixteenth-Century Portrait* (New York: Oxford University Press, 1988), 158.

43. *Institutes*, 1.7.5.

44. Michael J. McClymond, *Encounters with God: An Approach to the Theology of Jonathan Edwards* (Oxford: Oxford University Press, 1998), 21.

those of Augustine and Calvin. Further, Edwards refutes Locke on the crucial area of revelation. Revelation forms the warp and woof of Edwards's epistemology. As he himself observes, "The increase of learning and philosophy in the Christian world is owing to revelation: the doctrines of the word of God are the foundation of all useful and excellent knowledge."[45] This focus on revelation follows Calvin squarely. Ford Lewis Battles argues that Calvin's focus on knowledge at the beginning of the *Institutes* "emphasizes the centrality of revelation both in the structure and the content of Calvin's theology."[46] And, as argued above, at the center of Edwards's understanding of revelation is the doctrine of inspiration by the Holy Spirit.

THE HARMONY OF EDWARDS'S THOUGHT

Locke's understanding of inspiration sets the stage for Edwards—not by comparison, but by contrast. As David Laurence observes, the Bible is incapable of relating what Locke terms "actual knowledge" because it is written down. To be sure, the prophets' original inspiration counted for them as actual knowledge, but this does not extend to the written word. Also, the Bible can tell people what they are to believe, but "it cannot convey actual knowledge or understanding of those things in which people are to believe. . . . The Words of the Bible were one thing; religious truth was quite another thing."[47] Locke addresses inspiration in book 4, chapter 18, of his *Essay*. Here he places reason and the natural faculties above revelation. He writes, "For whatsoever Truth we come to the clear discovery of, from the Knowledge and Contemplation of our own *Ideas*, will always be certainer to us, than those which are conveyed to us by *Traditional Revelation*." Ignoring the noetic effects of original sin, Locke makes rea-

---

45. *The Works of Jonathan Edwards*, vol. 13, *The "Miscellanies," Entry Nos. a–z, aa–zz, 1–500*, ed. Thomas A. Schafer (New Haven: Yale University Press, 1994), 424–25.

46. *Institutes*, 1.1.1, note 1.

47. David Laurence, "Jonathan Edwards, John Locke, and the Canon of Experience," *Early American Literature* 15 (1980): 109–10.

son the arbiter of faith: "But yet nothing, I think, can, under that Title [Revelation from God], shake or over-rule plain Knowledge; or rationally prevail with any Man, to admit it for true, in a direct contradiction to the clear Evidence of his own Understanding."[48]

Locke further distinguishes the categories of faith and knowledge. In fact, Laurence notes, "In Locke's philosophy faith was not a kind of knowledge; it was the opposite of knowledge."[49] Knowledge asserts itself over faith and over revelation. In short, Locke's work posits the autonomy of reason, dismisses the Reformation principles of the authority and necessity of Scripture, and, as Laurence points out, initiates and fuels the higher criticism of the eighteenth century. Edwards could not disagree more with these conclusions.

In the middle of "The Mind," Edwards interjects a brief statement on inspiration. He observes, "The evidence of immediate inspiration that the prophets had when they were immediately inspired by the Spirit of God with any truth is *an absolute sort of certainty;* and the knowledge is in a sense intuitive, much in the same manner as faith and spiritual knowledge of the truth of religion." He draws an analogy between the inspiration by which the prophets received their messages and the illumination by which people today come to know spiritual knowledge. And just as the one who would know honey must taste it, so the verification of inspiration is in the experience of it. "The prophet has so divine a sense," explains Edwards, "such a divine disposition . . . that he sees as immediately that God is there as we perceive one another's presence when we are talking together face to face."[50] So the prophet, or the human author of Scripture, knows he is inspired when it happens.

Up to this point, Edwards appears to be following, to a certain degree, the logic of Locke by locating the verification of revelation in the prophet's experience. However, this is only partially the case.

48. Locke, *Essay Concerning Human Understanding,* 690–91 (emphasis original). Locke uses the term "Traditional Revelation" to refer to Scripture, and "Original Revelation" to refer to the prophet's own experience of inspiration.

49. Laurence, "Jonathan Edwards, John Locke, and the Canon of Experience," 110.

50. "The Mind," in *Scientific and Philosophical Writings,* 346 (emphasis added).

Edwards does not use the prophet's experience as the basis for accepting the veracity of the revelation. The prophet's experience validates it only for himself. The basis for accepting the veracity of Scripture is its self-attestation as inspired writing. Furthermore, in direct contradiction to Locke, Edwards argues that Scripture is the basis and source of all knowledge. These points will now be demonstrated from Edwards's writings.

First, Edwards strenuously affirms the absolute necessity and authority of Scripture in a series of miscellaneous observations collected and edited by John Erskine, entitled "Observations on the Facts and Evidences of Christianity." In a chapter addressing the authority and necessity of Scripture, Edwards poses the question, "Whether nature and reason alone can give us a right idea of God, and are sufficient to establish among mankind a clear and sure knowledge of his nature, and the relation we stand in to him, and his concern with us?" He answers that they cannot do so, and that they are not substitutes for revelation. In fact, reason has not only failed to obtain true knowledge, "but it affords no possibility of it."[51] Scripture, Edwards preached to his Northampton congregation, is "the fountain whence all knowledge in divinity must be derived."[52] While asserting the supremacy of Scripture, Edwards does not exclude other means of revelation, namely, general revelation and the Spirit's conviction.

In one of his earlier sermons preached at New York and probably preached again both during his time of pulpit supply at Bolton and during his tutorship at Yale, Edwards calls upon his audience to hearken to the fourfold voice of God. There is the written voice of God in Scripture, but also the voice of God in creation, providence, and the internal calling of the Spirit. He appeals to each of these in stressing the urgency of listening to God. "The voice of God in his Word," as he puts it, conveys far more explicit instruction, since it threatens, invites,

51. "Miscellaneous Observations on Important Theological Subjects," in *Works of Jonathan Edwards*, ed. Hickman, 2:475, 484.
52. "Christian Knowledge: or, The Importance and Advantage of a Thorough Knowledge of Divine Truth," in *Works of Jonathan Edwards*, ed. Hickman, 2:162.

entreats, warns, and directs. Edwards affirms the absolute necessity and authority of Scripture. He further maintains that "the Scriptures themselves are an evidence of their own divine authority."[53]

Calvin similarly affirms "that Scripture indeed is self-authenticated; hence, it is not right to subject it to proof and reasoning." Of course, this does not stop either Edwards or Calvin from pointing out that there are sufficient arguments to support the credibility of Scripture. Calvin stresses that to base the authority of the Scriptures on something external to the Scriptures would compromise their very authority; by definition, the authoritative Scriptures must be their own authority. He also notes that the reasons, arguments, or proofs that he does offer for Scripture's credibility are recognized only by those who "have embraced it devoutly as its dignity deserves." With these two points established, Calvin then proceeds to offer a series of arguments, based on Scripture's content, antiquity, fulfillment of prophecy, and preservation.[54]

Edwards follows a similar line of argumentation. Given the necessity of the new sense of the heart, reason and argumentation will not establish the authority of Scripture. Nonetheless, Edwards states that Scripture is agreeable to reason. John Gerstner highlights the aspects of Edwards's thought on Scripture that are concerned with answering the challenges of the nascent higher criticism of his day. He notes the way in which Edwards dealt with chronological or historical discrepancies, the synoptic problem, and even the ethical objections to such texts as the imprecatory psalms. However, Gerstner points out that the underlying foundation of Edwards's argumentation is verbal inspiration. He writes, "The Bible is the very word of God, as inerrant as if it were mechanically dictated (though it was not), and as unified as if it were written by the divine author only (though it was not)."[55]

---

53. "The Duty of Hearkening to God's Voice," in *The Works of Jonathan Edwards,* vol. 10, *Sermons and Discourses, 1720–1723,* ed. Wilson H. Kimnach (New Haven: Yale University Press, 1992), 441, 462.

54. *Institutes,* 1.7.5, 1.8.1, 1.8.2–13.

55. John H. Gerstner, *The Rational Biblical Theology of Jonathan Edwards,* 3 vols. (Powhatan, Va.: Berea Publications, 1991–93), 1:144–45.

Edwards subordinates evidences for Scripture to its own authority as divinely inspired, while nonetheless employing evidences. In
his sermons, he typically argues for any given point by first demonstrating that it is scriptural and then demonstrating that it is rational.
For instance, in "A Divine and Supernatural Light," Edwards argues first from biblical texts and then from reason for the necessity
of the spiritual and divine light.[56] This *modus operandi* reveals the
subordinate, albeit valid, role of reason and argument.

The content of Scripture itself argues for its veracity. In one of the
sermons from *A History of the Work of Redemption,* Edwards argues
that "the admirable consent and agreement" concerning the coming
of Christ "is, therefore, a clear and certain evidence of the divine authority of these writings." He goes on to entertain objections to the
historical nature and content of Scripture, concluding "that from
what has been said we may see much of the wisdom of God in the
composition of the Scripture of the Old Testament."[57] Edwards also
directly follows Calvin's point that the simplicity of Scripture proves
its authenticity. He speaks of an "unaccountable kind of enchant-
ment" in Scripture's record of history as opposed to other histories,
noting that Scripture "shines brighter with the amiable simplicity of
truth."[58] Edwards also appeals to fulfillment of prophecy as a proof
of Scripture's credibility in two lengthy entries in his "Miscellanies,"
entitled "Types of the Messiah" and "Fulfillment of the Prophecies
of the Messiah." The natural man, however, "not only do[es]n't receive them [the things of God], but he rejects them. . . . It appears all
quite tasteless, insipid, senseless, and foolish to him. . . . A natural
man and the knowledge of the things of God's Spirit are quite re-
pugnant and incompatible."[59] Like Calvin, Edwards affirms that
Scripture's rationality has a limited audience. In other words, they
are both preaching to the choir. However, this fails to detract from

56. Smith, *Jonathan Edwards Reader,* 118.
57. *The Works of Jonathan Edwards,* vol. 9, *A History of the Work of Redemption,* ed. John F.
Wilson (New Haven: Yale University Press, 1989), 283, 286.
58. *The "Miscellanies," Entry Nos. a–z, aa–zz, 1–500,* 202–3.
59. "A Spiritual Understanding of Divine Things," in *Sermons and Discourses, 1723–1729,* 71.

the validity of their arguments in and of themselves. The fact that only the regenerate appreciate their truth does not detract from their sufficiency to prove Scripture's truthfulness.

Edwards follows Calvin further in basing our confidence in the authority of Scripture on the witness of the Spirit. "The best way for our consciences not to be perpetually beset by the instability of doubt or vacillation," Calvin argues, "is in the secret testimony of the Holy Spirit."[60] This is, of course, a reference to the *internum testimonium Spiritus Sancti*, a subject fully developed later in this work. Here, however, it is important to note that the Spirit's witness to Scripture is predicated upon the Spirit's authorship of Scripture. In other words, assurance and illumination, as works of the Spirit, reflect another work of the Spirit, namely, inspiration. These works of the Spirit parallel one another, as Edwards argues in the selection from "The Mind" cited above. He observes that the knowledge that the prophets had because "they were immediately inspired by the Spirit of God," was, in fact, of "the same manner as faith and spiritual knowledge."[61] Similarly, in "A Spiritual Understanding of Divine Things," he observes that the Holy Spirit is the author of divine things, "either by inspiration of the Scripture or by saving illumination."[62] Scripture is divinely inspired and represents both the basis of knowledge and the source of knowledge. Consequently, Edwards concludes that "if there had never been any revelation . . . there would be endless disputes and abundance of uncertainty."[63]

CONCLUSION

Edwards's illustration of knowing about honey offers a fitting summary of his epistemology. He observes, "It is not he that has heard a long description of honey that can be said to have the greatest understanding of it, but he that has tasted." He then makes the con-

---

60. *Institutes*, 1.7.4.
61. *Scientific and Philosophical Writings*, 346.
62. *Sermons and Discourses, 1723–1729*, 71.
63. *The "Miscellanies," Entry Nos. a–z, aa–zz, 1–500*, 421–22.

nection to spiritual knowledge: "Now God has infused such a lively apprehension into the minds of the godly of divine things, as if they had tasted."[64] In this emphasis on knowledge entailing experience, one sees the influence of Locke's thinking on Edwards. Following McClymond, we should understand this "experience" as participation. Further, Edwards understood knowledge as covenantal. This conveys Edwards's idea of "greatest understanding" and recalls his distinction between notional and spiritual knowledge. Such a distinction does not propose two types of knowledge. Rather, it stresses the relationship that one has to knowledge. The one who possesses spiritual knowledge has the greatest knowledge; that is, he knows in relation to God. While one can see the influence of Locke, Berkeley, Malebranche, and the Cambridge Platonists on Edwards, it is clear that he was strongly influenced by Calvin and the Reformed tradition, as well.

Edwards makes the case that spiritual knowledge is about the things of God and also belongs to God. Hence, it is communicated by God via revelation. Because the Holy Spirit has a unique function in giving revelation, the Spirit plays a central role in Edwards's apologetic. Revelation is also central to Edwards's epistemology in that it speaks of things as they really are; one can have epistemological certainty because of the underlying ontological certainty.

The doctrine of inspiration emphasizes the role of the Spirit in the giving of Scripture. Here, too, Edwards follows the Reformed tradition. Yet, he incorporates his own penetrating reflection as he relates the unique *opera ad intra* of the Spirit to his unique *opera ad extra*. The Spirit of God provides the solid foundation for knowledge through the inspiration of Scripture, and, as developed in the next chapter, through illumination the Spirit enables one to see the harmony, excellence, and truth of Scripture.

64. *Sermons and Discourses, 1723–1729*, 76.

3

PERCEPTION: EDWARDS ON SEEING AND SENSING

The appearance of everything was altered: there seemed to be, as it were,

a calm, sweet cast, or appearance of divine glory, in almost everything.

God's excellency, his wisdom, his purity and love seemed to appear in everything;

in the sun, moon, and stars; in the clouds and blue sky; in the grass, flowers, trees;

in the water and all nature; which used greatly to fix my mind.

Jonathan Edwards, "Personal Narrative"

Edwards mediates philosophy and theology perhaps nowhere more clearly than in his doctrine of the new sense. Rich in sources from Sibbes, Owen, and Calvin, on the one hand, to Newton, Locke, and John Smith and the other Cambridge Platonists on the other, his discussion of the new sense of the heart manifests both Puritan and Enlightenment bearings. The new sense further underlines the prominence of the Holy Spirit in Edwards's apologetic by involving the doctrines of illumination and regeneration. Additionally, the new sense reveals his rather insightful psychology, which situates him well in contemporary discussions of the self and of the nature of faith and conversion. What follows explores each of these elements in an attempt to connect Edwards's fundamental epistemological concerns with his understanding of the Spirit's witness and the assurance of faith.

The New Sense in Context

Not surprisingly, Perry Miller locates the source and the primary contours of Edwards's understanding of the new sense in John Locke. Edwards, like other thinkers of the eighteenth century, was, according to Miller, one of Locke's prisoners. Unlike the others, however, Edwards managed to transcend Locke. Miller's high estimation of Edwards's improvement on Locke brings forth a rather infrequent exclamation point when he notes, "Edwards went beyond Locke, far beyond him!"[1]

Edwards went beyond Locke by including the emotions in his understanding of perception. Miller does not have in view here enthusiasm or emotive expression, but rather approbation or disapprobation. He writes, "To see is to have a sense; to have a sense is to have an inclination; and as a man inclines, he wills." Thus, Edwards articulates the new sense as a lived religion and not as a speculative religion. Miller emphasizes the empirical element of the new sense, reasoning that Edwards learned from Locke that "God works upon man through the daily shock of sensation." This leads Miller to the conclusion that, for Edwards, "Truth is in the seeing, not in the thing."[2] Hence, the new sense for Edwards, according to Miller, consists of perception and results in action, or "a determination of love and hate."[3]

Miller argues that Isaac Newton also influenced Edwards's understanding of the new sense. Newtonian physics functioned on a

1. Perry Miller, "The Rhetoric of Sensation," in *Errand into the Wilderness* (Cambridge, Mass.: Harvard University Press, 1956), 179.

2. Perry Miller, *Jonathan Edwards* (New York: William Sloane, 1949), 64, 56, 330.

3. Miller, "Rhetoric of Sensation," 179. Miller then claims, "For Edwards [this] was the most important achievement of his life and the key to his doctrine and practice" (p. 179).

number of levels in Edwards's apologetic. First and foremost, it provided a scientific or mechanical basis for God's government of the world, and thus for the moral government argument frequently employed by eighteenth-century apologists. The opening lines of Edmund Halley's memorial poem for Newton capture this thought:

> Lo, for your gaze, the pattern of the skies!
> What balance of the mass, what reckonings Divine!
> Here ponder too the laws which God,
> Framing the universe, set not aside
> But made the fixed foundations of his work.[4]

Miller concludes that Edwards made use of Newton's theory of atoms and his law of gravity in formulating his own understanding of the natural world. But Edwards also managed to go beyond Newton. The inevitable implication of Newton's mechanistic theory, although not drawn by Newton himself, is at best deism and at worst Hobbesian materialism. The apologetic argument gets turned on its head as the Newtonian-based argument for God's existence ends up making God unnecessary. Miller observes, "To suppose God the creator of the world, and then over and above that the stage-manager of gravity, was a way of disposing with God entirely."[5]

Edwards responds to the deists and the materialists by arguing for the necessity of God's intimate involvement in sustaining creation. In one of his earlier scientific notebooks, Edwards, thoroughly immersed in Newton's ideas, concludes a series of propositions and corollaries by asserting, "The constant exercise of the infinite power of God is necessary to preserve bodies in being."[6] The power necessary to bring beings into existence, reasons Edwards, remains necessary to keep beings in existence. Wallace Anderson notes that Ed-

---

4. Edmund Halley, "To the Illustrious Man Isaac Newton," trans. Leon J. Richardson, in *Sir Isaac Newton's Mathematical Principles of Natural Philosophy and His System of the World,* ed. Florian Cajori (Berkeley: University of California Press, 1960), xiii.

5. Miller, *Jonathan Edwards,* 93.

6. "Of Atoms," in *The Works of Jonathan Edwards,* vol. 6, *Scientific and Philosophical Writings,* ed. Wallace E. Anderson (New Haven: Yale University Press, 1980), 214.

wards's "position [is] that the mechanistic theory be taken merely as the form or manner in which the system of nature operates; it does not express the real causes by which natural events occur."[7]

More importantly for the present study, however, Newton also provides part of the impetus for the vision motif in Edwards. Anderson argues that Newton's *Opticks* profoundly influenced Edwards. From this work, Edwards not only gained an understanding of atomism and of gravity, but also of the nature of light rays, reflection, refraction, and vision. This appears conspicuously in three short essays from his student years at Yale. In his essay "Of Light Rays," Edwards offers detailed calculations of distances from stars and the sun in order to explicate the infinitesimal size of light rays. Edwards marvels at the findings and quickly concludes, "Hence the exquisite skill of the artificer whose fingers have formed these infinitely small bodies." He adjudges vision to be an exquisite sense. He then develops both of these themes in the essays "Beauty of the World" and "Wisdom in the Contrivance of the World."

In the former essay, he extols sight by drawing attention to the notion that one *sees* the beauty of this world. In fact, he argues that this provides a reason for living: "Hence the reason why almost all men, and those that seem to be very miserable, love life: because they cannot bear to lose the sight of such a beautiful and lovely world." In the last of these three essays, he reasons that the eye is "very evidential of the wisdom of God," and further acclaims the sense of sight.[8] Anderson's comments on another of Edwards's essays, "Natural Philosophy," may be appropriated to interpret Edwards's viewpoint in these three essays. Anderson observes that such passages in Edwards are not simply Christianizing science, "in the manner of Cotton Mather's *The Christian Philosopher.* Nor are they expressions of occasional and tangential spasms of religious piety. Edwards rather views the whole course of natural causes, as the scientist investigates them, in a theological setting."[9]

7. Anderson, editor's introduction to *Scientific and Philosophical Writings*, 46–47.
8. *Scientific and Philosophical Writings*, 304–7.
9. Anderson, editor's introduction to *Scientific and Philosophical Writings*, 49.

Edwards articulates his own conversion along the lines of this vision motif, as he recalls, "The appearance of everything was altered: there seemed to be, as it were, a calm, sweet cast, or appearance of divine glory in everything."[10] Edwards saw the same Connecticut River Valley before and after his conversion, yet there was a profound difference in his vision. This reinforces the perspective offered on Edwards's view of knowledge in chapter 2 above, and, once again, stresses the covenantal context. The object of one's knowledge or vision is the same for regenerate and unregenerate alike. The subject's relationship to the object, or one's perception of it, however, is quite different. This dynamic of continuity and discontinuity serves well in the formulation of Edwards's apologetic, for it both enables one to appeal to the beauty and wisdom that are evident in the world and also requires the Holy Spirit to affect the perception of the divine glory that inheres in the world.

One could argue that, for Edwards, the new sense does not assert a new metaphysical reality. Rather, the new sense enables a new relationship to, and gives a new perspective on, the reality that always has been present, but just not perceived. The new sense is a new way of seeing the world. In his literary strategy, sight functions as both a metonymy for sense (and vice versa) and a synecdoche for the other senses. Thus, Edwards, under the influence of Newton, elevates sight to a prominent role.

By drawing attention to Newton's influence on Edwards, Perry Miller points the way to exploring this aspect of the context of the new sense in Edwards. Miller, as mentioned above, also draws attention to Locke. But leaving the discussion at Newton, or, for that matter, at Locke, falls short of grasping the full context of the new sense and thus slights one's understanding of it. In other words, because Miller's data are too selective, his conclusions are problematic.

John E. Smith surveys the reading of Edwards that lies behind *Religious Affections*, the salient published work addressing the new sense.

---

10. "Personal Narrative," in *The Works of Jonathan Edwards*, vol. 16, *Letters and Personal Writings*, ed. George S. Claghorn (New Haven: Yale University Press, 1998), 793–94.

For the most part, his catalogue consists of seventeenth- and eighteenth-century Puritans and Nonconformists. The Cambridge Platonist John Smith also makes the list. John E. Smith observes, "Of very great interest is Smith's idea—expressed in the first discourse, 'The True Way or Method of Obtaining Divine Knowledge'—of a *spiritual sensation* by means of which the truths of religion are apprehended." Smith then notes, "Smith's inclusion of the element of 'sensation' in his doctrine of immediate knowledge is strikingly similar to the idea expressed by Edwards, and at the same time different from the position held by other illumination-type rationalists whose 'light' excluded the sensory element."[11] Edwards then employs the new sense in an apologetic fashion, following John Smith, against deistic notions of spiritual knowledge. This provides another key element in the context of the new sense in Edwards.

Miller's overstatement of the influence of Locke and particularly Newton on Edwards further complicates his thesis. Conrad Cherry was the first to advance this criticism against Miller's thesis. Cherry faults Miller for reading too much between the lines when it comes to their influence on Edwards. Perhaps most troubling for Miller's thesis is Cherry's observation that Miller subverts the essence of Edwards's understanding of the new sense. Cherry cites the following from Miller: "By maintaining a sharp distinction between 'mere notional understanding' and the sense of the heart, Edwards fully intended to subordinate understanding to feeling." Miller thus opens the door to interpreting Edwards as a mystic, as one who pitted the head against the heart, and as a forerunner to the anti-intellectual tradition. Cherry notes that "Edwards is always eager to avoid" such a subordination. He argues that "the sense of the heart is, in its very essence, an act of judgment, not an unconscious state of feeling."[12]

11. Editor's introduction to *The Works of Jonathan Edwards*, vol. 2, *Religious Affections*, ed. John E. Smith (New Haven: Yale University Press, 1959), 66. Smith refers to *Select Discourses by John Smith*, ed. Worthington (London, 1660). He further observes that "one of the longest single extracts quoted in the *Affections*" comes from Smith's *Discourses*.

12. Conrad Cherry, *The Theology of Jonathan Edwards: A Reappraisal* (Bloomington: Indiana University Press, 1990), 22–23.

The new sense is not simply an emotional reaction. Rather, according to Cherry, it is the overpowering of the self by the divine reality. This, as argued in chapter 2 above, may be better nuanced by noting that Edwards, by focusing on the affections, intended to bring together two things that were typically sundered, namely, the intellect or understanding and the will or heart. Instead of compartmentalizing human psychology, Edwards unifies it.[13] Cherry's main contribution here, however, is that he shifts the focus of the new sense away from anthropocentric concerns to its divine origins, a crucial element overlooked by Miller.

William Wainwright offers another serious criticism of Miller. It may be recalled that Miller represents Edwards as holding that "truth is in the seeing, not in the thing."[14] With this statement, Miller makes perception the arbiter of truth, which results in a subjective reading of the new sense. Wainwright counters by arguing that, according to Edwards, the idea of truth—defined as beauty, harmony, and consent in *The Nature of True Virtue*—inheres in the *thing* itself. Edwards "repudiates the suggestion that 'the idea we obtain by this spiritual sense could in no respect be said to be a knowledge or perception of anything besides what was in our own minds,' or that it is, 'no representation of anything without.'" Beauty and truth are both an "objective property of the things that have it."[15] He avoids Miller's selective approach and makes both *perception* and the *thing* important, thus avoiding a subjective reading of the new sense.

Roland Delattre puts forward a view that is similar to Wainwright's when he says that the concepts of beauty and sensibility are crucial

13. Eugene E. White documents what he terms the compartmentalization of the faculties bequeathed by the English Puritans to the Colonials in his *Puritan Rhetoric: The Issue of Emotion in Religion* (Carbondale: Southern Illinois University Press, 1972), esp. pp. 6–23. He observes that the interplay between the intellect and the will resulted in the development of the various models of conversion offered by the Puritans. This, he argues, lurked behind the controversy surrounding the Awakenings in the 1730s and 1740s and occupied Edwards's thoughts in his treatises on revival.

14. Miller, *Jonathan Edwards*, 330.

15. William Wainwright, "Jonathan Edwards and the Sense of the Heart," *Faith and Philosophy* 7 (1990): 46. Wainwright's quotations are from *The Nature of True Virtue*.

to understanding Edwards. He notes that beauty is not a type of escape or refuge for the personal and internal, "but a platform, and out of his [Edwards'] encounter with beauty he tries to move toward theological, philosophical, and moral clarity." Delattre then distinguishes between natural sensibility and spiritual sensibility, the latter, of course, being the new sense. He concludes, "Taken together, beauty and sensibility may be said to be the objective and subjective components of the moral or spiritual life. They must be taken and considered together, for they are essentially and internally related."[16] In other words, one distorts Edwards's view of perception or of the new sense when one views it in abstraction.

The work of Wainwright, Cherry, and Delattre paves the way for focusing on the theological context of the new sense. Terrence Erdt, following this path, argues that Edwards's understanding of the new sense is informed by Calvin's *sensus suavitatis*, which he develops in his discussion of faith in the *Institutes*. Erdt sets up his discussion by quoting the following from Calvin: "Indeed the Word of God is like the sun, shining upon all those to whom it is proclaimed, but with no effect among the blind. Now, all of us are blind by nature in this respect." The natural mind, in other words, is unable to see what is really there. Calvin then adds, "Accordingly, it cannot penetrate into our minds unless the Spirit, as the inner teacher, through his illumination makes entry for it."[17]

Calvin refers to this ability to see as a sense of sweetness or the *sensus suavitatis*.[18] Erdt continues by noting that the Holy Spirit enables this sense or perception: "The perception is the taste of a divine quality, 'the sure experience of godliness,' a 'practical knowledge [*practica notitia*] . . . doubtless more certain and firmer than any idle speculation' (I.xiii.13–14)." Edwards follows Calvin in asserting the existence of speculative knowledge, known naturally by

16. Roland Andre Delattre, *Beauty and Sensibility in the Thought of Jonathan Edwards: An Essay in Aesthetics and Theological Ethics* (New Haven: Yale University Press, 1968), 3.

17. John Calvin, *Institutes of the Christian Religion*, 2 vols., trans. Ford Lewis Battles, ed. John T. McNeill (Philadelphia: Westminster Press, 1960), 3.2.34.

18. Ibid., 3.2.15.

the senses, and spiritual knowledge, perceived only by the new sense, or, as Calvin terms it, the sense of sweetness. This also relates to Calvin's concept of spiritual knowledge. According to his doctrine of depravity, unregenerate humanity is unable to sense goodness, moral beauty, or spiritual knowledge. Hence, grace is necessary to change the disposition. Erdt concludes, "Just as Calvin found the *sensus suavitatis* to constitute knowledge beyond all the saints to fathom, Edwards proclaimed that 'it opens a new world to its view.'"[19] Erdt goes on to note that Edwards's fondness for the terms *heart, relish, taste,* and *sweetness* may be traced directly to Calvin.

As we have seen, John E. Smith brings Puritan writers to our attention as part of the context in which to understand Edwards's view of the new sense.[20] Jerald Brauer surveys the variegated forms of what he terms Puritan piety. Prior to his work, interpreters tended to view Puritan piety as a homogeneous entity, missing the diverse elements within it.[21] Recently, following Brauer's lead, Janice Knight has argued that reading Puritanism in its diversity helps us to understand Edwards's piety and the new sense. Edwards, she concludes, "articulated his theology at the intersection of a number of competing discourses."[22] The competing discourses reduce to two major factions: the Amesian preparationists, including such figures as William Perkins, Thomas Hooker, and Thomas Shepherd, and the Sibbesian consummationists, including John Owen, Thomas Goodwin, and John Cotton. Both lines influenced Edwards. In his *Medulla theologicae,* Ames argues that conversion consists of the outward call of the gospel, appealing mainly to the intellect, and the inward offer, which is "a kind of spiritual enlightenment, whereby the promises are presented to the hearts of men." Grace effects the passive reception of this offer by the will, as it is "the conversion of the

---

19. Terrence Erdt, *Jonathan Edwards: Art and the Sense of the Heart* (Amherst: University of Massachusetts Press, 1980), 11, 32.

20. Smith, editor's introduction to *Religious Affections*, 52–72.

21. Jerald C. Brauer, "Types of Puritan Piety," *Church History* 56 (1987): 39–58.

22. Janice Knight, *Orthodoxies in Massachusetts: Rereading American Puritanism* (Cambridge, Mass.: Harvard University Press, 1994), 211.

will [that] is the effectual principle in the conversion of the whole man."[23] Edwards follows Ames to a certain extent, as Ames's distinction between outward and inward calling is similar to Edwards's distinction between notional and spiritual knowledge. Edwards, however, as mentioned above, repudiates the separation of the will or heart from the intellect.

Here the influence of John Owen, one of the Sibbesians, comes into play. Owen's *Pneumatologia* profoundly influenced Edwards's *Religious Affections*.[24] Owen notes that the natural faculties are suitable for the outward call, as Ames terms it, or the preaching of the gospel. Yet the natural faculties cannot receive spiritual truth, Ames's inward offer, due to a natural impotency, which pollutes the intellect, and a moral impotency, which pollutes the will and the affections. Therefore, one *"cannot"* and *"will not"* receive spiritual things. Thus, he argues for "the *indispensable necessity* of a saving work of illumination on the mind to enable it to receive spiritual things spiritually."[25] Edwards's discussion of the will, the intellect, and the affections in *Religious Affections* may be traced directly back to Owen.

Further, one must consider the biblical context that lies behind both Edwards's Puritan sources and his own reflections. Throughout Scripture, sight and vision serve as metaphors for one's spiritual condition. Two New Testament texts illustrate this well, namely, the healing of the blind men in Matthew 20 and Paul's conversion narrative in Acts 9. In Matthew 20, Jesus heals two blind men on his way to his triumphant entry into Jerusalem (Matt. 21), indicating that the Jews are in a spiritually blind state, needing to have their eyes opened so that they might follow him (Matt. 20:34). And in

23. William Ames, *The Marrow of Theology*, trans. John Eusden (Grand Rapids: Baker, 1997), 158–59.

24. See Smith, editor's introduction to *Religious Affections*, 68–69. Smith notes that "in JE's 'Catologue' there is the following entry: 'Dr. Owen's [*Discourse on the Holy Spirit*] recommended by Mr. Halyburton to the young students of divinity in the University of St. Andrews above all human writings for a true view of the mystery of the gospel' (p. 3, col. 2)" (p. 69).

25. John Owen, *The Works of John Owen*, 16 vols., ed. William H. Goold (1850–53; reprint, Edinburgh: Banner of Truth, 1965–68), 3:266, 275 (emphasis original).

Paul's conversion in Acts 9, his vision of God is so intense that he loses his natural power of sight. But when Paul receives the Holy Spirit, the scales immediately fall from his eyes (Acts 9:19). Thus, his natural blindness depicts his spiritual blindness, and the recovery of his natural sight illustrates his receiving of spiritual sight.

Beyond these texts, numerous metaphorical references to blindness and sight fill the pages of Scripture, illustrating the idea that until the appropriation of the new sense, one cannot see spiritual realities. Edwards himself makes this observation in "Miscellanies," no. 123, "Spiritual Sight." Here he argues that vision exemplifies spiritual understanding, noting, "Hence we learn the reason, why regeneration is so often compared to opening the eyes of the mind, to calling out of darkness into marvelous light, enlightening the dark understanding, etc."[26] His sermons, the "Miscellanies," and the "Notes on the Bible" reflect his debt to this biblical material in the formation of his ideas. The sermon "A Divine and Supernatural Light" stands as a salient example.

This survey of the influence on Edwards from John Locke to the apostle Paul indicates the wide context out of which Edwards constructed his concept of the new sense. The juxtaposition of the theological context with the philosophical context is not intended to set one against the other. Rather, they are to be read in tandem. The full context reveals the full range of Edwards's intentions. Thus, he stresses divine agency, affirms both continuity and discontinuity between the regenerate and the unregenerate natural faculties, nuances the relationship between general and special revelation, and asserts a unified psychology of the self. In reference to divine agency, he puts forward the necessity of the work of the Spirit, or, as Calvin expresses it, "his [the Holy Spirit's] power alone thrives here."[27] The doctrines of regeneration and illumination delineate this work.

26. *The Works of Jonathan Edwards*, vol. 13, *The "Miscellanies," Entry Nos. a–z, aa–zz, 1–500*, ed. Thomas A. Schafer (New Haven: Yale University Press, 1994), 287.
27. Calvin, *Institutes*, 3.2.34.

THE NEW SENSE IN EDWARDS'S WRITINGS

There is a certain continuity between the faculties of the unregenerate and those of the regenerate, to the extent that the new sense entails the understanding and the will. Yet Edwards also asserts a discontinuity in that the new sense belongs exclusively to the regenerate. It alone enables the proper use of the intellect and the will. Further, the new sense stresses what can be properly known about God through Scripture and through creation. Following Calvin, Edwards affirms that the former must precede the latter if creation is to be read accurately. Finally, the new sense does not reflect a compartmentalized view of the head and the heart. Rather, the new sense brings the two together. In his "Miscellanies," *Religious Affections*, and "Personal Narrative," Edwards demonstrates each of these points.

The early entries in the "Miscellanies" prefigure Edwards's mature thought on the new sense, as found in *Religious Affections*. In entry no. 123, Edwards defines spiritual sight or understanding (later to be termed "the new sense") aesthetically, as spiritual sight results in a "certain sweet motion of the mind that I call benevolence," which delights in the harmony and proportion of ideas.[28] The natural person is destitute of such ideas, and one realizes them only when the disposition of one's mind is changed. Edwards pursues this theme in entry no. 141. In this rather short entry, he continues the theme of harmony, noting that spiritual understanding, like "a musical ear," distinguishes the harmonious from the unharmonious. He also notes that "the unsanctified mind is not capable of" such perceptions.[29] Schafer observes that the essence of these two entries is captured in the doctrine of the sermon "A Spiritual Understanding of Divine Things."[30] The

28. *The "Miscellanies," Entry Nos. a–z, aa–zz, 1–500*, 286. Edwards develops this theme in "The Nature of True Virtue," in *The Works of Jonathan Edwards*, vol. 8, *Ethical Writings*, ed. Paul Ramsey (New Haven: Yale University Press, 1989), esp. pp. 539–49. Entry no. 123, according to Thomas Schafer, dates between September 1724 and June 1725.

29. *The "Miscellanies," Entry Nos. a–z, aa–zz, 1–500*, 297–98. Entry no. 141, according to Schafer, dates between September 1724 and June 1725.

30. See Schafer, editor's introduction to *The "Miscellanies," Entry Nos. a–z, aa–zz, 1–500*, 49–50.

doctrine is, "There is a spiritual understanding of divine things, which all natural and unregenerate men are destitute of."[31]

Edwards also connects spiritual understanding to the new sense in entry no. 782. He begins this lengthy entry by distinguishing within human knowledge between what is speculative and what is sensible. The latter involves apprehension, and is a function of the heart and will. Edwards then divides sensible knowledge into that which is obtained naturally and that which is obtained spiritually. Edwards argues that certain spiritual things are agreeable to human nature. "Persons are capable of sensible knowledge of things of religion," he says, "of themselves." However, he quickly adds, "But yet by reason of the natural stupidity of the soul . . . men will never attain any very considerable sense of them without the influence of the Spirit of God assisting the natural faculties of human nature and impressing a lively sense of them." This, Edwards explains, is a work of the Spirit within the natural or unregenerate person that impresses upon him "the force of natural arguments," and in it "consists the whole of the common work of the Spirit of God in man." Given the deficiency of this natural sensible knowledge, it requires the work of the Spirit.

Edwards now proceeds to define spiritual sensible knowledge, or that which is known by the new sense. He states, "The spiritual work of the Spirit of God, or that which is peculiar to the saints, consists in giving the sensible knowledge of the things of religion with respect to their spiritual good or evil, which indeed does all originally consist in a sense of the spiritual excellency, beauty, or sweetness of divine things." Hence, the new sense is "an ideal and sensible apprehension of the spiritual excellency of divine things." Add to this the notion that it is a work of the Spirit, and that it "does depend on and presuppose those things that are natural in religion [natural sensible knowledge] . . . as this may be needful to prepare the mind for a sense of its spiritual excellency."[32]

---

31. *The Works of Jonathan Edwards*, vol. 14, *Sermons and Discourses, 1723–1729*, ed. Kenneth P. Minkema (New Haven: Yale University Press, 1997), 72.

32. "Miscellanies," no. 782, in *The Philosophy of Jonathan Edwards from His Private Notebooks*, ed. Harvey G. Townsend (Eugene: University of Oregon Monographs, 1955), 122–25.

Edwards reveals his mature thought on these ideas in *Religious Affections*. Specifically, the fourth sign of genuine religious affections explicates his doctrine of the new sense. Edwards vividly notes that "holy affections are not heat without light." In other words, Edwards eschews enthusiasm as the essence of the new sense. Instead, holy affections "arise from some information of the understanding, some spiritual instruction that the mind receives, some light or actual knowledge." But, as he teaches elsewhere, such understanding or apprehending of spiritual things is "peculiar to the saints." He then offers his definitive understanding of the new sense:

> We come necessarily to this conclusion, concerning that wherein spiritual understanding consists; viz. that it consists in a sense of the heart, of the supreme beauty and sweetness of the holiness or moral perfection of divine things, together with all that discerning and knowledge of things of religion, that depends upon, and flows from such a sense. Spiritual understanding consists primarily in a sense of heart of that spiritual beauty.

He goes on to explain what he means by "sense": "I say, a sense of heart; for it is not speculation [intellect] merely that is concerned in this kind of understanding: nor can there be a clear distinction made between the two faculties of understanding and will." The new sense not only knows and beholds, but also relishes and delights. And, as elsewhere, Edwards here also affirms that the new sense is supernaturally implanted as a work of the Spirit. Edwards further likens the new sense to sight—and to yet another sense, *taste*. This spiritual taste, or holy disposition, develops within the regenerate as a habit of the mind, "which will teach and guide a man in his actions"—which is to say, one is led by the Spirit.[33]

Edwards applies this paradigm to his own conversion, which he conveys in his "Personal Narrative." He defines his conversion as a new disposition, or the "new sense of things." After his conversion, he notes, "the appearance of everything was altered," and he could see

---

33. *Religious Affections*, 266, 270, 272, 281, 283.

the "appearance of divine glory" in everything. He also contrasts his experiences after his conversion to those prior. He notes, "They were of a more inward, pure, soul-animating and refreshing nature. Those former delights, never reached the heart; and did not arise from any sight of the divine excellency of the things of God." He likens the new sense both to sight and to taste. He exclaims that the former delights did not have "any taste of the soul-satisfying, and life-giving good, there is in them."[34] Calvin illustrates conversion by combining these two senses: "And man's understanding, thus beamed by the light of the Holy Spirit, then at last truly begins to taste those things which belong to the kingdom of God, having formerly been quite foolish and dull in tasting them."[35]

Sight, however, receives prominence in Edwards's narrative, and as he develops this sense, he uses it to unite general revelation and Scripture. Again, this is similar to Calvin in that it reflects Calvin's notion that Scripture provides the spectacles for one to see, and hence to read, nature aright.[36] Despite his reading of Edwards's narrative as an untrustworthy account, Holbrook draws attention to the formative nature of the Connecticut River Valley on Edwards's thought. Just as Anderson notes that Edwards's scientific forays were put in a theological context, so Holbrook notes that Edwards took impressions from nature—from the sky, trees, fields, water, etc., all of which he recounts in the "Personal Narrative"—and "interpreted the impressions for these realities in theological terms." Edwards, Holbrook goes on to demonstrate, further plumbs what spiritual realities can be seen in nature through his extensive use of typology. "Newton's world," quips Holbrook, "was looked on with a regenerate eye."[37]

34. *Letters and Personal Writings,* 793–95.

35. Calvin, *Institutes,* 3.2.34.

36. Calvin refers to Scripture as spectacles in *Institutes,* 1.6.1. He draws upon the image throughout his discussion of the relationship of Scripture to a proper knowledge of God (see 1.10.1., 1.14.1).

37. Clyde Holbrook, *Jonathan Edwards, The Valley and Nature: An Interpretative Essay* (Lewisburg, Pa.: Bucknell University Press, 1987), 33, 75.

The New Sense and Regeneration
and Illumination

The new sense, first and foremost, is a work of the Holy Spirit. As such, it corresponds to regeneration and illumination. These doctrines were crucial to the overall theology of the Reformation. Calvin, Luther, and Zwingli all emphasized this aspect of the Spirit's work. In his essay on hermeneutics delivered to the Convent at Oetenbach in 1522, Zwingli introduced the notion that one must be *"theodidacti,* that is taught of God," in order to understand spiritual things. For Zwingli, to be taught of God means to be taught by the Holy Spirit. The Spirit must illuminate Scripture if it is to be understood correctly, or if it is to be taken as the word of God. As Zwingli rhetorically states, "Even if you hear the gospel of Jesus Christ from an apostle, you cannot act upon it unless the heavenly Father teach and draw you by the Spirit. The words are clear; enlightenment, instruction and assurance are by divine teaching without any intervention on the part of that which is human."[38]

The doctrine of illumination was also central to Luther, who treated it more extensively than Zwingli. A corollary to Luther's central principle of *sola Scriptura* is the notion of the perspicuity of the Word of God, or *claritas Scripturae.* In his *Bondage of the Will,* Luther replies to Erasmus's contention that the Scriptures are not clear. He notes that such a claim was spread by the Sophists and by Satan, who "used these unsubstantial spectres to scare men off reading the sacred text, and to destroy all sense of its value, so as to ensure that his own brand of poisonous philosophy reigns supreme in the church." Luther does acknowledge that there are obstacles that sometimes make it difficult to understand the Scriptures. He summarizes them as "our own linguistic and grammatical ignorance" and (because of human depravity) our "own blindness and dullness." These things impede what he terms the internal

---

38. Ulrich Zwingli, "On the Clarity and Certainty of the Word of God," in *Zwingli and Bullinger,* ed. G. W. Bromiley (Philadelphia: Westminster Press, 1953), 89, 82. See also W. P. Stephens, *Zwingli: An Introduction to His Thought* (Oxford: Oxford University Press, 1992), 30–36.

perspicuity of Scripture. He writes, "If you speak of *internal* perspicuity, the truth is that nobody who has not the Spirit of God sees a jot of what is in the Scriptures." He continues, "The Spirit is needed for the understanding of all Scripture and every part of Scripture."[39] Thus, Luther emphasizes the necessity of the Holy Spirit's illumination.

With regard to Calvin, Jaroslav Pelikan notes, "It has been observed that 'in reading Calvin one may soon come to think that his favorite descriptive word for the Spirit is "Teacher." ' "[40] In his commentary on John, Calvin observes that "Christ gives the Spirit another title—that He is the Teacher of truth (*magister veritatis*). From this it follows that until we have been inwardly taught by Him all our minds are held by vanity and falsehood." Without the Spirit, Christ "is unknown and incomprehensible."[41] Similarly, he comments on 1 Corinthians 2:1–11, "Having concluded that all men are blind, and having deprived the human mind of the power to rise up to knowledge of God, Paul now shows how the faithful are delivered from this blindness, viz., by the Lord honouring them with a special enlightenment of the Spirit."[42] Finally, in his commentary on Ephesians he observes, "Until we have been taught by the Spirit our master, all that we know is folly and ignorance. Until the Spirit of God has made it known to us by a secret revelation, the knowledge of our divine calling exceeds the grasp of our minds."[43]

39. Martin Luther, *The Bondage of the Will*, trans. J. I. Packer and O. R. Johnston (Westwood, N.J.: Revell, 1957), 71–74.

40. Jaroslav Pelikan, *The Christian Tradition*, vol. 4, *Reformation of Church and Dogma (1300–1700)* (Chicago: University of Chicago Press, 1983), 187. He quotes H. Jackson Forstman, *Word and Spirit: Calvin's Doctrine of Biblical Authority* (Stanford: Stanford University Press, 1962), 75.

41. John Calvin, *The Gospel According to Saint John 11–21 and the First Epistle of John*, trans. T. H. L. Parker, ed. D. W. Torrance and T. F. Torrance (Grand Rapids: Eerdmans, 1961), 82–83.

42. John Calvin, *The First Epistle of Paul the Apostle to the Corinthians*, trans. John W. Fraser, ed. D. W. Torrance and T. F. Torrance (Grand Rapids: Eerdmans, 1960), 57.

43. John Calvin, *The Epistle of Paul the Apostle to the Galatians, Ephesians, Philippians and Colossians*, trans. T. H. L. Parker, ed. D. W. Torrance and T. F. Torrance (Grand Rapids: Eerdmans, 1965), 134.

Similar remarks may be found in Calvin's *Institutes*. He writes, "The same Spirit, therefore, who has spoken through the mouths of the prophets must penetrate into our hearts to persuade us that they faithfully proclaimed what had been divinely commanded." Then he adds, "Until he illumines their minds, they ever waver among many doubts."[44] Calvin also refers to Augustine as sharing a similar view: "But Augustine so recognizes this inability of the reason to understand the things of God that he deems the grace of illumination no less necessary for our minds than the light of the sun for our eyes."[45]

Two main ideas are evident in Calvin's view of illumination. First, the illumination of the Holy Spirit is necessary to convict one of the truth of the gospel and of one's need for it. Second, the Holy Spirit has the ongoing ministry of confirming the truth of the gospel to believers. Calvin understands the Spirit's role of illumination in accordance with his soteriology, which emphasizes the total depravity of mankind and thus the need for divine action to turn people to God. Illumination reflects the doctrine of regeneration and vice versa. Calvin, as the systematizer of the Reformation, brings the idea of illumination to its clearest expression.

In order for the illumination of the Holy Spirit to work efficaciously, two things are necessary. First, there must be the Word, or the revelation, to be illumined. Second, there must be the regenerated person to receive the illumination. Calvin writes, "It will not be enough for the mind to be illumined by the Spirit of God unless the heart is also strengthened and supported by his power."[46] Because the entire person is corrupted by sin, the whole individual needs to be renewed by the Spirit. As sin mortifies, regeneration vivifies. Calvin also argues that regeneration not only involves conversion, but brings into its purview the life that follows. Regeneration produces the desire "to live in a holy and devoted manner," and enables one to "begin to live to God."[47]

44. Calvin, *Institutes*, 1.7.4.
45. Ibid., 2.2.25.
46. Ibid., 3.2.33.
47. Ibid., 3.3.3.

Calvin, Edward Dowey argues, uses illumination as the term to "describe in general the inner work of the Spirit."[48] Thus, illumination reflects regeneration.

It should also be noted that illumination is not viewed in the Reformed tradition as imparting any secret or new revelation. As Calvin writes, "The Spirit, promised to us, has not the task of inventing new and unheard of revelations, or of forging a new kind of doctrine, to lead us away from the received doctrine of the gospel, but of sealing our minds with that very doctrine that is commended by the gospel."[49] Edwards concurs: "This spiritual light is not the suggesting of any new truths, or propositions not contained in the Word of God." That, Edwards notes, is the function of inspiration; instead, illumination "gives a due apprehension of those things that are taught in the Word of God."[50]

John Owen represents the Puritan reflections on illumination and regeneration which, along with the reflections of the Reformers, influenced Edwards's thought. In his *Pneumatologia*, Owen defines regeneration as "a new, spiritual, supernatural, vital principle or habit of grace, infused into the soul, the mind, will, and affections, by the power of the Holy Spirit, disposing and enabling them in whom it is unto spiritual, supernatural, vital acts of faith and obedience."[51] Here he establishes that regeneration affects the whole person, that it is a work of the Holy Spirit, and that it results in sanctified living. He also refers to regeneration as both a moral suasion, since it involves conviction of truth, and a physical operation, since it involves the transformation of the individual.[52]

This transformation extends to the entire individual—mind, heart, and affections. Thus, the Holy Spirit operates on these faculties of

48. Edward A. Dowey Jr., *The Knowledge of God in Calvin's Theology,* 3d ed. (Grand Rapids: Eerdmans, 1994), 175.

49. Calvin, *Institutes,* 1.9.1.

50. Jonathan Edwards, "A Divine and Supernatural Light," in *A Jonathan Edwards Reader,* ed. John E. Smith, Harry S. Stout, and Kenneth P. Minkema (New Haven: Yale University Press, 1995), 110.

51. *Works of John Owen,* ed. Goold, 3:329.

52. Ibid., 316.

the soul. The will is principally dead in sin, necessitating its vivifi-
cation. The natural mind is blind, so there must be the opening of
our eyes and the communication of *"light* unto our minds." Here,
Owen's doctrine of regeneration looks similar to the doctrine of illumination. In fact, earlier, though still in reference to regeneration,
Owen distinguishes the work of the Spirit at conversion from the
work of the Spirit in inspiration. The Spirit's work of producing "immediate influence and impression" on the mind should be distinguished from the "prophetical inspirations of old." Illumination is
more likely to be confused with inspiration than with regeneration.
Yet, Owen so formulates his doctrine of regeneration as to bring out
its connection to illumination. Finally, similar to Calvin, Owen
teaches that regeneration starts a work that continues in one's life
to God. Owen concludes his discussion of regeneration by noting
that the power received in regeneration proceeds in "sanctification
and holiness."[53]

THE NEW SENSE AND APOLOGETICS

Edwards's doctrines of regeneration and illumination play a crucial role in his treatment of apologetics and epistemology. In a manuscript entitled "Concerning Efficacious Grace," Edwards begins by
observing, "If ever men are turned from sin, God must undertake
it; that it is his doing that must determine the matter; that all that
others can do, will avail nothing, without his agency."[54] The work
of God in effecting regeneration is undertaken by the Holy Spirit
and results in the one converted partaking of the divine nature
(2 Peter 1:4).[55] In *Original Sin,* Edwards observes that the "change
of state" that is necessary in regeneration demonstrates the extent
of human depravity resulting from the Fall. Regeneration "signifies

53. Ibid., 333, 318–19, 336 (emphasis original).
54. "Concerning Efficacious Grace," in *The Works of Jonathan Edwards,* 2 vols., ed. Edward Hickman (1834; reprint, Edinburgh: Banner of Truth, 1974), 2:543.
55. Ibid., 2:543, 564. Edwards writes in "Miscellanies," no. 396, that "this Holy Spirit of
God, is that divine nature spoken of, II Pet. 1:4, that we are made partakers of through the
gospel" (*The "Miscellanies," Entry Nos. a–z, aa–zz, 1–500,* 462).

a change of the mind," turning it from sin to God and true virtue, so that "men come to have the character of true Christians." Regeneration involves not just the new birth, but "a resurrection to a new divine life."[56] Edwards defines illumination in his "Miscellanies" specifically as "that spiritual light that is let into the soul by the Spirit of God discovering the excellency and glory of divine things."[57] In this way, the Holy Spirit "helps us to receive the revelation in the word."[58] And Edwards states, "There is none that teaches like God."[59] But Edwards does not always keep regeneration and illumination distinct. In the entry quoted above, he goes on to note that while illumination "directly evidences the truth of religion to the mind," it also "sanctifies the reasoning faculty and assists it to see the clear evidence there is of the truth of religion in rational arguments." It accomplishes the latter "two ways, viz., as it removes prejudices and so lays the mind more open to the force of the arguments, and also secondly, as it positively enlightens and assists it to see the force of rational arguments."[60] John Gerstner, reflecting on the relationship of regeneration to illumination in the theology of Edwards, concludes that they are part of "Edwards' soteriological 'pre-established harmony.'"[61] So one expects to find fluid movement between the two doctrines. The regenerated and illuminated person, absent the natural prejudices against divine truth, sees and senses spiritual things.

Returning to "Concerning Efficacious Grace," we find that Edwards, having established that regeneration is a radical transforma-

---

56. *The Works of Jonathan Edwards,* vol. 3, *Original Sin,* ed. Clyde A. Holbrook (New Haven: Yale University Press, 1970), 361–63, 365.

57. "Miscellanies," no. 628, in *Philosophy of Jonathan Edwards from His Private Notebooks,* ed. Townsend, 251.

58. Unpublished sermon manuscript on Matthew 13:5–6, cited in John Gerstner, *The Rational Biblical Theology of Jonathan Edwards,* 3 vols. (Powhatan, Va.: Berea Publications, 1991–93), 1:186.

59. Unpublished sermon manuscript on Job 36:22, cited in Gerstner, *Rational Biblical Theology of Jonathan Edwards,* 188.

60. "Miscellanies," no. 628, in *Philosophy of Jonathan Edwards from His Private Notebooks,* ed. Townsend, 251.

61. Gerstner, *Rational Biblical Theology of Jonathan Edwards,* 3:168.

tion that involves partaking of the divine nature, goes on to distinguish the unregenerate from the regenerate by noting that without the indwelling Spirit, "a natural man has no degree of that relish and sense of spiritual things, or things of the spirit, and of their divine truth and excellency, which a godly man has."[62] In a later version of these thoughts, entitled "Treatise on Grace," he continues this approach by noting that "the sense of things of religion that a natural man has, is not only not to the same degree, but nothing of the same nature with that which a true saint has."[63] Edwards here employs the same language applied to the new sense. This is expressly the case in "A Divine and Supernatural Light." In this sermon, Edwards shifts easily from illumination to regeneration to the new sense. He discusses illumination, differentiating it from inspiration, and discusses regeneration, expressing how it transforms one's faculties.[64]

The divine light immediately given by God is illumination; the "indwelling vital principle" implanted by the Holy Spirit that enables one to receive the light is a result of regeneration. Both fall under the purview of the new sense. Edwards links illumination to the new sense when he writes, "He that is spiritually enlightened truly apprehends and sees it, or has a sense of it."[65] He links both regeneration and illumination to the new sense when he states, "Hence the work of the Spirit of God in regeneration is often in Scripture compared to the giving a new sense, giving eyes to see . . . opening the eyes of them that were born blind, and turning from darkness unto light."[66] So the new sense, according to Edwards, incorporates the doctrines of regeneration and illumination. In referring to regeneration and illumination as the new sense, Edwards is not entirely without precedent. Janice Knight speaks of "striking rhetorical and doctrinal similarities between Sibbes, Cotton, and

---

62. "Concerning Efficacious Grace," 2:564.

63. "Treatise on Grace," in *Selections from the Unpublished Writings of Jonathan Edwards*, ed. Alexander B. Grosart (Ligonier, Pa.: Soli Deo Gloria, 1992), 22.

64. "A Divine and Supernatural Light," 109–10.

65. Ibid., 108, 111.

66. *Religious Affections*, 206.

Edwards." She then cites selections from each to prove her point. She notes that Sibbes states, "There is [in the holy heart] a sweet relish in all divine truths . . . a spiritual taste, which the Spirit of God put into the soul of his children." Then she turns to Cotton, who speaks of finding "some sweet relish in the Ordinances [of Scripture]."[67]

At the heart of Edwards's understanding of illumination, following in the Puritan and Reformed tradition, is the view that the Spirit enlightens the mind and opens the eyes to the truth of revelation already given. Illumination especially enables one to see or apprehend the gospel. On the periphery, but present, is the notion that illumination is an ongoing experience in the saint's reading and understanding of revelation. The doctrine of illumination intersects with the doctrine of regeneration, which is the Spirit's work of revivifying one who is dead in sin. Regeneration transforms the individual in totality, making him a new creation, resulting in a new nature. In other words, regeneration involves a dispositional change. Illumination, properly speaking, is the light seen by the one who is able, through regeneration, to see.

The new sense encompasses both doctrines. Further, Edwards speaks of the new sense as a shorthand designation for all aspects of the Spirit's work in conversion, all aspects of change that are wrought at conversion, and all aspects of the new life that follow conversion. Understanding Edwards's theological heritage as well as his own doctrine of the new sense is crucial to understanding the role of the new sense in his apologetics.

The apologetic implications of the new sense are evident in the relationship of the new sense to nature. Conrad Cherry's work brings this out. In *Nature and Religious Imagination,* he returns to themes he introduced in his work on Edwards's theology. One such theme is the revelation of the beauty of nature. Cherry succinctly states Ed-

---

67. Knight, *Orthodoxies in Massachusetts,* 205–6. Her quotations are from *The Complete Works of Richard Sibbes,* 7 vols. (Edinburgh: James Nichol, 1862–64), 2:34, and John Cotton, *Christ the Foundation of Life* (London, 1651), 135.

wards's thesis in the *Two Dissertations:* "The world is beautiful to the extent that it reflects the beauty of human virtue, and human virtue is beautiful insofar as it reflects the benevolence of God. Such is the nature of things." But, Cherry notes, "sin has added a loud discordant note to the inner harmony of man and the outer regularity of the universe." Thus, conversion is necessary. The crucial evidence that conversion has occurred is that one apprehends spiritual knowledge, because that can only be the result of illumination, and that of course is tantamount to the new sense. Edwards, Cherry maintains, is always careful to insist upon the necessity of the work of the Spirit. He notes, "The illumination provided by God's Spirit strikes to the center of the human self and supplies a new foundation of knowing." The new sense provides "the vision of the whole self in a whole world," reflecting, quoting Edwards, "the symmetry and beauty in God's workmanship."[68]

The beauty, harmony, and excellence, however, are there in the world itself, and so Edwards can employ both nature and one's perception of it in his sermons and treatises to develop an apologetic for the reality of divine and spiritual truth. The wisdom of God, Edwards argues, is visible in "the contrivance of the world." The resultant vision, deriving from the new sense, reveals the reality that is present. Further, from the perspective of the new sense, Edwards can appeal to the apologetic import of general revelation. Employing the thought of Romans 1, the evidence of God in the "contrivance of the world" proves sufficient to condemn humanity.[69]

Since conversion is necessary to apprehend spiritual knowledge, one can almost say that one needs the new sense to understand the new sense. Thus, Edwards's notion of the new sense faces the problem of circularity. William Wainwright addresses this problem directly. He concludes, however, that Edwards escapes circularity: "Justifications of spiritual perception aren't circular in the sense that

68. Conrad Cherry, *Nature and Religious Imagination: From Edwards to Bushnell* (Philadelphia: Fortress Press, 1980), 54, 58, 62.
69. Jonathan Edwards, "Wisdom in the Contrivance of the World," in *Scientific and Philosophical Writings,* 307–10.

they employ premises which explicitly or implicitly assert that spiritual perceptions are reliable." This represents Edwards's position in *Religious Affections*. Wainwright adds, "Nor are they circular in the sense that they employ premises which can *in principle* only be known to be true by those who rely on their spiritual sense." Wainwright acknowledges that there is a causal connection between justification of belief and spiritual perceptions. Sin, he reasons, "blinds us to the [rational] evidence's force." Consequently, spiritual perception overtakes the inclination to discount the rational persuasion presented by the sheer force of creation and theistic metaphysics. Nevertheless, the "justificatory process itself" does not depend upon spiritual perceptions.[70] Rather, the justificatory process itself rests on the theistic metaphysics underlying the perception.

The new sense is a belief-producing mechanism, to be sure, but it is neither the source nor the justification of the belief. The new sense as an apologetic appeals not to itself, but to that which it enables one to see, as the warrant of its credibility. This way in which the new sense operates may be clarified by drawing an analogy to faith. John Murray's discussion of faith illustrates this well. He observes, "Faith is trust. Trust presupposes an object. An object evokes trust when there is an antecedent judgment of the mind that the object is trustworthy." He then cites B. B. Warfield, who adds, "The *saving power* of faith resides thus not in itself, but in the Almighty Saviour on whom it rests. . . . It is not faith that saves, but faith in Jesus Christ."[71] Understanding the new sense in this way avoids the problem of circularity and also reveals the proper place of the new sense in Edwards's apologetic.

The work of William P. Alston proves helpful in understanding Edwards's concept of the new sense. Alston argues that sense perception is a reliable source of true beliefs. "Any access we have to

70. Wainwright, "Jonathan Edwards and the Sense of the Heart," 56–57.
71. John Murray, "Faith," in *The Collected Writings of John Murray*, vol. 2, *Select Lectures in Systematic Theology* (Edinburgh: Banner of Truth, 1977), 237, 260. The citation is from Warfield's "The Biblical Doctrine of Faith," in *Biblical Doctrines* (New York: Oxford University Press, 1929), 504.

the physical world," he declares, "ultimately rests on sense perception." How could sense perception possibly be proved unreliable, since it is necessarily used to establish its own reliability or unreliability? In other words, he takes the circularity argument against sense perception and turns it around. He does so, not to prove that sense perception is perfectly reliable, but to prove that it is basically reliable. Further, he observes, "We find ourselves relying on the practices under investigation for the facts adduced in support of the reliability of those practices." He concludes by arguing for the "rationality of supposing sense perception to be reliable." He acknowledges, "It would be much more satisfying to produce a direct demonstration of the truth of the proposition that sense perception *is reliable.*"[72] But he cannot muster such an argument, nor does he think it is possible to do so. In the end, Alston can only posit, at best, probability. Nevertheless, he does establish what he calls the practical rationality of relying on sense perception. Edwards enhances this argument and safeguards the reliability of one's sense perception by arguing that the new sense is a work of God and does not leave the recognition of truth up to the individual alone. Thus, Edwards escapes the limitation of probability that plagues Alston's view.

Leon Chai further explores this angle by noting that the new sense transcends subjectivity, and, for that matter, circularity, by appealing to an external source of knowledge. Without such a source, "piety becomes purely subjective." Edwards's careful emphasis on an external source of knowledge in his discussion of the new sense "leads to a demonstrative certainty about points of religious doctrine." Contemporary Enlightenment philosophers shared his aspirations for certainty. In fact, the quest for certainty characterized much of the Enlightenment mood, from Descartes to Locke. Chai observes that Locke purported to find certainty in "intuitive knowledge." This does not satisfy Edwards, due to its subjectivity and neglect of the noetic

72. William P. Alston, *The Reliability of Sense Perception* (Ithaca, N.Y.: Cornell University Press, 1993), 13–15, 125, 133.

effects of sin. Instead, Edwards rests the certainty of religious truth upon experience. The irony here is that Locke's concept of sensation in the end is too internal. But for Edwards, as Chai notes, "sensation implies the existence of something external to the mind." And this knowledge "is essentially propositional in nature. It consists, we are told, of a new way of understanding Christian doctrine."[73]

By viewing the new sense as one's perception of spiritual reality, Edwards deals with the knotty relationship of subject to object. Unlike Locke and others entangled in this matter, Edwards does not rely on the individual's sense to navigate through it. Instead, he relies upon the Holy Spirit to effect the ability to perceive aright, and he relies upon theistic metaphysics, or the spiritual reality that is perceived.

Thoroughly immersed in his Puritan and Reformed background, Edwards approaches the Enlightenment's challenge to knowledge from the perspective of, and informed by, the biblical teaching on illumination, regeneration, and the new sense. Thus, he brings theology to bear upon philosophy and, in the process, makes a valuable contribution to the problem of knowledge. His contribution consists in his acknowledgment of the subject's involvement in the process of knowing. He does not posit a naïve neutrality on the part of the knower. The subject moves from a relationship of prejudiced hostility to spiritual knowledge to one of assent to it and trust in it. Further, Edwards stresses the role of revelation in the process of knowing. Finally, he emphasizes the necessity of the work of the Holy Spirit in enabling one to come to knowledge.

One further aspect of the relationship of the new sense to apologetics has to do with the nature of faith. The Reformers defined saving faith as entailing *notitia, assensus,* and *fiducia.*[74] Faith involves knowledge of the facts of the gospel (*notitia*), the assent of the will

73. Leon Chai, *Jonathan Edwards and the Limits of Enlightenment Philosophy* (Oxford: Oxford University Press, 1998), 35, 29, 33.

74. For a discussion of this in Calvin, see *Institutes,* 3.2. Regarding Calvin's view, see also Paul Helm, *Varieties of Belief* (London: George Allen & Unwin, 1973), 101–17. For a con-

(*assensus*), and profound trust (*fiducia*). Edwards describes the new sense in a way that not only presents a unified self, but also extricates faith from the horns of the false dilemma of the head versus the heart. The new sense serves apologetics by transcending this dilemma and demonstrating sensitivity to the complexities of faith. Edwards's conception of the new sense requires that there be propositional or notional content to one's faith. It further requires that there also be trust in this content. And this, Edwards argues, is brought about by the work of the Spirit.

CONCLUSION

While it may be inaccurate to assert that the new sense *is* Edwards's apologetic, the new sense is nevertheless a crucial part of it. Like his understanding of knowledge, his reflections on perception led him down many different paths. From Locke he appropriated the new sense as a simple idea, that is, as something known through the senses. For Edwards, the new sense is produced by God working through the senses. From Newton he learned to illustrate the new sense as a new way of seeing the world. And from the Cambridge Platonists he learned to utilize the new sense as a polemic against the deists. Yet, as Chai notes, Edwards was not mastered by his sources. Rather, he mastered them.[75] Edwards demonstrates this especially by bringing biblical teaching and his theological context to bear upon the philosophical problem of perception. Drawing especially upon Calvin and Owen, Edwards bases his understanding of perception upon the doctrines of regeneration and illumination, both of which he incorporates in his concept of the new sense. This gives the work of the Holy Spirit a prominent place in Edwards's apologetic.

---

temporary Reformed perspective on this view of faith as entailing *notitia, assensus,* and *fiducia,* see Robert L. Reymond, *A New Systematic Theology of the Christian Faith* (Nashville: Nelson, 1998), 726–29.

75. See Chai, *Jonathan Edwards and the Limits of Enlightenment Philosophy,* 22.

Having earlier examined Edwards's view of knowledge, in this chapter we have explored the ways in which one comes to perceive knowledge through the new sense. Edwards himself, however, acknowledges that affections can sometimes be misleading.[76] Thus, the stage is set for yet another provocative element of Edwards's apologetic, namely, the Spirit's work of assurance.

76. *Religious Affections*, 279.

4

ASSURANCE: EDWARDS
ON TESTIMONY (1)

The gospel of the blessed God do[es]n't go abroad a begging for its evidence, so much as
some think; it has its highest and most proper evidence in itself.

Jonathan Edwards, *Religious Affections*

Sometime in 1636, Thomas Shepherd asked John Cotton if a
Christian should find assurance of his conversion in the promises
contained in Scripture, or if he should wait for "a more full and
clearer Revelation of the spirit." Or, as he restated the matter,
"Whether this revelation of the spirit, is a thing beyond and above
the woord." Shepherd was not looking for advice in order to take
his position on this issue. He had already arrived at one, and in
the letter he let Cotton know that in his view "the spirit is not separated from the woord but in it and is ever according to it." Cotton, not entirely satisfied with Shepherd on this point, preferred
to nuance Shepherd's view. He replied, "Though I consent to you,
that the spirit is not separated from the word, but in it, and ever
according to it: yet above, and beyond the letter of the word it

reacheth forth comfort, and power to the soule, though not above the sence, and Intendment of the Word."[1]

This exchange marked the beginning of the Antinomian Controversy in the American colonies.[2] It also presents the issues pertaining to the doctrine of assurance, or the *internum testimonium Spiritus Sancti.* What is the relationship between the Spirit's internal witness and the Word? This chapter explores three main aspects of this question. First, Calvin's understanding of the *internum testimonium* provides the broad context and serves as a good starting point for understanding Edwards's contribution. Next, the revivals of the 1740s reveal the immediate context in which Edwards engages this issue. Finally, Edwards's own understanding of assurance is examined with a view to delineating the apologetic angle that Edwards brings to this doctrine.

Alvin Plantinga, appropriating Edwards's thought on assurance, regards this as one way in which Christian beliefs may be warranted. It may be recalled from chapter 3 that Edwards's understanding of the new sense, and hence of perception, emphasizes that God works through the senses, resulting in a new way of seeing his world and Word. In Plantinga's language, the new sense cures our epistemic capacities from sin's maleficence. Plantinga then explains the connection of the new sense to assurance. The Spirit enables one to see the beauty of the gospel, "whereupon she infers that they are in fact divine and hence to be believed."[3] The perception occasions the formulation of belief, but is itself not the warrant for the belief, as three other elements are put forth as warrant. First, there is the word, or the propositional truth of Scripture. Second, there is assurance.

1. "Thomas Shepherd to John Cotton," in *The Antinomian Controversy, 1636–1638: A Documentary History,* ed. David D. Hall, 2d ed. (Durham: Duke University Press, 1990), 25–26, 30 (spelling original).

2. For a synopsis of the Antinomian Controversy, see David D. Hall's introduction to *The Antinomian Controversy,* 3–23, and Samuel T. Logan, "Antinomian Controversy," in *Dictionary of Christianity in America,* ed. Daniel G. Reid et al. (Downers Grove, Ill.: InterVarsity Press, 1990), 69.

3. Alvin Plantinga, *Warranted Christian Belief* (Oxford: Oxford University Press, 2000), 305.

Third, there is faith itself. This chapter argues that Edwards utilizes assurance as the warrant for Christian belief, which places assurance at the center of his apologetic. *Assurance,* as used here, is *the internal witness of the Holy Spirit to the absolute certainty and objective truth of Christianity.* As perception is grounded in the reality of the thing perceived and not in the one perceiving, so assurance is not to be construed as a mystical or subjective exchange.

CALVIN'S DOCTRINE OF THE *INTERNUM TESTIMONIUM SPIRITUS SANCTI*

It will prove helpful here to look back at Calvin in order to see his influence on Edwards. Calvin ultimately grounds the authority, veracity, and warrant of Scripture in the witness of the Spirit, while at the same time using subordinate proofs and rational arguments. He states, "The testimony of the Spirit is more excellent than all reason. For as God alone is a fit witness of himself in his Word, so also the Word will not find acceptance in men's hearts before it is sealed by the inward testimony of the Spirit."[4] In the same section of the *Institutes,* Calvin also refers to the Spirit's testimony as "secret." As I. John Hesselink observes, Calvin "first developed this idea of the internal witness into a distinctive doctrine." Hesselink further interacts with the two criticisms of Calvin's view, namely, its circularity and its subjectivity. Hesselink admits that in one sense it is indeed circular. However, it also follows a biblical pattern of arguing for Scripture's authenticity and also, in the words of Karl Barth, is a "logical circle."[5] If one appeals to an external authority to establish the authority of Scripture, then one undermines the very authority that one endeavors to establish. Scripture, as Calvin concludes, must be self-authenticating.

4. John Calvin, *Institutes of the Christian Religion,* 2 vols., trans. Ford Lewis Battles, ed. John T. McNeill (Philadelphia: Westminster Press, 1960), 1.7.4.

5. I. John Hesselink, *Calvin's First Catechism, A Commentary* (Louisville: Westminster John Knox Press, 1997), 179, 182. The quotation of Barth is from his *Church Dogmatics,* I, 2 (Edinburgh: T. & T. Clark, 1956), 535.

Hesselink also interacts with the charge of subjectivism, based on Calvin's use of the terms "internal" and "secret." If abstracted, this teaching does lend itself to an existential or subjective interpretation of this work of the Spirit. Calvin, however, intends no such abstraction, for the Spirit testifies to an objective Scripture, not to an isolated, subjective experience. That is, Calvin's full teaching on this point is *Spiritus cum verbo* ("Spirit with the Word"). Hesselink argues that there is a connection between the internal testimony of the Spirit and the Spirit's witness to the divine origin of Scripture. He writes:

> Actually, there are four different facets to the one "testimony" of the Spirit: (1) the certainty of Scripture; (2) the certainty of salvation; (3) the certainty of our divine adoption; (4) the certainty of the divine authority of the Word, which offers the promise of adoption. Ultimately, however, there are not two or four distinct witnesses (*testimonia*) of the Spirit but one.[6]

Calvin does not intend for the *internum testimonium* to be abstracted; neither does he intend "internal" and "secret" to be interpreted as "mystical." To be sure, there is a subjective element in that the witness is to the individual. Yet this witness is linked both to the Spirit's witness to the authority of Scripture that is inherent because of its inspiration, and to the Spirit's witness to one's own appropriation of the truths of the gospel, or the assurance of faith. According to Calvin, the various aspects of the Spirit's witness are better viewed as parts that are necessarily linked to, and contribute to, the whole. Viewing the internal testimony of the Spirit in its full context enables one to gain a better understanding of how assurance functions, not only in Calvin, but also in the Reformed and Puritan tradition, and especially in Edwards.

Additionally, understanding the relationship of assurance to faith also proves beneficial. First, Calvin views faith as dispositional in character, not merely as intellectual. Faith is "more of the disposi-

6. Hesselink, *Calvin's First Catechism*, 183.

tion than of the understanding." He further says, "Now we shall possess a right definition of faith if we call it a firm and certain knowledge of God's benevolence towards us, founded upon the truth of the freely given promise in Christ, both revealed to our minds and sealed upon our hearts through the Holy Spirit." A number of elements here deserve attention. First, Calvin defines faith as knowledge and refers to the mind and mental activity. True to his understanding of spiritual knowledge, however, such knowledge is "more of the heart than of the brain."[7] Again, according to Calvin, faith is both intellectual and dispositional.

Further, Calvin identifies the grounds that establish such knowledge as firm and certain.[8] These grounds are, first, the objective truth of the promises contained in Scripture and, second, the testimony of the Spirit. Calvin draws attention to two specific functions of the Holy Spirit. First, the Spirit reveals the truth of the promises of Scripture to one's mind. Second, the Spirit seals such truths upon one's heart. T. H. L. Parker makes a crucial observation at this point, noting that it is not that one derives assurance from faith itself, but from the object of faith.[9]

It now remains to connect faith to assurance in Calvin's thought. Joel Beeke argues that, according to Calvin, faith "possesses assurance at its very nature. Assurance, certainty, trust—such is the essence of faith."[10] For example, Calvin connects faith and assurance in his commentary on 1 Corinthians 2:12, noting that this text is "abundantly clear" in its refutation of the Sophists who would

7. Calvin, *Institutes*, 3.2.8.

8. This accords with William Bouwsma's contention that to understand Calvin's theology, one must place Calvin against the background of the crisis of knowledge in the Renaissance. Calvin, Bouwsma observes, is concerned with the human capacity to have any certainty of knowledge in the process of establishing the certainty of one's knowledge of God ("Calvin and the Renaissance Crisis of Knowing," *Calvin Theological Journal* 17 [1982]: 190–211; see also David Steinmetz, *Calvin in Context* [Oxford: Oxford University Press, 1995], 23–39).

9. T. H. L. Parker, *Calvin: An Introduction to His Thought* (Louisville: Westminster John Knox Press, 1995), 82.

10. Joel Beeke, *The Quest for Full Assurance: The Legacy of Calvin and His Successors* (Edinburgh: Banner of Truth, 1999), 38.

deny any confidence in assurance, positing instead that one should be plagued by doubt. Calvin replies, "Here, however, the Apostle declares in general terms, that the elect have the Spirit given them, by whose testimony they are assured that they have been adopted to the hope of eternal salvation." He then adds, "Hence we may know the nature of faith to be this, that conscience has from the Holy Spirit a sure testimony of the good-will of God towards it, so that, resting upon this, it does not hesitate to invoke God as a Father." This faith that is assurance also leads to more knowledge. Commenting on Paul's words, "That we may know the things that are given us by Christ," Calvin notes, "The word *know* is made use of to express more fully the assurance of confidence. Let us observe, however, that it is not acquired in a natural way, and is not attained by the mental capacity, but depends entirely upon the revelation of the Spirit."[11] Spiritual knowledge is given by the Spirit. It is made accessible through the Spirit's work of regeneration and illumination (the new sense), and witness is borne to it by the Spirit—culminating in confident belief or certain knowledge. Edward Dowey Jr. brings these strands together by stating, "The objective revelation is there, or 'out there' in Scripture, which is *autopiston,* self-authenticating. But it is 'self' authenticating only to those who have been empowered by the Spirit to perceive this authentication."[12]

In summary, for Calvin, the *internum testimonium Spiritus Sancti* is not a subjective, ineffable experience. Rather, it is a witness to the truthfulness of revelation, and it provides one with confidence in the certainty of the knowledge of God. Further, it includes several particular functions of the Holy Spirit: the giving of revelation, the illuminating of revelation, and the bearing witness to revelation. Joel Beeke traces the development of Calvin's doctrine of assurance in

11. John Calvin, *Calvin's Commentaries,* vol. 20, *Commentary on the Epistles of Paul the Apostle to the Corinthians,* trans. and ed. John Pringle (reprint, Grand Rapids: Baker, 1996), 112–13.

12. Edward A. Dowey Jr., *The Knowledge of God in Calvin's Theology,* 3d ed. (Grand Rapids: Eerdmans, 1994), 108.

the Puritan and Reformed tradition, arguing for a basic agreement in substance, while allowing for minor differences.[13]

One significant step in the development traced by Beeke is the statement on assurance in the Westminster Confession of Faith. Chapter 18 of the confession begins the discussion of assurance by observing that true believers "may in this life be certainly assured that they are in the state of grace." Such certainty is not a "bare and probable persuasion," but is grounded on "an infallible assurance of faith, founded upon the divine truth of the promises of salvation, the inward evidence of those graces unto which these promises are made, the testimony of the Spirit of adoption witnessing with our spirits that we are the children of God."

The Confession up to this point agrees with Calvin's teaching. In the third article of this chapter, however, the Confession nuances Calvin's connection of assurance to faith: "This infallible assurance doth not so belong to the essence of faith." The assurance waxes and wanes—or, in the words of the Confession, it may be "shaken, diminished, and intermitted"—as one neglects the means of grace. Yet, believers who lack assurance are "never utterly destitute of that seed of God, and life of faith."[14] In essence, the Confession acknowledges that there are varying degrees of assurance, while holding that all who have faith also have some assurance.

John Murray helps to explain the Confession's teaching. He observes that assurance is a reflex act or a secondary act of faith. As such, it does not belong to faith's essence. This, however, "is not to be confused with any lack of certitude respecting the object of faith. Every believer is assured of God's reality and the truth of the gospel."[15] The certainty, Murray argues, belongs to faith, whereas

13. Beeke, *Quest for Full Assurance,* 3–4. For a full discussion of the merits of Beeke's conclusions, as well as other interpretations, such as those advanced by R. T. Kendall and M. Charles Bell, see D. A. Carson, "Reflections on Christian Assurance," *Westminster Theological Journal* 54 (1992): 3–5.

14. Chapter 18, "Of Assurance of Grace and Salvation," in *The Westminster Confession of Faith* (Glasgow: Free Presbyterian Publications, 1976), 75–79.

15. John Murray, "The Assurance of Faith," in *The Collected Writings of John Murray,* vol. 2, *Select Lectures in Systematic Theology* (Edinburgh: Banner of Truth, 1977), 266. See also Joel

assurance is a witness or testimony to that certainty. Murray then exhorts believers to cultivate assurance through the means of grace. This follows the thought of many of the English Puritans, perhaps exemplified most poignantly in the studies on casuistry, or cases of conscience produced throughout the sixteenth and seventeenth centuries, which were attempts to arrive at assurance. This quest was not lost on the American colonies.

Before moving on to the colonies, however, it is important to make one final observation on Calvin's thought. While, to a certain degree, Calvin's teaching on the *internum testimonium Spiritus Sancti* is to be equated with the doctrine of assurance, these two cannot be entirely equated. This may explain some of the differences between Calvin and his successors. On the one hand, assurance (perhaps especially in its popular understanding) is more anthropocentric, as it is one's response to the work of God or is contingent upon one's existential state as a Christian. Murray's designation of assurance as a reflex act expresses this notion well. This understanding leads to a more subjective conception of assurance.

The *internum testimonium Spiritus Sancti* likewise involves the individual, for the Spirit testifies *to* someone. It is, on the other hand, theocentric (or, more accurately, pneumatocentric), as it is contingent not upon one's experiential state, but upon the Spirit's testimony to the gospel, which is God's promise in Christ, that it is in fact true.[16] As the Puritan divines developed this idea, they brought the Spirit's testimony to bear upon one's daily experiences of living

---

R. Beeke, "Personal Assurance of Faith: The Puritans and Chapter 18.2 of the *Westminster Confession,*"*Westminster Theological Journal* 55 (1993): 1–30. Beeke argues that the Westminster divines put equal emphasis on each of the three elements of assurance—"faith in God's promises, inward evidences of grace, and the witness of the Spirit" (p. 28).

16. For Edwards's discussion of assurance as it relates to the experiences of the Christian life, see his appendix to *The Life of David Brainerd*. Edwards concludes that "in him [Brainerd] we have an instance of one that possessed as constant and unshaken assurance through the course of his life, after conversion" (*The Works of Jonathan Edwards*, vol. 7, *The Life of David Brainerd*, ed. Norman Pettit [New Haven: Yale University Press, 1985], 505). For issues concerning the interpretation of Edwards's biography of Brainerd, see Pettit's introduction.

the Christian life, while preserving the notion that assurance is present "in principle" in all who possess faith.

As argued below, Edwards's understanding of assurance on some points reflects post-Reformation developments. On other points, his understanding of assurance squares with Calvin's treatment of the *internum testimonium Spiritus Sancti*, and from this stance Edwards advances his apologetic. Specifically, Edwards learned from Calvin, in the words of Dowey, that "the word is the Scripture, the oracles of God objectified—previously inspired and recorded. The Spirit's testimony is the present subjective illumination by which alone the Scripture is recognized for what it is. . . . These two elements are not to be separated from one another. They are functionally one term."[17] While Calvin's understanding of assurance and the development of that understanding within the Puritan and Reformed tradition serve as the larger context for understanding Edwards's views on assurance, the immediate context was shaped by the revivals and the responses to them in eighteenth-century New England.

ENTHUSIASM, RATIONALISM, AND REVIVALISM

While there was a formal settling of some of the issues related to the Antinomian Controversy in the writing and adopting of the Cambridge Platform (1649), many of the issues continued to ferment under the surface and reemerged during the revivals that occurred during the first half of the eighteenth century in New England.[18] The issues that historians focus on today, such as confessional subscription and purity, the involvement of lay preaching, cooperation between denominations, and extra-ecclesiastical evangelism and preaching, while of concern to Edwards, were not necessarily at the center of his thought and writings on the revivals and revivalism.[19]

17. Dowey, *Knowledge of God in Calvin's Theology*, 117.

18. See Williston Walker, *The Creeds and Platforms of Congregationalism* (New York: Pilgrim Press, 1991), 157–237.

19. For a representative earlier work, see Edwin Gaustad, *The Great Awakening in New England* (Gloucester, Mass.: Peter Smith, 1965). For a more recent work, see Frank Lambert, *Inventing the "Great Awakening"* (Princeton: Princeton University Press, 1999). For a

Edwards's chief concern, as reflected in *The Treatise Concerning Religious Affections* (1746), was how to evaluate whether religious conversion was genuine. John E. Smith states that Edwards "struggled with the central question of Puritan Protestantism: How shall the presence of the divine Spirit be discerned?" Edwards found this perennial religious question in the revivals, and he set out to offer an "acute and detailed treatment of the central task of defining the soul's relation to God."[20]

Three major writings—*A Faithful Narrative* (1736), *The Distinguishing Marks of a Work of the Spirit of God* (1741), and *Some Thoughts Concerning the Revival* (1742)—many detailed letters, and numerous sermons and lectures preceded the publication of *Religious Affections,* and together these works constitute Edwards's reflections on revivalism. It is important to examine his understanding of the Spirit's work, as he mediates the two factions emerging from the revivals: the enthusiasts, who advocated and promoted extremes, whose chief proponent was James Davenport; and the rationalists, whose quintessential representative, Charles Chauncey, disdained the revivals and all those involved with them. C. C. Goen cites a letter from 1742 expressing the exasperation of a Presbyterian minister in Boston, John Moorhead, who was caught between the horns of this dilemma: "God direct us what to do, particularly with *pious zealots* and *cold, diabolical opposers.*" As Goen notes, "If that prayer had an answer, it lay with Jonathan Edwards."[21]

Edwards's mediating of these factions is seen in both his critique of Davenport in *The Distinguishing Marks* and his critique of Chauncey in *Some Thoughts Concerning the Revival.* In articulating his understanding of the Holy Spirit's witness, Edwards avoids mys-

brief discussion of the problem of revivalism for confessionalism, see D. G. Hart, "Revivals, Presbyterians and," in *Dictionary of the Reformed and Presbyterian Tradition in America,* ed. D. G. Hart and Mark A. Noll (Downers Grove, Ill.: InterVarsity Press, 1999), 216–18.

20. Editor's introduction to *The Works of Jonathan Edwards,* vol. 2, *Religious Affections,* ed. John E. Smith (New Haven: Yale University Press, 1957), 1.

21. Cited in the editor's introduction to *The Works of Jonathan Edwards,* vol. 4, *The Great Awakening,* ed. C. C. Goen (New Haven: Yale University Press, 1972), 64 (emphasis Goen's).

ticism and its overemphasis on the dynamic activity of the Spirit. In mysticism, the Spirit works beyond, or even without, the restrictions of the Word.[22] Yet Edwards also avoids rationalism, which does not leave room for the working of the Spirit. This rationalism reflected the nascent deistic tendencies among the Colonials that would eventually blossom into Unitarianism.[23] Both extremes, mysticism and rationalism, according to Edwards, have an inaccurate view of the work of the Holy Spirit. Because of the controversy surrounding the revivals, Edwards's writings on the Spirit's work have an apologetic angle to them.

Edwards presents a succinct treatment of the Spirit's work in conversion, with an emphasis on assurance, in *The Distinguishing Marks*. His goal in this work, following 1 John 4:1, is to test the spirits, in order "to shew what are the true, certain, and distinguishing evidences of a work of the Spirit of God, by which we may proceed

22. The extreme element of the New Lights manifested itself in the infamous book-burning incident in the streets of New London in 1743. As Sidney Ahlstrom observes, "These extremes were Davenport's last" (*A Religious History of the American People* [New Haven: Yale University Press, 1972], 285). Only a year later, Davenport recanted his excesses in his *Confessions and Retractions* (1744). Eventually, Ahlstrom adds, he was able to "return to favor among the more moderate revivalists" (p. 286). For an account of Davenport's activities and his retraction, see Richard L. Bushman, ed., *The Great Awakening: Documents on the Revival of Religion* (Chapel Hill: University of North Carolina Press, 1989), 45–55.

23. Chauncy was initially favorable to the revivals and irenic toward Edwards. However, he quickly drew battle lines between his understanding of God's work among people and that of the revivalists, and in 1743 he published *Seasonable Thoughts on the State of Religion in New England*, a rebuttal and repudiation of Edwards and the revival (see Edwin Gaustad, *The Great Awakening in New England* [Chicago: Quadrangle Books, 1968], 80–101, and Amy Schrager Lang, "'A Flood of Errors': Chauncey and Edwards in the Great Awakening," in *Jonathan Edwards and the American Experience*, ed. Nathan O. Hatch and Harry S. Stout [Oxford: Oxford University Press, 1988], 160–73). Chauncey, an Arminian, stressed human involvement—especially of the rational processes—in conversion. Mark Noll observes that Chauncey and his colleague Jonathan Mayhew "found in Enlightenment trends from Europe an antidote to what they considered the overheated supernaturalism of the revivals" (*A History of Christianity in the United States and Canada* [Grand Rapids: Eerdmans, 1992], 98). Bruce Kuklick discusses Chauncey's movement, noting that "breaking with Old Calvinism, he rejected eternal damnation and acknowledged that everyone would be saved" (*Churchmen and Philosophers: From Jonathan Edwards to John Dewey* [New Haven: Yale University Press, 1985], 80). He also discusses Chauncey's disbelief in the divinity of Christ and notes that "by 1820 Boston and its locale were 'Unitarian' rather than Calvinist in religious philosophy" (p. 81).

safely in judging of any operation we find in ourselves, or see in others." He then discusses negative signs, or those evidences, activities, or phenomena that are not indicative of the work of the Spirit. He then turns to "the sure, distinguishing, Scripture evidences and marks of a work of the Spirit of God."[24]

The first sign involves raising one's esteem of Christ. This leads one to confess an orthodox Christology, viewing Christ as the Son of God, God come in the flesh, and as Savior. The second sign involves an awakening of the conscience, or a conviction of sin. This would not be produced by the devil, reasons Edwards, for this runs counter to Satan's operations. The last sign evidencing the work of the Spirit is a sincere love for God and others. The first two signs emphasize aspects of the Spirit's witness, or the doctrine of assurance.

Concerning the third sign, Edwards writes: "That spirit that operates in such a manner, as to cause in men a greater regard to the Holy Scriptures, and establishes them more in their truth and divinity, is certainly the Spirit of God." "The Prince of Darkness," Edwards argues, would never lead people to the sun. He also observes here the lack of the primacy of Scripture within the mystical strain, or among the enthusiasts. He notes, "And accordingly we see it common in enthusiasts, that they depreciate this written rule, and set up the light within, or some other rule above it."[25] This leads to the fourth sign: "If by observing the manner of operation of a spirit that is at work among a people, we see that it operates as a spirit of truth, leading persons to truth, convincing them of those things that are true, we may safely determine that 'tis a right and true spirit." This Spirit "operates as a spirit of truth: he represents things as they are indeed: he brings men to the light; for whatever makes truth manifest, is light." The Holy Spirit, through the work of regeneration and

24. *The Great Awakening*, 227, 248.
25. Ibid., 253–54. Edwards repeats this caution in the application section. There he states that such things as impressions or impulses of "immediate significations from heaven" are to be understood as the Spirit's work of inspiration. But, despite the claims of the enthusiasts, such works ceased with the prophets and apostles of old. This is not how the "gracious influences of the Spirit of God on the hearts of the saints operate" (p. 278).

illumination, "removes our darkness and brings us to the light, un-deceives us, and convinces us of the truth." Edwards does not teach that the Spirit works independently of Scripture or provides new revelation. And he does not teach that the Spirit substantiates revelation or makes it true. Rather, the Spirit reveals the truth of Scripture to one who previously did not see such truth. In short, the Spirit of truth makes "persons more sensible of what is really true."[26] The Spirit is his own witness, which makes his work in conversion self-authenticating.

Edwards elaborates on this position in *Religious Affections*. The fourth of twelve signs of a truly spiritual or divine affection is that one is "enlightened, rightly and spiritually to understand or appre-hend divine things." This, as discussed above in chapter 3, leads to Edwards's notion of the new sense, or the spiritual understanding or taste of the beauty of divine excellence. Edwards further elabo-rates on this idea in the fifth sign of true religious affections: "Truly gracious affections are attended with a reasonable and spiritual con-viction of the judgment, of the reality and certainty of divine things." This certain persuasion or conviction is "reasonable." That is, it is "a conviction founded on real evidence, or upon that which is a good reason, or just ground of conviction." Such a conviction is reason-able in the light of education and rational arguments, but what ul-timately makes it reasonable is that it is "spiritual." This is what dis-tinguishes the natural person's beliefs or convictions from those of one who truly has gracious affections. He concludes: "There is such a thing as spiritual belief or conviction of the truth of the things of the gospel, or a belief that is peculiar to those who are spiritual, or who are regenerated, and have the Spirit of God, in his holy com-munications, and dwelling in them as a vital principle."[27] This pro-vides the grounds for certainty.

The revivals, in one sense, brought to the surface the credibility of the truths of Christianity. Edwards took advantage of the occa-

26. Ibid., 254–55, 261.
27. *Religious Affections*, 266, 291, 295–96.

sion to articulate the necessity of a particular work of the Spirit, understood in the Reformed tradition as the *internum testimonium Spiritus Sancti,* which enables one to perceive and apprehend the truth of the gospel. His exposition of this doctrine began in the revival treatises. His ideas found further expression in the controversy surrounding the Lord's Supper.

Assurance and the Lord's Supper

The issue of assurance arose in Edwards's debate with his congregants over who should be admitted to the Lord's Supper.[28] In one sense, this ecclesiastical controversy was not only a continuation of the debate between the Old Lights and the New Lights, but a continuation of the Antinomian Controversy of the previous century. At issue was the Puritan discussion of visible sainthood.[29] Edmund Morgan traces the history of this notion from its roots in the Donatist controversy of the early church, through the Reformation and the attempts to establish a pure church, to the English Puritans and Colonial Congregationalists who sought a body of true saints, or, in the words of Puritan John Field, a "congregatione of the faythfull called and gathered out of the worlde by the preaching of the gospel."[30]

A development much closer to the time of Edwards was the institution of the halfway covenant at Northampton by his grandfather, Solomon Stoddard. This modified church membership qualifications by allowing those who had been baptized, but were apparently unregenerate, to present their children to the church for

28. For a discussion of the Lord's Supper controversy at Northampton and Edwards's eventual dismissal, see Stephen J. Nichols, *Jonathan Edwards: A Guided Tour of His Life and Thought* (Phillipsburg, N.J.: P&R Publishing, 2001), 125–37.

29. Edwards himself defines *visible sainthood* in "Miscellanies," no. 345: "[By] VISIBLE CHRISTIANS must be meant being Christians in what is visible, or in what appears, or in what is outward. To be a Christian really, is to have faith and holiness and obedience of heart. To be outwardly a Christian is to have outward faith, that is, profession of faith, and outward holiness in the visible life and conversation."

30. Edmund Morgan, *Visible Saints: The History of a Puritan Idea* (New York: New York University Press, 1963), 31.

membership.[31] However, the real issue at Northampton, as David Hall argues, had to do not with the sacrament of baptism, but with the sacrament of the Lord's Supper. In Hall's view, Stoddard—and Edwards, for that matter—inherited a rather complex paradox: "on the one hand the doctrine of election and its practical corollary, that Christians underwent a work of grace which enabled them to know if they were saved; on the other, the imperative of baptism, entering into the disciplinary watch of the church and relying on a routinized holiness for assurance of salvation."[32] We should have full assurance, yet we can never be too wary of hypocrisy, self-deception, or less than genuine religious affections. This double edge applied to the problem of introspection, leading either to abstaining or to participating in the Lord's Supper. The wave of new converts during the revivals heightened the tension.

Stoddard and Edwards each proposed his own solution to this difficult problem. The former "came to feel that unnecessary scruples about assurance of salvation stood in the way of attendance at the Lord's Supper."[33] Consequently, he eliminated regeneration as necessary for admission to communion, allowing everyone who was baptized to participate.[34] At first, and for quite some time, Edwards held Stoddard's position. However, he begin to articulate a different one. For instance, in the "Miscellanies," no. 462, he wrote that all those who come to the Lord's Table "must be Christians really," and must "examine and prove themselves, whether or no they believe the gospel with all their hearts, or are

31. This was, by all accounts, the majority position of those present for the Cambridge Platform; however, as J. Cooper points out, "a minority of dissenters prevented the elders from adding the provision to the *Cambridge Platform*" ("Half-Way Covenant," in *Dictionary of Christianity in America*, ed. Reid, 505).

32. Editor's introduction to *The Works of Jonathan Edwards*, vol. 12, *Ecclesiastical Writings*, ed. David D. Hall (New Haven: Yale University Press, 1994), 35.

33. Ibid., 39.

34. Hall notes that while Stoddard advocated such views as early as 1679, he did not publish them until 1700 in *The Doctrine of Instituted Churches*. This was followed by *The Inexcusableness of Neglecting the Worship of God* (1708) and *An Appeal to the Learned* (1709) (editor's introduction to *Ecclesiastical Writings*, 40–41).

heartily convinced of the truth of it."[35] Then in 1749 he wrote to
his publisher and friend in Scotland, John Erskine, of "a great dif-
ficulty [that] has arisen between me and my people, relating to
qualifications for communion at the Lord's table." He notes that
he formerly conformed to Stoddard's practice, but "I dared no
longer to proceed in the former way." He even goes on to predict
that "this affair will issue in a separation between me and my
people."[36] His prediction came true, as he was dismissed from
Northampton on June 22, 1750.

What is crucial for the purposes of the present study is the way
in which Edwards works out his ideas of assurance in this context.
In order to engage the issue between himself and his congregation,
he published *An Humble Inquiry* in 1749.[37] In the final part of the
treatise, Edwards answers a number of potential objections to his
view, and in the middle of these objections he answers questions related to certainty, visibility, and assurance.

One objection is: "If sanctifying grace be a requisite qualification
in order to persons' due access to Christian sacraments, God would
have given some 'certain rule'" to determine such. Edwards replies,
"God has given some certain rule, which can only be known by the
subject himself, and can only be known by others through profession and visibility of grace operative in one's life." This objection addresses the question of a minister's knowledge of someone's standing before God. Edwards's answer reinforces the view that while
assurance provides certainty for the individual Christian, it cannot
serve as the rule for others.

---

35. *The Works of Jonathan Edwards*, vol. 13, *The "Miscellanies," Entry Nos. a–z, aa–zz, 1–500*,
ed. Thomas A. Schafer (New Haven: Yale University Press, 1994), 503. Edwards publicly revealed these views in his sermon preached on March 21, 1731, "Self-Examination and the
Lord's Supper," in *The Works of Jonathan Edwards*, vol. 17, *Sermons and Discourses, 1730–1733*,
ed. Mark Valeri (New Haven: Yale University Press, 1999), 262–75.

36. *The Works of Jonathan Edwards*, vol. 16, *Letters and Personal Writings*, ed. George S.
Claghorn (New Haven: Yale University Press, 1998), 271.

37. The full title of the work was *An Humble Inquiry into the Rules of the Word of God, Concerning the Qualifications Requisite to a Complete Standing and Full Communion in the Visible
Christian Church*. See *Ecclesiastical Writings*, 165–348.

Edwards then directs his attention to the objection that the individual coming for communion cannot have knowledge of his right to lawful participation, but "only an opinion and probable hopes," which does "not warrant his coming." His answer is that the warrant for one's coming to the table is Scripture. He adds that "no natural man knows the Scriptures to be the Word of God; that although such may think so, yet they don't *know* it; and at best they have a doubtful opinion. . . . No natural man is thoroughly convinced, that the Scriptures are the Word of God."[38] Turning that point around, one could argue that one who is spiritual, as opposed to one who is natural, can know with certainty.

In fact, Edwards does explicitly state this, arguing that while the unregenerate can only posit probable opinion, the regenerate "have certain knowledge of this." This leads him to entertain an objection concerning doubt. He answers this objection by noting that Christians may experience doubts regarding their spiritual state. He quickly points out that such doubts "are not owing to the Word of God"; instead, their source is the neglect of one's spiritual life. He even relies on Stoddard to prove his point: "Mr. Stoddard often taught his people, that assurance is attainable, and that those who are true saints might know it, if they would, i.e. if they would use proper means and endeavors in order to it."[39]

Edwards further addresses these issues in *Misrepresentations Corrected,* a book-length reply to Solomon Williams, Edwards's cousin and a follower of Stoddard, who actively criticized Edwards's view.[40] Edwards observes that Williams sets up the criterion of moral sincerity as the qualification for communion. Finding such a construct problematic, Edwards reiterates that the requisite is saving grace, which can be known with certainty. Williams's own quotation of William Perkins bears this out, so Edwards quotes Williams as writ-

38. Ibid., 291–93.

39. Ibid., 294, 298–99.

40. Solomon Williams, *The True State of the Question Concerning the Qualifications Necessary to Lawful Communion in the Christian Sacraments, Being an Answer to the Reverend Jonathan Edwards* (Boston: S. Kneeland, 1751).

ing, "We agree with Mr. Perkins, 'that a man in this life may ordinarily be infallibly certain of his salvation.'" Edwards also adds the comments of Stoddard: "There is no necessity that the people of God should lie under darkness and temptation; they may obtain assurance." The lack of assurance is due not to God, his operations, or his ordering of things, but rather to one's slothfulness. The doctrine of assurance, Edwards concludes, "has a tendency in the end to that solid peace and comfort . . . and that, and not the saint's perplexity, is properly the effect of this doctrine."[41] In the communion controversy, Edwards moves from a discussion of assurance as the *internum testimonium Spiritus Sancti* to engage the understanding of assurance in the experiences of the Christian life. Nevertheless, the witness of the Spirit is presented as providing the certainty of the knowledge of divine and spiritual truths. This again separates the unregenerate from the regenerate, those with the Spirit from those without. The communion writings add to Edwards's teaching that the Spirit alone provides such certainty.

Finally, we should consider the sermon series entitled "The Threefold Work of the Holy Ghost." Edwards bases this sermon on John 16:8 and understands the threefold work of the Spirit to be the conviction of sin, of righteousness, and of judgment. He stresses the necessity of this work, given the stupefying effects of sin upon humanity's noetic capacities. Here he also asks the significant question that lies in the background throughout his revival treatises and his communion writings: "How may it be known whether the concerns that persons are under about the state of their souls are from the Spirit of God?" In other words, how does one recognize a work of the Spirit? He offers a rather lengthy answer, which he sums up like this: "Whatsoever convictions and awakenings are agreeable to truth" are from the Spirit.

This answer appears to beg the question, until he clarifies what he means: "When convictions are thus according to truth, etc. they are according to the word of God." Later he adds that the Holy Spirit

41. *Ecclesiastical Writings*, 494.

is the author of "real conviction of the truth of the gospel" and that he enables the regenerate to "see what ground and reason there is to believe." He then concludes this line of thought: "The Holy Spirit, when he enters, he lets in that divine light that discovers truth, and makes it appear as truth and shows the way of salvation, which appears and makes itself known by its own intrinsic evidence, which it carries with it."[42] An essential point here is that the Spirit's work of conviction is "its own intrinsic evidence." Thus, assurance emerges in Edwards's thought as providing warrant for Christian belief, as the grounds and evidence for belief, and as the basis for knowing that belief to be certain and true. In short, assurance is an absolute sort of certainty, at the center of Edwards's apologetic.

"AN ABSOLUTE SORT OF CERTAINTY": ASSURANCE AND THE JUSTIFICATION OF BELIEF

While it is somewhat anachronistic to impose upon Edwards the idea that assurance justifies belief, and thus provides certain knowledge, he does speak of assurance and its related notions in a rather contemporary fashion. He serves well as a modern-day interlocutor in discussions of religious epistemology. Edwards and his *Religious Affections* often get transported at least to the beginnings of the twentieth century and placed in dialogue with William James and his *Varieties of Religious Experience*. These two works, the argument goes, present a uniquely American psychology of religion by offering an existential description or descriptions of religious experience. This thesis, however, is flawed.

According to William James, religious truth, like all truth, is better spoken of as *truths*.[43] Note well the plural. Religious truth is

---

42. *The Works of Jonathan Edwards*, vol. 14, *Sermons and Discourses, 1723–1729*, ed. Kenneth P. Minkema (New Haven: Yale University Press, 1997), 388, 390–91, 406–7. As in his other treatments of assurance, Edwards here notes how the Spirit enables one to see the fitness in God's plan and enables a "sweet harmony now between the soul and the gospel" (p. 409).

43. James offers this summary definition of truth: "Our account of truth is an account of truths in the plural, of processes of leading, realized in rebus, and having only this quality in common, that they pay" (*Pragmatism*, ed. Bruce Kuklick [Indianapolis: Hackett, 1981], 98).

about religious experience, and so his work on the sociology of religion, *Varieties of Religious Experience,* offers a descriptive survey of religious experiences. These experiences are meaningful to the subject, but nothing more. In this scenario, James attributes the warrant for belief to the belief itself. This belief is understood as the religious experience. James, however, mistakenly regards the belief as justification for itself. In doing so, he misreads Mrs. Edwards's retelling of her conversion. James excerpts a major portion of Sarah Edwards's account of her conversion in order to offer empirical evidence that religious ideals foster the highest sentiments of human nature. James finds in her testimony, as in many other accounts of similar experiences from a variety of religions, the character of "saintliness." The first characteristic is the sense of an "Ideal Power." He then notes, "In Christian saintliness this power is always personified as God; but abstract moral ideals, civic or patriotic utopias, or inner versions of holiness or right may also be felt as the true lords and enlargers of our life." This sense of power leads to "fundamental inner conditions [which] have characteristic practical consequences," such as piety and charity.[44]

Various accounts of saintliness, Sarah's included, may use different terms deriving from particular aspects of religion. According to James, no one religion is better than the others, and religion itself is more of human origin than divine origin. This misreads Sarah's testimony, as it is taken out of the context in which Edwards places it in *Some Thoughts Concerning the Revival.* Edwards presents the testimonies of Sarah and others as *a posteriori* evidences that the revivals are a work of God. Earlier in the treatise, however, Edwards goes to great lengths to establish that Scripture is the only valid, and therefore the primary and constitutive, evidence that something is the work of the Spirit.[45] The testimonies are supplemental to, and reflective of, this foundational evidence.

---

44. William James, *The Varieties of Religious Experience: A Study in Human Nature* (1902; reprint, New York: The Modern Library, 1994), 298–300.

45. *The Great Awakening,* 296.

James also misreads Mr. Edwards. James refers to him at times favorably, at other times critically. In each case, however, he misses Edwards's entire point. According to James, Edwards's new sense, resulting from conversion, is presented as "warrant [for] one's belief in a radically new substantial nature," so that the new sense by which one perceives is evidence of regeneration. James argues, however, that Edwards's evidence of the new sense fails to warrant such belief: "Throughout Jonathan Edwards's admirably rich and delicate description of the supernaturally infused condition, in his Treatise on Religious Affections, there is not one decisive trait, not one mark, that unmistakably parts it off from what may possibly be only an exceptionally high degree of natural goodness." James uses Jonathan Edwards, as he uses Sarah Edwards, as evidence that religious experience is ultimately a natural phenomenon. James then turns to the doctrine of assurance, or, as he prefers to call it, the "assurance-state." The assurance-state is deeper and more compelling than the faith-state and leaves one with "the certainty of God's 'grace,' 'justification,' or 'salvation.'" This is "an objective belief that usually accompanies the change in Christians." He adds that this state "is the sense of perceiving truths not known before." James then cites Edwards's testimony of his conversion and his new sense and new perception of the world. James concludes that the assurance-state is on a par with a photism, that is, "pseudo-hallucinatory luminous phenomena."[46]

James not only misreads Edwards, but misreads the Christian understanding of assurance. The belief or so-called religious experience is not the warrant. The warrant is the *internum testimonium Spiritus Sancti,* which is a witness to the Word. The Word is a witness to the event. The event and the Word, then, are objective truth. In other words, Edwards is not appealing to subjective experience as the warrant for his belief. Rather, he is appealing to the absolute certainty derived from the Spirit's ministry of assurance. The Spirit enlightens, regenerates, illuminates—gives the new sense to—the individ-

46. James, *Varieties of Religious Experience,* 252, 263, 272–76.

ual, and then the Spirit assures the individual of the truthfulness of the gospel or of the reality of the gospel. Again, James misses Edwards's whole point about assurance.

The ideas of James have led to the modern-day notion that religious experiences are privately beneficial, but publicly meaningless. That is, religious experiences, and hence religious propositions, are not communicable. So-called Wittgensteinian fideism, or the neo-Wittgensteinian view of religious language, entrenches such conceptions. [47] D. Z. Phillips, a leading proponent of this view, does not advocate an explanation of religion or of religious language and belief. Rather, he is concerned to discuss the philosophizing that religious concepts call for. Philosophers contend that for believers "the answers come from *within* religion, they presuppose the framework of Faith, and therefore cannot be treated as *evidence* for religious belief." But philosophers search "for evidence or reasons for religious beliefs *external* to belief itself," and if such evidences were to be found, they would "constitute the grounds of religious belief." This dilemma expresses the problem of a purely theoretical belief in God and, according to Phillips, the establishment of meaningless criteria to evaluate religious truths. Hence, Phillips calls upon philosophers to concentrate on "the question of what kind of philosophical enquiry the concept of divine reality calls for."[48] Phillips finds the solution in Wittgenstein. Borrowing Wittgenstein's notion of

47. For representative statements of the neo-Wittgensteinian theory of religious language, see D. Z. Phillips, *Faith and Philosophical Enquiry* (London: Routledge, 1970), and Paul Van Buren, *The Edges of Language* (New York: Macmillan, 1972). For a brief summary of this view, see John Hick, *Philosophy of Religion*, 4th ed. (Englewood Cliffs, N.J.: Prentice Hall, 1990), 96–99. Hick challenges this view by observing, "Indeed, the basic criticism that has been made of the Neo-Wittgensteinian theory of religious language is that it is not (as it professes to be) an account of normal or ordinary religious language use but rather is a proposal for a radical new interpretation of religious utterances. In this new interpretation, religious expressions are systematically deprived of the cosmic implications that they always have been assumed to have" (p. 98). Another vocal critic of this view is Alasdair McIntyre, who argues that such an understanding of religious assertions precludes the ability to disprove them.

48. D. Z. Phillips, "Faith, Skepticism, and Religious Understanding," in *Contemporary Perspectives on Religious Epistemology*, ed. R. Douglas Geivett and Brendan Sweetman (Oxford: Oxford University Press, 1992), 81–82.

lebensform ("contexts in life"), Phillips contends that religious propositions are meaningful only within the context of the religious community, or *Lebensform,* to which those propositions belong.

Also, Norman Malcolm borrows Wittgenstein's notion of *Sprach-
spiel* ("language games"). Malcolm says, "One of the primary
pathologies of philosophy is the feeling that we must *justify* our lan-
guage-games. We want to establish them as well grounded." He
points out the flaw in this by referring to Wittgenstein: "But we
should consider here Wittgenstein's remark that a language-game
'is not based on grounds. It is there—like life.' Within the language-
game," he continues, "there is justification and lack of justification,
evidence and proof."[49] But outside the language-game or context
of life, there is groundlessness. As Wittgenstein quips, "The diffi-
culty is to realize the groundlessness of our believing."[50]

This digression on James and the neo-Wittgensteinian theory of
religious language shows that Edwards's concept of assurance as
warrant differs from other views of the role of assurance. If assurance is an isolated activity, cut off from everything external and entirely a dynamic experience of an individual or even of a particular
religious community, then James's assertion that it is nothing more
than an overly enthusiastic psychological experience, or the neo-
Wittgensteinian assertion that it is merely a linguistic construct,
holds. However, this is not how Edwards presents assurance. He
does not offer it as an isolated, individualistic, or existential notion.
His discussion of assurance is entirely informed by the related doctrines of the work of the Holy Spirit, as discussed in previous chapters, namely, inspiration, illumination, and regeneration. And this is
the backdrop against which we can best read Edwards on assurance.

In his discussion of the fifth sign of genuine religious affections,
Edwards offers a detailed treatment of assurance. His summary
statement is: "Truly gracious affections are attended with a reason-

---

49. Norman Malcolm, "The Groundlessness of Belief," in *Contemporary Perspectives on
Religious Epistemology,* ed. Geivett and Sweetman, 98. Malcolm quotes Wittgenstein, *On Certainty,* ed. G. E. M. Anscombe and G. H. Von Wright (Oxford: Blackwell, 1969), no. 559.

50. Wittgenstein, *On Certainty,* no. 166.

able and spiritual conviction of the judgment, of the reality and certainty of divine things." He expounds upon the notion of certainty: "All those who are truly gracious persons have a solid, full, thorough, and effectual conviction of the truth of the great things of the gospel." Such persons need no longer content themselves with opinion, rely on probability, or be consumed with doubt. Rather, they have unalterable beliefs. "That all true Christians have such a kind of conviction of the truth of the things of the gospel," Edwards continues, "is abundantly manifest from the Holy Scriptures." He proceeds to quote numerous biblical references proving his point. This leads him to contrast his understanding of conviction with "divine discoveries, which are affecting but not convicting."[51] These affections are false because they do not arise from the truth of Scripture, unlike genuine affections. So the first thing to note about Edwards's understanding of assurance, though he does not use that word here, is that it is conviction or persuasion that is in fact true.

Edwards then argues that conviction or persuasion must be "reasonable." He explains: "By reasonable conviction, I mean a conviction founded on real evidence, or upon that which is a good reason, or just ground of conviction." He then explores ways in which the reasonableness can be established. First, he considers education, concluding that this does not suffice. He argues that a conviction of the truth of Christianity that is based on education or on the opinions of others is "no better than the Mahotmen's conviction." He continues, "The Mahotmens are strongly persuaded of the truth of the Mahotmen religion, because their forefathers, and neighbors, and nation believe it." That belief, no matter how compelling to the individual, or no matter if it is perceived as truth, is not, in Edwards's words, "owing to truth, but to education."[52]

Second, he considers reason or evidences, or rationalism. He writes, "I suppose none will doubt but that some natural men do yield a kind of assent of their judgments to the truth of the Chris-

---

51. *Religious Affections*, 291–93.
52. Ibid., 295.

tian religion, from the rational proofs or arguments that are offered to evidence it." He then proceeds to offer what he takes as biblical examples illustrating his point. Hence—and this appears oxymoronic—truly reasonable convictions are spiritual convictions. The reasonableness of the conviction derives from the fact that the conviction is spiritual. Such a spiritual conviction is necessarily exclusive: "'Tis evident that there is such a thing as a spiritual belief or conviction of the truth of the things of the gospel, or a belief that is peculiar to those who are spiritual." By "spiritual conviction," Edwards intends to encompass many of the ministries of the Holy Spirit. So he argues that those who are spiritual are those "who are regenerated, and have the Spirit of God, in his holy communications, and, dwelling in them as a vital principle."

To support his view, he cites 1 John 5:10, "He that believeth on the Son of God hath the witness in himself."[53] This witness is the *internum testimonium Spiritus Sancti,* or assurance. While this is peculiar to the regenerate, it is not on a par with, to use Edwards's example, the Muslim's belief, even though the two may be equally compelling in terms of the individual's perceptions. What ultimately makes the Christian belief truth, according to Edwards, is the truth of God's Word, which underlies and grounds the belief.

As may be recalled from chapter 2, Edwards speaks of inspiration as possessing an "absolute sort of certainty."[54] So, too, when one encounters the truth of the gospel in the Word, through the Spirit's work of regeneration, illumination, and witness, one has an absolute sort of certainty or a certain, unalterable conviction of truth. Arguing that this is Paul's teaching in 2 Corinthians 4, Edwards states: "Nothing can be more evident than that a saving belief of the gospel, is here spoken of, by the Apostle, as the mind's being enlightened, to behold the divine glory of the things it exhibits."[55]

53. Ibid., 296.
54. "The Mind," in *The Works of Jonathan Edwards,* vol. 6, *Scientific and Philosophical Writings,* ed. Wallace E. Anderson (New Haven: Yale University Press, 1980), 346.
55. *Religious Affections,* 298.

He then concludes his treatment of the fifth sign with a lengthy discussion of the ways in which this conviction of the mind is both direct and indirect. By "direct," he refers to the direct evidence of the new sense itself. "The divine glory and beauty of divine things is in itself," he argues, "real evidence of their divinity, and the most direct and strong evidence." This again is called a reasonable conviction, because it comes from the new sense. So he concludes that this "belief and assurance is altogether agreeable to reason." But just as truly reasonable convictions are those that are spiritual ones, so reasonable assurance is that which is spiritual, or of the Spirit. However, the natural mind cannot apprehend this truth or see this excellence. So Edwards observes, "There are very many of the most important things declared in the gospel, that are hid from the eyes of natural men." On the other hand, "as soon as ever the eyes are opened to behold the holy beauty and amiableness that is in divine things, a multitude of most important doctrines of the gospel, that depend on it (which all appear strange and dark to natural men), are at once seen to be true."[56] Spiritual conviction enables one to see rightly.

In fact, he argues that one cannot get beyond probability unless he "may come to a reasonable solid persuasion and conviction of the truth of the gospel, by the internal evidences of it, in the way that has been spoken, viz. by a sight of its glory."[57] Christian belief is true because of the self-attesting claims of Scripture. Edwards does not imply here that the self-attestation of Scripture is in some way linked to one's response, for he argues, in keeping with the Calvinistic understanding, that Scripture's self-attestation is an objective attribute. Edwards here emphasizes the subject's ability to perceive the true nature of Scripture as divinely given. In other words, he is careful to distinguish between the self-attestation of Scripture and the internal witness of the Spirit to Scripture.

56. Ibid., 298, 301.
57. Ibid., 303.

John Murray offers some helpful observations on this distinction. He notes that because Scripture is the word of God, "it must be self-evidencing, self-authenticating, autopistic." But if this is the case, "why is not faith the result in everyone to whom [Scripture] is addressed?" He answers by citing 1 Corinthians 2:14 concerning the blindness that accompanies man in his natural state. Murray then observes:

> It is here that the doctrine of the internal testimony of the Holy Spirit enters. And this doctrine is to the effect that, if faith in the Word of God is to be induced, there must be the interposition of another supernatural factor, a supernatural factor not for the purpose of supplying any deficiency that inheres in the Scripture as the word of God, but a supernatural factor directed to our need.

According to Murray, the self-attestation of the Word and the internal testimony of the Spirit work together in bringing one to see Scripture as God-given. This is referred to as *fides generalis*, defined as "the belief that Scripture is the Word of God."[58]

This internal evidence is not on the level of probability. As Edwards notes, it is "unreasonable to suppose, that God has provided for his people, no more than probable evidences of the truth of the Gospel."[59] Rather, God "has with great care, abundantly provided, and given them, the most convincing, assuring, satisfying, and manifold evidence of his faithfulness in the covenant of grace." Edwards adds here the covenantal context to knowledge. It is important to note, however, that Edwards does not view assurance itself as the

---

58. John Murray, "Faith," in *Collected Writings of John Murray*, vol. 2, *Select Lectures in Systematic Theology* (Edinburgh: Banner of Truth, 1977), 242–43, 254. The Westminster Confession of Faith, 1.4–5, likewise states that the authority of Scripture depends wholly upon God's own testimony to it, that is, its self-attestation. The confession then states, "Our full persuasion and assurance of the infallible truth and divine authority thereof, is from the inward work of the Holy Spirit, bearing witness by and with the word in our hearts."

59. *Religious Affections*, 303. Edwards may have John Locke in view here. Locke ascribed probability to belief, especially religious belief, since it is not quite on the level of knowledge. See Paul Helm, *Varieties of Belief* (London: George Allen & Unwin, 1973), 85–100. This will be addressed further in chap. 5 below.

justification or warrant for belief. This builds upon Edwards's distinction between notional knowledge and spiritual knowledge. He distinguishes the two, not in order to differentiate two types of knowledge, but to distinguish clearly between one's relationship to knowledge without the Spirit and with the Spirit. He then offers his final conclusion concerning direct evidence: "The gospel of the blessed God do[es]n't go abroad a begging for its evidence, so much as some may think; it has its highest and most proper evidence in itself."[60]

This leaves Edwards with the question of the role of evidences. He carefully establishes his parameters by noting that evidences play a subordinate, yet "prized and valued," role for non-Christian and Christian alike. They "are not to be neglected, but highly prized and valued; for they may be greatly serviceable to awaken unbelievers, and bring them to serious consideration, and to confirm the faith of true saints." But he quickly adds, "Though what was said before remains true, that there is no spiritual conviction of the judgment, but what arises from an apprehension of the spiritual beauty and glory of divine things."[61] His line of thinking here further establishes the thesis that Edwards advances assurance as an apologetic.

The new sense not only evidences itself directly via assurance, but also evidences itself indirectly. That is, "a view of divine glory" both "removes the hindrances of reason" and "positively helps reason." The removal of hindrances consists in the reversal of the noetic effects of sin on the rational processes. Salvation removes the prejudices of the mind against spiritual truth and has a sanctifying effect upon the faculty of reason. Edwards illustrates this point by differentiating the persuasive power that "Christ's miracles had to convince the disciples, from what they had to convince the Scribes and Pharisees: not that they had a stronger reason, or had their reason more improved; but their reason was sanctified, and those blinding prejudices . . . were removed."[62] The unregenerate person, in Ed-

60. *Religious Affections*, 304, 307.
61. Ibid., 307.
62. Ibid.

wards's view, is at enmity with the truth of the gospel. This again brings in the covenantal context of knowledge.

Following Paul in Romans 1, Cornelius Van Til argues that the problem with people is that they are covenant breakers, suppressing and rebelling against the knowledge of God.[63] Edwards likewise articulates the view that what distinguishes Christians from non-Christians in seeing the truth of the gospel is not one's reasoning capacities, but one's covenantal relationship to the gospel. The new sense not only removes the mind's prejudices, but it positively enables the mind to see things more clearly. For Edwards, this amounts to seeing things in their harmonious relations.

Harmony, or fitness, is crucial to Edwards's overall thought. The harmony between Creator and creature serves as the basis of many of his ideas. Samuel T. Logan argues that fitness is the central theme of *The End for Which God Created the World*, *The Nature of True Virtue*, and *The History of the Work of Redemption*. In the first two treatises, fitness applies to ethics or virtue, in that actions which are truly virtuous involve "a harmony between the will of the creator and the will of the creature." In the third treatise, Edwards's philosophy of history is that the "plethora of historical details which constitute the story of man and his world" harmonize with the single, predestined plan of God.[64] Here fitness continues to be a central theme in terms of Edwards's understanding of salvation. Conversion enables one to see the harmony of the world, to see all things coalesce in the divine glory. Just as the light of the sun enables one to see the objects of the earth more clearly, so the light of the divine glory within enables one to see "the truth and reality of divine things."[65]

---

63. See Cornelius Van Til, *Christian Apologetics* (Nutley, N.J.: Presbyterian and Reformed, 1976), 57. Summarizing Van Til's idea and commenting on it, Greg Bahnsen notes, "Seeking to suppress his knowledge of the truth about God . . . their thinking and attempts to gain knowledge can be reduced to absurdity. This biblical insight is at the heart of Van Til's presuppositional defense of the faith" (*Van Til's Apologetic: Readings and Analysis* [Phillipsburg, N.J.: P&R Publishing, 1998], 182).

64. Samuel T. Logan Jr., "The Doctrine of Justification in the Theology of Jonathan Edwards," *Westminster Theological Journal* 46 (1984): 48–49.

65. *Religious Affections*, 308.

Edwards's comments discussed here need to be seen in the context of *The Distinguishing Marks of a Work of the Spirit of God.* In that treatise, he argues that the Holy Spirit works to enable spiritual conviction. Also, the ideas drawn here from *Religious Affections* resonate with much of what Edwards wrote throughout his life. In an early entry in his "Miscellanies" on faith, he writes of the testimony of the Spirit: "There may undoubtedly be such a thing as is called the testimony of faith, and a certainty of faith that is different from reason, that is, is different from discourse by a chain of arguments, a certainty that is given by the Holy Spirit."[66] As he does in the fifth sign of *Religious Affections,* he argues that this confidence is unalterable, derives solely from the Spirit, and is different from reason and evidences. However, he continues to nuance this difference by observing, "Yet such a belief may be altogether agreeable to reason, agreeable to the exactest rules of philosophy." The agreeableness, or fitness, is only known through the Spirit's work.

Edwards next tries to show that such reasoning is not nonphilosophical, arguing, "No man should deny that such an idea of religion may possibly be wrought by the Holy Spirit." His logic is that spiritual truths are spiritually discerned; spiritual knowledge is known through the "testimony of the Spirit."[67] Later he continues this line of thought, writing that the immediate work of the Holy Spirit enables one to understand and see the truth of spiritual things. Here he reasons that "the sanctified mind is let into the spiritual world, or has those ideas . . . which an unsanctified mind is not capable of, or is easily receptive of those ideas."[68] On another occasion, Edwards elaborates on the ministry of the Spirit's testimony by calling attention to the work of the Spirit in drawing one to salvation. The Spirit

66. "Miscellanies," no. aa, in *The "Miscellanies," Entry Nos. a–z, aa–zz, 1–500,* 177.
67. Ibid., 178.
68. "Miscellanies," no. 141, in *The "Miscellanies," Entry Nos. a–z, aa–zz, 1–500,* 297. Here Edwards also stresses harmony, observing, "The holy mind does, and safely may, reject for false everything in divinity that is not harmonious. The soul distinguishes as a musical ear; and besides, holiness itself consists in spiritual harmony; and whatever do[es]n't agree with that, as a base to a treble, the soul rejects" (p. 298).

first "convince[s] them that 'tis best to seek [grace]," and then the Spirit offers "conviction of the worth of the reward."[69]

As discussed above, assurance, for Edwards, does not function as the truth itself. Assurance is a witness to the truth, which is the gospel as recorded in Scripture and reflects the harmony and fitness of God's plan for the world. Assurance enables one to see that Scripture is indeed truth. Additionally, it enables one to see the harmony, fitness, and excellence of God's plan. This preserves the self-authenticating nature of the warrant for Christianity. It also preserves the authority of Scripture, for the Spirit is the only appropriate witness to it. This also distinguishes Edwards's thought from the neo-Wittgensteinian theory of religious experience or a sociological approach to religious experience that grants "truth" to experiences or propositions within the boundaries of a particular religious community, but denies that truth extends beyond the community. Edwards also engages other facets of contemporary epistemological discussion, especially pertaining to religious epistemology.

One particular dimension of contemporary discussion to which Edwards speaks concerns postmodernist Richard Rorty. Rorty opts for solidarity, as opposed to objectivity, as the basis of knowledge. In *Philosophy and the Mirror of Nature,* he says that if we adopt a Deweyan conception of knowledge, "then we will not imagine that there are enduring constraints on what can count as knowledge, since we will see 'justification' as a social phenomenon rather than a transaction between 'the knowing subject' and 'reality.'" He also recommends that we see "truth as, in James's phrase, 'what it is better for us to believe,' rather than as 'the accurate representation of reality.'" He continues, "Or to put the point less provocatively, they [positivists and pragmatists] show us that the notion of 'accurate representation' is simply an automatic and empty compliment which we pay to those beliefs which are successful in helping us do what we want to do."[70]

69. "Miscellanies," no. 116, in *The "Miscellanies," Entry Nos. a–z, aa–zz, 1–500,* 283.
70. Richard Rorty, *Philosophy and the Mirror of Nature* (Princeton: Princeton University Press, 1979), 9–10.

In his essay "Solidarity or Objectivity?" Rorty grounds any sense of objectivity or justification of belief or truth in solidarity, that is, in the consent of communities. The desire of these communities is "for as much intersubjective agreement as possible, the desire to extend the reference of 'us' as far as we can." Truth statements are purely intersubjective or community-based because there is "no independent test of the accuracy of correspondence"; there is "no God's-eye standpoint."[71] In sum, Rorty's version of postmodernism aims at undermining Enlightenment or modernist rationalism by challenging the notion of objectivity.[72]

Edwards likewise stands as a critic of Enlightenment rationalism, although he views it from its beginnings, instead of from its demise. He does not simply seek to undermine the idea of objectivity. To be sure, his covenantal understanding of knowledge leads him to reject the assumption that humanity can be unbiased and to reject the idea that humanity will, on the basis of its rational capacities, attain certain knowledge and truth. In his view, one either is at enmity with the truths of the gospel or sees the beauty and harmony of the gospel. The problem of knowledge is not to discover or find it, but to overcome one's prejudices against genuine spiritual knowledge. And this overcoming of prejudices is a work of the Spirit. Edwards's critique of Enlightenment epistemology differs from Rorty's in that Edwards does not jettison an "accurate representation of reality," nor does he preclude a basis or ground for justifying belief. The truth of Christianity may belong to the Christian community, but the community

71. Richard Rorty, *Objectivity, Relativism, and Truth* (Cambridge: Cambridge University Press, 1991), 23, 6.

72. The literature on postmodernism is vast, and the issue lies far beyond the scope of this work. For engaging critiques of postmodernism by evangelicals, see Brian D. Ingraffia, *Postmodern Theory and Biblical Theology* (Cambridge: Cambridge University Press, 1995), and D. A. Carson, *The Gagging of God: Christianity Confronts Pluralism* (Grand Rapids: Zondervan, 1996), 57–137. For a favorable perspective on postmodernism and contemporary apologetics, see Phillip D. Kenneson, "There's No Such Thing as Objective Truth and It's a Good Thing, Too," in *Christian Apologetics in the Postmodern World*, ed. Timothy Phillips and Dennis Okholm (Downers Grove, Ill.: InterVarsity Press, 1995), 155–70, and the essays in *The Nature of Confession: Evangelicals and Postliberals in Conversation*, ed. Timothy Phillips and Dennis Okholm (Downers Grove, Ill.: InterVarsity Press, 1996).

is not the warrant for the belief. The warrant is provided by the Spirit's testimony to the truth of Scripture and by the harmonious correspondence of the truth of Scripture with God's plan for the world.

This stance enables Edwards to judge those who are outside of the Christian community as not having the truth and not knowing reality. Gerald McDermott devotes much attention to Edwards and the question of non-Christian religions. While he may conclude that Edwards was more charitable toward non-Christian religions than he really was, he does uncover a significant element in Edwards's thought.[73] Focusing on Islam, or, "Mahometanism," as Edwards referred to it, McDermott draws attention to some significant writings of Edwards on revelation and truth. Countering the deists, who, according to McDermott, "were claiming the capability of human reason to discover the truths of natural religion, which alone are sufficient for salvation," Edwards turns to revelation. He acknowledges elements of truth in non-Christian religions; such truths, however, "came not from unassisted reason but from revelation, by tradition from the ancient founders of nations or from the Jews." Edwards teaches that "reason can never produce true religion," and "human nature is such that it tends to pervert what little religious truth it is given and turn it into idolatry."[74]

These ideas are found in Edwards's short writing, "Mahometanism Compared with Christianity—Particularly with Respect to Their Propagation." Edwards concludes by noting that Christianity lays an exclusive claim "to be a religion revealed by God," and that Mahometan religion confirms Christianity to be a revealed religion. This serves as a "great demonstration of the ex-

73. McDermott interprets Edwards's "dispositional ontology" as allowing for salvation beyond explicit faith in Christ and the gospel. See his "A Possibility of Reconciliation: Jonathan Edwards and the Salvation of Non-Christians," in *Edwards in Our Time: Jonathan Edwards and the Shaping of American Religion,* ed. Sang Hyun Lee and Allen C. Guelzo (Grand Rapids: Eerdmans, 1999), 193–95.

74. Gerald R. McDermott, "The Deist Connection: Jonathan Edwards and Islam," in *Jonathan Edwards's Writings: Text, Context, Interpretation,* ed. Stephen J. Stein (Bloomington: Indiana University Press, 1996), 44.

treme darkness, blindness, weakness, childishness, folly, and madness of mankind in matters of religion, and shows how greatly they stand in need of a divine guide, and in need of divine grace and strength for their help, such as the gospel reveals."[75] Edwards's view is that Christianity is objectively true and that other religions, while containing borrowed truths, are false. And once again he stresses the Spirit's enablement to grasp the truth.

We may conclude, then, that Edwards, like postmodernism, repudiates the Enlightenment claim to neutrality and the alleged ability of human rationality to arrive at certainty of knowledge. Unlike postmodernism, however, he does not limit the truth of Christianity merely to being a truth within a community that does not offer an accurate and incontestable view of reality for all. Instead, he insists that Christianity is in fact an accurate representation of reality and that, while it does of course belong to the Christian community, its truth is not restricted to the boundaries of that community.

Leon Chai interprets Edwards's relationship to the Enlightenment slightly differently. For him, Edwards has an affinity with Enlightenment methodology; that is, he adopts Locke's understanding of cognition, Malebranche's view of ideas, and Leibniz's thinking on causation. Chai further speaks of Enlightenment philosophy's complex and problematic relation to contemporary discussions. He then notes, "Clearly, the epistemic certainty once deemed necessary has ceased to seem indispensable. In many instances, we now recognize the impossibility of obtaining that certainty." This is not necessarily due to postmodern critiques of the Enlightenment; the Enlightenment brought this upon itself. The reason is that, despite its best efforts to do so, the Enlightenment, as represented by Locke, Malebranche, and Leibniz—and Descartes, for that matter—could not escape inference. Hence, Enlightenment rationality cannot claim absolute certainty of knowledge without acknowledging certain *a*

---

75. "Miscellanies," no. 1334, dated 1748 by Thomas Schafer (see McDermott, "Deist Connection," 47). It is printed in *The Works of Jonathan Edwards*, 2 vols., ed. Edward Hickman (1834; reprint, Edinburgh: Banner of Truth, 1974), 2:491–93.

priori conditions, circumstances, or inferences. Chai argues that statements with inferences embody their own justification; "hence there is at least the possibility that it [the statement] might not be true." So, he concludes, "analysis based on rational inferences inevitably leads to epistemic uncertainty," and he calls for "a new attitude toward knowledge."[76]

According to Chai, Edwards failed to find certainty in *Religious Affections,* "The Mind," and *Freedom of the Will.*[77] For instance, with respect to *Religious Affections,* Chai notes that the "sort of epistemic certainty [Edwards] craves is, ultimately, unattainable." This is so because no evaluation of piety can transcend the subject. Consequently, "without an external source, piety becomes purely subjective."[78]

But Chai misreads Edwards's understanding of the nature and function of assurance. While assurance is experienced by the subject, it is not produced by the subject. Rather, it is impressed upon the subject by an external source, namely, the Spirit. Additionally, the Spirit's assurance corresponds to the truth of an external source, namely, Scripture. Chai fails to put Edwards's understanding of assurance in its Calvinistic or Reformed context. As demonstrated above, Calvin argued against the idea that assurance is subjective. To be sure, the Spirit's witness is internal, but that internal witness has an external ground. It is the testimony of the Spirit to the individual, not the testimony of the individual to himself.

Whether or not one finds this line of reasoning compelling, this is the framework within which Edwards operates. These two factors, that the Spirit is an external witness and that the Spirit witnesses to Scripture, mitigate Chai's conclusion that Edwards was too bound up in Enlightenment methodology to acknowledge the failure of his arguments. Henry May concurs with this judgment against Chai's

---

76. Leon Chai, *Jonathan Edwards and the Limits of Enlightenment Philosophy* (Oxford: Oxford University Press, 1998), x, 118–19.

77. Ibid., 114. While calling Edwards's methodology or argumentation a failure, Chai nevertheless intends to read Edwards charitably, on the grounds that he was limited by the philosophical tools of his day.

78. Ibid., 35.

interpretation. Writing much earlier than Chai, May observes, "Despite his eager appropriation of Locke and Newton and Hutcheson for his own purposes, he was not a man of the moderate, rational English Enlightenment of his day. Indeed he was the most powerful enemy of that way of thought."[79]

As is especially evident in the revival treatises, Edwards adamantly opposes the rationalistic approach of the deists to discovering truth, especially religious truth. "I am of the mind," Edwards writes, "that mankind would have been like a parcel of beasts with respect to their knowledge in all important truths, if there never had been any such thing as revelation in the world." Edwards is not referring to general revelation, as he makes clear: "The increase of learning and philosophy in the Christian world is owing to revelation: the doctrines of the Word of God are the foundation of all useful and excellent knowledge."[80] In a culture that proposed reasonableness as the criterion of truth, Edwards proposes revelation and the Spirit's witness to that revelation as an accurate representation of reality. Far from being a child of the Enlightenment, Edwards stands as a critic of the Enlightenment by turning the focus away from humanity to God as the source of all truth and knowledge. In the contemporary discussion of the so-called collapse of the Enlightenment and the death of modernity, Edwards's criticisms ring prophetic.

Michael McClymond interprets Edwards's apologetic as a balance of subjective and objective elements. He emphasizes that Edwards was "far more concerned about the subjective dimension of Christianity than were Paley or Butler. His teaching on the spiritual sense placed him closer to Schleiermacher and other theological romantics than to those more prosaic and earthbound defenders of the faith." McClymond does refine his argument by finally seeing Edwards as a proponent of a *via media* between the distant and objectified God and apologetics of Paley and the subjectified and mys-

79. Henry F. May, *The Enlightenment in America* (Oxford: Oxford University Press, 1976), 49.

80. "Miscellanies," no. 350, in *The "Miscellanies," Entry Nos. a–z, aa–zz, 1–500*, 424–25.

tical God and apologetics of Schleiermacher. These different views do not "compete in Edwards." Rather, "Edwards falls into both categories." McClymond's interpretation hinges upon seeing Edwards as bringing together the cognitive and the affective in a holistic response to God; to "prove" Christianity amounts to little if one cannot "appreciate" the truths proved. So, McClymond makes the case that Edwards "stated unequivocally that the perception of the divine 'excellency' is the highest and most reliable of all evidences for God." He further argues, "Regeneration is the epistemological foundation of Edwards' entire religious outlook."[81]

McClymond's interpretation has much to be commended. Unlike Chai, he finds Edwards clearly recognizing the snares of Enlightenment thought for Christian apologetics. He stresses the apologetic role of perception and the new sense of Edwards. He even goes so far as to argue that such perception is Edwards's ultimate apologetic. However, by focusing on the conjunction of the cognitive and affective aspects of the human response as the solution to the impasse between rationalistic deism and mystical liberalism, McClymond makes Edwards's apologetic anthropocentric. On the one hand, this charge is difficult to sustain. McClymond himself declares, "Edwards's lifework might be seen as a massive attempt to . . . reestablish a theocentric perspective within a culture increasingly alienated from God."[82] On the other hand, McClymond argues that Edwards arrives at such a perspective by stressing perception. This puts undue stress on the subject and obscures the centrality of the Holy Spirit in Edwards's apologetic.

McClymond's thesis might be improved if, rather than arguing that regeneration is Edwards's epistemological foundation, he argued that revelation is its basis. Regeneration then enables one to see the truth of revelation. The epistemological foundation, however, is not the perception of revelation, but revelation itself. Both

81. Michael J. McClymond, *Encounters with God: An Approach to the Theology of Edwards* (Oxford: Oxford University Press, 1998), 105–6, 108, 111.
82. Ibid., 112.

revelation and the perception of it are given by the Spirit. Likewise, the basis of certainty is not the perception that one has or the new sense, but assurance or the Spirit's witness. In other words, McClymond's emphasis on perception, which amounts to a bringing together of the cognitive and affective elements of human nature in order to bring about "a certain way of looking at all things, based on a way of looking at certain things," neglects a full-orbed perspective that encompasses the various functions of the Spirit, especially the function of the Spirit as the witness that provides certainty.[83]

Another aspect of contemporary epistemology to which Edwards speaks is Alvin Plantinga's concept of warrant. One of the essential elements of Plantinga's view is that belief in God is properly basic. By *properly*, he means that it is justifiable, given "for a person at a time if (a) he is violating no epistemic duties and is within his epistemic rights in accepting it then and (b) his noetic structure is not defective by virtue of his then accepting it."[84] Plantinga has since developed his proposal into the thesis that "a belief has warrant [that which makes true belief knowledge] if it is produced by cognitive facilities functioning properly (subject to no malfunctioning) in a cognitive environment congenial for those faculties according to a design plan successfully aimed at truth."[85] This proposal has two major components. First, there is the notion of proper function— the proper function of one's epistemic equipment in the right epistemic environment. Second, there is the notion of a design plan, or a set of specifications for the functioning of a thing, the way a thing is supposed to work. The key—or, as Plantinga puts it, "the best way for one to have warrant"—is proper function. Plantinga further notes that his notion of proper function as warrant results in at best a high

83. Ibid., 111.
84. Alvin Plantinga, "Reason and Belief in God," in *Faith and Rationality: Reason and Belief in God,* ed. Alvin Plantinga and Nicholas Wolterstorff (Notre Dame, Ind.: University of Notre Dame Press, 1983), 79.
85. Alvin Plantinga, *Warrant and Proper Function* (Oxford: Oxford University Press, 1993), viii–ix.

statistical or objective probability and that it is most plausible in the context of a supernaturalistic metaphysics.[86]

In the latest installment of his discussion of warrant, *Warranted Christian Belief,* Plantinga argues that "Christian belief is produced in the believer by the internal instigation of the Holy Spirit, endorsing the teachings of Scripture, which is itself divinely inspired by the Holy Spirit. The result of the work of the Holy Spirit is *faith.*" These three elements—the Word of God, faith, and internal instigation—provide warrant for belief. Plantinga derives these from the thought of Aquinas, Calvin, and Edwards. By "internal instigation," Plantinga has in view what has been presented in this study as the Spirit's witness or assurance, and he depends on Edwards for his ideas. The internal instigation depends not only upon the Spirit's work of inspiration, but also upon the Spirit's work of regeneration. As Plantinga observes, "Regeneration is a matter of curing both intellectual and affective disorders." Regeneration enables one's epistemic equipment to function properly. He then concludes that the internal instigation of the Holy Spirit "enables the believer to see the glory and beauty of the gospel, whereupon she infers that they are in fact divine and hence to be believed."[87]

Plantinga's interpretation of Edwards further counters McClymond's emphasis on perception in his understanding of Edwards's apologetic. Plantinga argues, "It isn't by way of perception of God that Christians come to hold their characteristic beliefs, and the warrant those beliefs have for them is not perceptual warrant." Instead, warrant comes from "the Bible, the internal instigation of the Holy Spirit, and faith."[88] That Plantinga utilizes Edwards in this way shows the relevance of Edwards to contemporary epistemological discussion. Additionally, Plantinga's most recent work, which is so dependent upon Calvin and Edwards, serves as a healthy rejoinder to his earlier work. Edwards's apologetic points to the necessity

86. Ibid., 237.
87. Plantinga, *Warranted Christian Belief,* 290, 303, 305 (emphasis original).
88. Plantinga, *Warrant and Proper Function,* 43.

of both a theistic metaphysics and a theistic epistemology undergirded by the Spirit's work of inspiration, regeneration, and assurance. As Plantinga is currently arguing, the Spirit's witness provides warrant for Christian belief. Building upon Plantinga's position, one could argue that the Spirit's witness provides absolute certainty.

Affections Can Be Misleading: The Problem of Self-Deception

Edwards, like all Puritans, was well aware of the power and danger of self-deception.[89] In his discussion of assurance, Edwards acknowledges that the potential for hypocrisy is so great that one can not only deceive others, but deceive oneself as well. Early in his discussion of the fifth sign, Edwards observes that "some persons, under high affections, and a confident persuasion of their good estate, have that, which they very ignorantly call a seeing the truth of the Word of God, and which is very far from it." What they really see, he argues, is not the truth of the gospel, but a delusion. He then concludes, "Therefore those affections which arise from no other persuasion of the truth of the Word of God than this, arise from delusion, and not true conviction."[90] Edwards argues that self-deception arises when, as the word itself suggests, the affections arise from the self, not from the witness of the Spirit to something external, such as Scripture. This underscores Edwards's point that the Spirit's testi-

89. It is more accurate to say that Edwards grew into such awareness. In *The Distinguishing Marks*, he records: "I once did not imagine that the heart of man had been so unsearchable as I find it is. I am less charitable, and less uncharitable, than once I was. I find more things in wicked men that may counterfeit, and make a fair show of piety, and more ways that the remaining corruption of the godly may make them appear like carnal men, formalists and dead hypocrites, than once I knew of" (*The Great Awakening*, 285). His suspicions grew after he left Northampton and reflected back on the revivals and his own interpretations of events as presented in his earlier revival writings. In a letter to Thomas Gillespie, a fellow revivalist on the other side of the Atlantic, dated July 1, 1751, Edwards writes, "There was a very glorious work of God wrought in Northampton, and there were numerous instances of saving conversion; though undoubtedly many were deceived, and deceived others; and the number of true converts was not so great as was then imagined" (*Letters and Personal Writings*, 384).

90. *Religious Affections*, 294–95.

mony is not to be understood as subjectivity. Positively, Edwards emphasizes the reliability of genuine spiritual conviction as he clarifies the role of the individual in assurance.

Referring to *Religious Affections,* Ava Chamberlain observes, "Edwards' aim in this treatise was specifically to discriminate between gracious and counterfeit affections in order to establish a firm foundation for personal assurance." Edwards was fighting a war on two fronts, against Chauncey's Arminian rationalism and New Light extremist enthusiasm. The latter consisted of emotional exuberances that were mistaken as effects of the Spirit. Edwards assessed such activity as "the hypocrite's error . . . to use them [epiphenomenal experiences] as evidence of conversion and as the foundation for assurance." However, because of the emphasis that Edwards placed on the affections, the resultant "experimental religion inadvertently encouraged not only antinomianism and enthusiasm but also a more moderate form of hypocrisy that resulted when assurance was grounded on immediate experience."[91] Chamberlain concludes that Edwards's achievement in *Religious Affections* consisted in ameliorating this dilemma by arguing for long-term Christian practice as opposed to momentary, immediate experiences. Thus, he retooled the Puritan idea of sanctification by combining the vigilance of the old order with the new revivalism.

However, Chamberlain's understanding of Edwards's doctrine of assurance is too narrow. "According to Edwards," she asserts, "Christian practice was the locus of assurance."[92] By treating assurance simply as a human response to the work of God in one's life, she fails to see that assurance is produced by the Spirit, as the equivalent to Calvin's *internum testimonium Spiritus Sancti.* Edwards does relate assurance to one's Christian experiences, in order to assess whether one is in fact regenerate. He argues that the more one obeys the demands of the gospel, and the longer one lives a life of obedi-

91. Ava Chamberlain, "Self-Deception as a Theological Problem in Jonathan Edwards's 'Treatise Concerning Religious Affections,'" *Church History* 63 (1994): 546, 550, 555.
92. Ibid., 553.

ence, the greater one's sense of assurance will be. Chamberlain is right to draw attention to Edwards's view on the relationship of the life of obedience, or sanctification, to justification—that is, the relationship of faith to works.

However, for Edwards, assurance is more than an outgrowth of Christian experiences. It also encompasses the Spirit's testimony to the truthfulness of Scripture and the gospel, which is produced within the regenerate and accompanies the new sense. This witness produces certain knowledge. Edwards brings these two ideas together in *Religious Affections,* avoiding both antinomianism and hypocrisy. Thus we see that *Religious Affections* presents a crucial component in Edwards's apologetic.

George Marsden hints at such an understanding when he portrays Edwards as fashioning Puritanism, through the catalyst of the revivals, as a viable option in the emerging modern world. He argues that Edwards steers clear of "the mistake, so common today, of making human nature and human psychology the primary focus of theological analysis." Marsden then observes, "This trend had already begun in Edwards' day, shifting theological analysis from looking at God to looking at human responses to God." He concludes that Edwards "always made crystal clear that God is the central focus in religious experience."[93] This clear focus on God guides Edwards's treatment of assurance in *Religious Affections.* With this in view, we will now see how Edwards treats assurance negatively, as self-deception or hypocrisy, in *Religious Affections.*[94]

Edwards says that there are different means of self-deception, or, as he puts the matter, "many ways whereby some are deceived." The first is by misinterpreting "the common enlightenings of the Spirit of God" as a "conviction of truth of the great things of religion." Edwards has in view something akin to Luther's distinction between

93. George M. Marsden, "Jonathan Edwards Speaks to Our Technological Age," *Christian History* 4 (1985): 27.

94. Edwards frequently warns against hypocrisy and self-deception. For instance, he warns against "the comforts of hypocrites" in his concluding application of "God Makes Men Sensible of Their Misery," in *Sermons and Discourses 1730–1733,* 172.

the external perspicuity and the internal perspicuity of Scripture. Scripture is externally clear to all humanity because it is a human book, yet as a divine book it is internally clear only to those who possess the Spirit of God. Similarly, one may have a sense of one's sin and attendant misery due to sin, yet lack a "sense of the beauty and amiableness of the moral and holy excellency that is in the things of religion." If that be the case, one has "no spiritual conviction of their truth."[95]

There is another danger that relates to the Awakenings and the excesses of the enthusiasts. Edwards refers to these phenomena as "extraordinary impressions which are made on the imaginations of some persons, in the visions, and immediate strong impulses and suggestions that they have, as though they saw sights, and had words spoken to 'em." Such activities, Edwards acknowledges, "may, and often do beget a strong persuasion of the truth of invisible things." Yet he quickly adds, "The general tendency of such things, in their final issue, is to draw men off from the Word of God, and to cause them to reject the gospel." Before they reach their final issue, however, such things instill "a confident persuasion of the truth of some things that are revealed in the Scriptures; however their confidence is founded in delusion, and so nothing worth."[96]

In part 2 of *Religious Affections*, discussing what do not count as signs of truly gracious affections, Edwards addresses hypocrisy. He states that those who are "deceived with false discoveries and elevations" miss the true nature of assurance. They mistake their "impulses and supposed revelation . . . about their good estate [as] the witness of the Spirit; entirely misunderstanding the nature of the witness of the Spirit." Such self-deception is like a delusional madness that would lead one to believe confidently that he is a king and maintain such belief "against all manner of reason and evidence."[97] Edwards's point is that genuine witness is not a matter of the self's

95. *Religious Affections*, 308–9.
96. Ibid., 309.
97. Ibid., 173–74.

own determination or sentiment. Rather, genuine witness, or assurance, comes from the correspondence of the witness to reality or to certainty and truthfulness. Edwards advocates a lifetime of Christian practice as evidence of truly gracious affections, rather than immediate, short-term experiences that may not last and therefore lack any gracious work. In other words, he advocates a by-your-fruits-you-will-know approach to verifying the truthfulness of religious notions and experiences. That is, if one's life corresponds to one's profession, then one can derive genuine assurance. He also maintains—and this is the crucial point that relates to his apologetic—that assurance produces certainty because it is the Spirit who testifies to the individual, and this testimony is to the truthfulness of the things of God's Word.

Edwards's treatment of self-deception further demonstrates that he did not intend assurance to be understood in a subjective manner. Rather, he treats assurance as a reference point outside of oneself that provides one with certain knowledge. As *The Oxford Companion to Philosophy* recognizes, "Puritan faith runs throughout his philosophy, where all explanation ends in God."[98] Once again we see that Edwards is a consummate critic of Enlightenment thought, which sought its reference point in humanity. The gracious affections, he argues, "which the saints are subjects of, and the effects of God's Spirit which they experience, are entirely above, altogether of a different kind from anything that men find within themselves by nature, or only in the exercise of natural principles."[99]

The context of Edwards's thought here in *Religious Affections* serves to distinguish between and to elucidate his two uses of assurance. He is primarily discussing assurance of one's salvation, not the *internum testimonium Spiritus Sancti*. These two types of assurance, though distinct, nonetheless contribute to one another and coalesce. In fact, Edwards himself moves from one to the other in his discus-

98. *The Oxford Companion to Philosophy*, ed. Ted Honderich (Oxford: Oxford University Press, 1995), 711.

99. *Religious Affections*, 205.

sion of the fifth sign. Given the potential for self-deception, the first type of assurance (confidence of one's own conversion) is precarious without the second type of assurance (confidence in Scripture as truth, through the *internum testimonium Spiritus Sancti*) at work buttressing it. The first type of assurance is by definition subjective and derivative, and is insufficient to provide warrant for the belief itself. But the second type of assurance, which is neither subjective nor derivative, does provide warrant for belief. This second type of assurance produces and grounds one's faith; the first type confirms one's faith. Consequently, Edwards introduces the *internum testimonium Spiritus Sancti* in his argumentation in *Religious Affections* as a necessary and sufficient cause of assurance. Plantinga brings together both types of assurance and captures their relationship well: "Faith is a matter of a sure and certain knowledge, both revealed to the mind and sealed to the heart . . . consist[ing] in the right sorts of affections; in essence, it consists in loving God above all and one's neighbor as oneself."[100]

CONCLUSION

In conclusion, according to Edwards, assurance is the culmination of a number of different operations of the Spirit, including inspiration (the giving of Scripture) and regeneration and illumination (the giving of the new sense in order to "see" Scripture). Assurance is based on the Spirit's witness or testimony to the truth of the gospel and to the harmony of that gospel, as revealed in Scripture, with God's plan for redemption. That harmony or fitness also extends to the soul participating in that plan. The Spirit's testimony convinces one of the certainty and truthfulness of Scripture. The internal witness of the Spirit is related to, but distinct from, Scripture's self-attesting nature. Scripture's self-attestation is an objective attribute of Scripture, due to its divine origin, that is unaffected by one's response to it. The internal witness of the Spirit is a witness to Scrip-

100. Plantinga, *Warranted Christian Belief*, 323.

ture, but it is directed at the individual, who, because of the Fall and the noetic effects of sin, is prejudiced against it. The Spirit's witness then enables the subject to perceive Scripture as divinely given.

In articulating these ideas, Edwards followed Calvin and the Reformed doctrine of the *internum testimonium Spiritus Sancti*. The exigencies of the Awakenings and the controversy regarding the Lord's Supper at Northampton provided the context and the impetus for Edwards's exposition of the doctrine of assurance. Additionally, since he stood at the beginning of the Enlightenment, he dealt with the biblical teaching on assurance from the perspective of the epistemological discussions of the time. As an apologist, he brought together both his theological concerns and his philosophical interests in formulating his view. In the end, he concluded that assurance, or the witness provided by the Spirit to Scripture, which is predicated upon the self-attestation of Scripture, is the sole source of certainty regarding the truth of Christianity. Only the Spirit's ministry of conviction provides justification of one's belief as true knowledge, reflective of the true, spiritual reality. In articulating this, Edwards countered deism, offered an apologetic against non-Christian religions, and even contributed to epistemological issues of our day, such as the postmodern critique of knowledge and Plantinga's views on proper epistemic function and warrant.

In other words, assurance, as internal testimony, is an absolute certainty and is at the center of Edwards's apologetic and epistemology. He advances a revelation-centered view of knowledge (as argued in chapter 2), stresses the necessity of the new sense in terms of one's relationship to that knowledge (as argued in chapter 3), and emphasizes the Holy Spirit's testimony as the source of certainty concerning that knowledge (as argued in this chapter). Especially given the fact that the Spirit's *internum testimonium* is by definition internal, the question that remains is, How does one make a defense of the faith to those without the Spirit? In other words, does the Spirit's testimony function externally as an apologetic? This question leads us to the next chapter.

5

VERIFICATION: EDWARDS ON TESTIMONY (2)

And reasoning is only of use to us in consequence of the paucity of our ideas,
and because we can have but very few in view at once. Hence it is evident
that all things are self-evident to God.

Jonathan Edwards, "The Mind"

Samuel Hopkins records a rather curious conversation that he had with George Whitefield about Jonathan Edwards in 1770. After a few comments about the tendencies of New England ministers, Whitefield quipped, "Is it not surprising, and much to be regretted, that good Mr. Edwards should deny the witness of the Spirit?" Hopkins replied, "I did not know that he had. What do you understand sir by the witness of the Spirit?" Whitefield's pause caused Hopkins to surmise that he was searching, unfruitfully, for an answer, so Hopkins advanced one: "Do you mean by it an impression upon the imagination, by some immediate communication from the Spirit, that your sins are forgiven and that you are a child of God?" "No," said Whitefield, "that does not express my opinion." Hopkins then advanced another option: "Do you then mean an influence of the Spirit of God, exciting such a love for God and Jesus Christ, such clear views of their character, as that the subject of it knows from experience and from Scripture, that he is a child of God and an heir of salvation?" Whitefield declared that this "accords more with [my] views." Hopkins concluded the exchange by exclaiming, "This is that witness of the Spirit for which Mr. Edwards pleads, in distinction from the former, which he represents as a form of enthusiasm."[1]

This exchange highlights both the essence of Edwards's teaching on assurance and the problem that it raises for apologetics. Three aspects of his teaching are evident here. First, assurance does not have any affinity with the experience of the enthusiasts. Hence, it is not subjective or emotive. Second, the Spirit's witness enables one to see the truth in Scripture concerning God and his redemptive activity, which is "out there," or objective. Finally, the subject engages these "clear views" by experience. Again, as Edwards says, he who would know the sweetness of honey must taste it.

These ideas highlight the remaining problem with Edwards's apologetic. If one can arrive at certainty of knowledge about God, his world, and his work only through the witness of the Spirit, which entails the experience of regeneration or the new sense, then how can anyone be shown the truth of Christianity apart from such an experience? How can one make a case for Christianity to others, if the only way for others to know it is true is through firsthand experience? This problem faces not only Edwards, but, in a sense, any apologetic system that asserts the self-authenticating nature of Christianity as the foundational presupposition or reference point for any and all predication. So exploring Edwards on these issues, and also engaging him in contemporary discussions, will inform the present state of apologetics and philosophy of religion.

Below is an account of the role of testimony in the acquisition of knowledge. This will provide a helpful backdrop to Edwards's un-

---

1. *The Works of Samuel Hopkins, D.D.*, 3 vols. (Reprint, Boston: Doctrinal Book and Tract Society, 1854), 1:87. For Hopkins's further exposition on assurance, see 1:519–34.

derstanding of assurance as testimony or evidence of a warranted belief. Some of the conversations started in the previous chapter will be continued and expanded here. Next, Edwards's apologetic method will be explored, making use of his strategy of showing how his ideas are first scriptural and secondly reasonable. Finally, the implications of these issues will be brought together to summarize his understanding of assurance as an apologetic. If assurance is the only basis on which one can claim certainty, as argued in the previous chapter, then does it necessarily follow that assurance is the only possible basis on which one can offer an apologetic? This chapter answers affirmatively, by arguing that central to the apologetics of Edwards is the proclamation of the testimony that God has given of himself.

TESTIMONY AND KNOWLEDGE

Contemporary epistemological discussions acknowledge the important role that testimony plays in one's acquisition and justification of knowledge. As J. L. Austin observes, "The statement of an authority makes me aware of something, enables me to know something, which I shouldn't otherwise have known. It is a source of knowledge."[2] C. A. J. Coady adds that "testimony is very important in the formation of much that we normally regard as reasonable belief," and "our reliance upon it is extensive."[3] He goes on to demonstrate the pervasiveness of testimony in the social and physical sciences. Yet, he is hard-pressed to find many in the history of epistemology who grant a significant role to testimony. One person he does find, however, is Thomas Reid. Reid argues for the function of testimony not only in the area of scientific knowledge, but also in other areas. Coady then concludes, "By now it will, I hope, have become clear that we are greatly indebted to testimony

2. J. L. Austin, "Other Minds," cited in C. A. J. Coady, *Testimony: A Philosophical Study* (Oxford: Oxford University Press, 1992), 3.
3. Coady, *Testimony*, 8–9.

at the level of both common sense and theory for much of what we usually regard as knowledge."[4]

Coady is not the only contemporary philosopher to take his cue from Thomas Reid. Alvin Plantinga also speaks of his debt to Reid when he notes, "The position I shall develop is broadly Reidian; the global outline of Thomas Reid's epistemology seems to me to be largely correct."[5] Plantinga follows Reid specifically with regard to the role of testimony. He also concurs with Coady's assessment that philosophers too quickly discount testimony in the formation of beliefs and the acquisition of knowledge. As Plantinga observes, "The Enlightenment looked down its rationalistic nose at testimony and tradition, comparing them invidiously with science; but, without learning by testimony, clearly, science would be impossible."[6]

Before examining Plantinga's view further, it will be helpful to return to Coady's exposition of Reid's view of testimony. Citing a selection from Reid's *Essays on the Intellectual Powers of Man,* Coady argues that Reid's understanding of testimony "is connected with the very idea of objectivity via the concept of what is public." He continues, "The judgments of others constitute an important, indeed perhaps the *most* important, test of whether my own judgments reflect a reality independent of my subjectivity."[7] This is especially the case in scientific knowledge, as Reid illustrates by supposing that a scientist conducts an experiment that produces a certain result. Before he rests confident in his findings, however, he submits the process to his colleagues for verification. "If the judgement of his friend agrees with his own, especially if it be confirmed by two or three able judges, he rests secure of his discovery without further examination." If, however, the judgment of his colleague is not in accordance with his findings, then "he is brought back into a kind

4. Ibid., 13.

5. Alvin Plantinga, *Warrant and Proper Function* (Oxford: Oxford University Press, 1993), x. In addition, see Robert Audi's discussion of testimony in *Epistemology: A Contemporary Introduction to the Theory of Knowledge* (London: Routledge, 1998), 130–48. Audi finds much that is commendable in both Coady's and Reid's work on epistemology.

6. Plantinga, *Warrant and Proper Function,* 77.

7. Coady, *Testimony,* 12.

of suspense, until the part that is suspected undergoes a new and more rigorous examination."[8]

Reid argues that testimony, or, as in this case, even the opinion of others, plays a stronger role in the acquisition of knowledge than inductive reasoning and experimentation. The reason is that the testimony of others may correct faulty perceptions or confirm accurate perceptions that one has. Reid explains: "The wise Author of nature hath planted in the human mind a propensity to rely upon this evidence [testimony] before we can give a reason for doing so. . . . If children were so framed as to pay no regard to testimony or to authority, they must, in the literal sense, perish for a lack of knowledge."[9] Reid does not endorse a naïve view of testimony. On the contrary, he acknowledges, "When we grow up, and begin to reason about them, the credit given to human testimony is restrained and weakened, by the experience we have of deceit."[10] Reid refers to the counteracting principles of veracity and credulity. The first is the propensity, given by the Supreme Being, to tell the truth and to believe what one hears as truth. The other principle, which is also given by the Supreme Being, is credulity, which acknowledges the possibility of deception by others. Yet, while human authority is attenuated by instances of equivocation and lying, "the authority of human reason is only weakened by them, but not destroyed."[11] Reid also distinguishes between testimony that is given by one's senses and that which is given by others. While the two are analogous, Reid attributes more warrant to the testimony derived from one's senses.[12] Despite these two caveats, testimony derived from others is a major source of knowledge, according to Thomas Reid.

8. Thomas Reid, *Essays on the Intellectual Powers of Man,* cited in Coady, *Testimony,* 12.

9. Reid, *Essays on the Intellectual Powers of Man,* in *Thomas Reid's Inquiry and Essays,* ed. Ronald Beanblossom and Keith Lehrer (Indianapolis: Hackett, 1983), 282.

10. Thomas Reid, *An Inquiry into the Human Mind on the Principles of Common Sense,* cited in Keith Lehrer, *Thomas Reid* (London: Routledge, 1989), 74.

11. Beanblossom, *Thomas Reid's Inquiry and Essays,* 95.

12. Lehrer, *Thomas Reid,* 73–74.

Plantinga, while commending Reid's epistemology and his emphasis on testimony, mitigates testimony as warrant for belief on two counts. "First, testimony is ordinarily parasitic on other sources of belief so far as warrant goes." It is not a first-order source, but derives from the original experience of others. The second problem with testimony is that "there is a cognitively superior way," namely, eyewitness experience. So Plantinga concludes, "Testimonial evidence is indeed evidence; it is not always the evidence of choice." Plantinga then turns to perception as part of the cognitively superior way. Nonetheless, Plantinga shares Reid's view of testimony: "Testimonial evidence is indeed evidence; and if I get enough and strong enough testimonial evidence for a given fact . . . the belief in question may have warrant enough to constitute knowledge."[13] This raises the question of the nature of assurance as testimony in Edwards's thought.

Reid, like Kant, was awakened from his dogmatic—or, at least his epistemological—slumbers by David Hume's argument that certainty of knowledge is impossible. Unlike Kant, however, Reid decided to reexamine John Locke in order to refute Hume. Reid found Locke's emphasis on sensation objectionable because it tends to emphasize the subject in the process of knowing to the detriment of the object. Locke, in other words, emphasizes sensation rather than the thing sensed, perception rather than the thing perceived. To counter Locke's point, Reid points to the role of testimony given by others, as mentioned above. Then he offers a simple illustration which draws into question Locke's and also Hume's understanding of perception. Reid was largely unsatisfied with Locke's view that ideas are the only object of thought. He saw that Descartes bequeathed such a perspective to Locke, who in turn gave it to Berkeley and then to Hume. Lehrer sums up Reid's strategy by noting, "Reid took Hume's work to have proven that the major assumption of Berkeley's philosophy, that what is before the mind is always some idea, would

13. Plantinga, *Warrant and Proper Function*, 87–88, 82.

lead to absurdity. So Reid rejected that assumption and undertook the construction of an alternative system."[14]

In Reid's alternative system, external objects are assumed to exist and are taken as the basis of one's perception. The illustration he offers is of the table, perceived from different angles at different distances. Reid observes, "Let the table be placed successively in as many of those different distances and positions as you will or in them all; open your eyes and you shall see a table precisely of that apparent magnitude, and that apparent figure, which the real table must have in that distance and in that position." He then concludes, "Is not this a strong argument that it is the real table you see?"[15] However the table is looked at, it appears just as a real table would appear. Thus, according to Reid, the object of knowledge is not ideas, but material, external entities. With respect to testimony and perception, Reid finds Locke wanting.

Edwards does not follow Reid *per se* as much as he criticizes Locke. In "The Mind," he examines a number of ways that one comes to knowledge. He considers that which is learned by demonstration, through sensation, and by reasoning. First, Edwards argues that "we are certain of many things upon demonstration, which yet we may be made more certain through more demonstration," yet one cannot have absolute certainty through demonstration.[16] "Nor are our senses certain in anything at all," he notes, concluding, "We are in danger of being deceived by our senses in judging of appearances by our experience in different things, or by judging where we have had no experience of the like."[17] As for reasoning, Edwards holds that much of what we know through reasoning is *a priori*. In other words, Edwards finds difficulties in all of the ways in which we ar-

14. Lehrer, *Thomas Reid*, 3.

15. Beanblossom, *Thomas Reid's Inquiry and Essays,* 179.

16. Jonathan Edwards, "The Mind," in *The Works of Jonathan Edwards,* vol. 6, *Scientific and PhilosophicalWritings,* ed. Wallace E. Anderson (New Haven: Yale University Press, 1980), 339.

17. Ibid., 369–70.

rive at knowledge. Yet he maintains that there is knowledge, and that one can know it with certainty.

At the end of "The Mind," Edwards recorded a number of inchoate "subjects to be handled," which his untimely death prevented him from handling. One of these subjects has to do with certainty and assurance. While he does not give a full-fledged treatment to these matters, he does sketch some important contours. First, he rehearses the role that demonstration and reasoning play in one's assurance or certainty. He also hints at the resolution to the problem of arriving at certainty when he indicates his intention to explain "how God's sight only is infinitely clear and strong." He makes a similar statement earlier in "The Mind," when he writes, "And reasoning is only of use to us in consequence of the paucity of our ideas, and because we can have but very few in view at once. Hence it is evident that all things are self-evident to God." On the one hand, Edwards affirms something quite close to Berkeleyan idealism, which finds the basis of the existence of all things in divine perception. On the other hand, and especially when this quotation is taken in its context, Edwards affirms that all knowledge finds its basis in God, for "God is truth itself." Truth may be defined as "the consistency and agreement of our ideas with the ideas of God."[18]

It is possible to arrive at certainty, Edwards argues, only through God's self-disclosure. The idea that "all things are self-evident to God" means that he alone can bear witness to the certainty of all things. On this basis, one can perceive through the senses accurately and reason correctly. Yet, contrary to Reid, this is not left to the laws of nature ordained by the Author of nature, or to the faculties of reason given by the Supreme Being. Rather, Edwards insists on the necessity of special revelation and the work of the Holy Spirit.

Edwards appeals to testimony, but this testimony is given by God, who testifies through the world and the Word. This further serves to differentiate Edwards from Reid. Two significant areas of difference emerge. First, Edwards does not grant the possibility of one's epistemic

18. Ibid., 388, 341–42.

capacities functioning properly apart from a regenerative work of the Spirit. Second, Edwards reflects on the nature of the one testifying, namely, God himself. Edwards utilizes assurance as a testimony to the truth of Christianity that not only convinces the individual assured, but also enables the individual to proclaim the truth of Christianity on the basis of such testimony. The end of such a proclamation is to convince one of the truth. Edwards, as argued above, does not pretend that such convincing comes apart from the regenerative work of the Spirit. It does not come, either, apart from the proclamation of the Word. Edwards reveals his methodology of proclaiming God's testimony by appealing to the self-attestation of Scripture and also to its reasonableness. The order is important, and it reflects Edwards's view of the role of evidences, rationality, and rationalism. Next we will consider these two elements in the methodology of Edwards's apologetic.

'TIS SCRIPTURAL AND 'TIS RATIONAL: THE METHODOLOGY OF EDWARDS'S APOLOGETIC

Commenting on *Freedom of the Will,* Paul Ramsey points to the "two pillars" of Edwards's thought: "the proof from biblical revelation and the proof from reason."[19] Revelation is the fundamental and primary pillar. In this, Edwards followed the Reformed tradition. Michael McClymond notes, "In accordance with the Reformed tradition and such earlier figures as Calvin, Edwards saw the Bible as self-authenticating and asserted that its teachings and very words strike the mind as God-given."[20] In chapter 2 above, numerous passages in Edwards's writings, such as "The Duty of Hearkening to God's Voice," were presented to show that Edwards derives Scripture's authority from its claim to be the word of God.[21] He also ar-

19. Editor's introduction to *The Works of Jonathan Edwards,* vol. 1, *Freedom of the Will,* ed. Paul Ramsey (New Haven: Yale University Press, 1957), 8.

20. Michael J. McClymond, *Encounters with God: An Approach to the Theology of Jonathan Edwards* (Oxford: Oxford University Press, 1998), 97.

21. *The Works of Jonathan Edwards,* vol. 10, *Sermons and Discourses, 1720–1723,* ed. Wilson H. Kimnach (New Haven: Yale University Press, 1992), 438–50.

gues similarly in a number of entries in his "Miscellanies," such as one on the literary style of Scripture. Here Edwards observes the simple style of the text and concludes, "It shines brighter with the amiable simplicity of truth. There is something in the relation that at the same time very much pleases and engages the reader, and evidences the truth of the fact."[22] Edwards does not appeal to a text *per se*, but to the style of Scripture, as evidence of its truthfulness.

Edwards argues similarly with regard to John's Apocalypse: "Indeed this book of the Revelation is full of such strokes, that for their naturalness exceed all human invention or imitation, and denote a knowledge of nature beyond what ever I saw anywhere in human writings."[23] He later concludes, "The being of God is evident by the Scriptures, and the Scriptures themselves are an evidence of their own divine authority."[24] Consequently, Edwards, in his sermons, offers proof for his arguments by claiming that they are scriptural, on the assumption that what is scriptural is true.

In his sermon "A Divine and Supernatural Light," Edwards first shows what the divine light is and then shows how it is immediately given by God. He then argues that this doctrine is true, first by showing that it is scriptural and second by showing that it is rational. In the section demonstrating that the doctrine is scriptural, Edwards does not defend the text or appeal to any evidence in support of it. Instead, he simply quotes or refers to a number of texts as authoritative.[25] That is how he characteristically presents his biblical material. Similarly in *Concerning the End for Which God Created the World*, he discusses both what reason teaches concerning this matter and what Scripture teaches. He discusses reason first, but notes, "Indeed, this affair [God's end for the world] seems properly to be an

22. "Miscellanies," no. 6, in *The Works of Jonathan Edwards*, vol. 13, *The "Miscellanies," Entry Nos. a–z, aa–zz, 1–500*, ed. Thomas A. Schafer (New Haven: Yale University Press, 1994), 203.

23. "Miscellanies," no. 195, in *The "Miscellanies," Entry Nos. a–z, aa–zz, 1–500*, 335.

24. "Miscellanies," no. 333, in *The "Miscellanies," Entry Nos. a–z, aa–zz, 1–500*, 410.

25. *The Works of Jonathan Edwards*, vol. 17, *Sermons and Discourses, 1730–1733*, ed. Mark Valeri (New Haven: Yale University Press, 1999), 417–19.

affair of divine revelation."[26] Again, Edwards exposits the text without defending its authority. This is the approach he ordinarily follows in his other treatises.

Edwards may appear to be speaking to an audience that grants Scripture its authority. However, this is not entirely the case. As mentioned in chapter 2, the veracity of Scripture was being challenged in Edwards's day, primarily by deistic attacks on the necessity of special revelation and on the credibility of accounts of miraculous events.[27] Thus, one cannot just assume that Edwards's audience would automatically grant Scripture its authority. As will be seen below, Edwards does sometimes counter challenges to Scripture. In fact, as Douglas Sweeney observes, "One recent estimate suggests that more that 25 percent of Edwards's 'Miscellanies,' the most famous of his private theological and philosophical notebooks, treated either deism itself or the issues raised by deists."[28] However, there is a point at which Edwards does not pretend to establish the authority of Scripture, and this accounts for his mere positing of its authority, rather than trying to prove it as his starting point. In his day, there was also an awareness of other cultures and of non-Christian religions and their scriptures.[29] In other words, one cannot assume that Edwards and his audience were unaware of the challenges of pluralism. Although it may not

26. *The Works of Jonathan Edwards,* vol. 8, *Ethical Writings,* ed. Paul Ramsey (New Haven: Yale University Press, 1989), 419.

27. John Redwood documents and explores the impact of deism on British thought and life in *Reason, Ridicule and Religion: The Age of Enlightenment in England, 1660–1750* (Cambridge, Mass.: Harvard University Press, 1976). Deism also affected the American colonies. See James Turner, *Without God, Without Creed: The Origins of Unbelief in America* (Baltimore: Johns Hopkins University Press, 1985). Turner argues that deism did not influence America until after the Revolutionary War; however, its earlier effects were real.

28. Douglas A. Sweeney, "Edwards, Jonathan," in *Historical Handbook of Major Biblical Interpreters,* ed. Donald McKim (Downers Grove, Ill.: InterVarsity Press, 1998), 309.

29. Gerald McDermott gives much attention to this area of Edwards's thought. His work shows the extent to which there was an awareness of non-Christian religions and scriptures in the eighteenth century. See "A Possibility of Reconciliation: Jonathan Edwards and the Salvation of Non-Christians," in *Edwards in Our Time: Jonathan Edwards and the Shaping of American Religion,* ed. Sang Hyun Lee and Allen C. Guelzo (Grand Rapids: Eerdmans, 1999), 173–202.

have had a pronounced influence, pluralism was nonetheless present in his day. Finally, in his day there were various individuals who, for one reason or another, rejected the Scriptures.

Edwards engages such a person in his sermon "The Unreasonableness of Indetermination in Religion." He considers various things that some persons have left unresolved or undetermined, including their attitude toward Scripture. He writes, "Some never come to any determination whether the Scriptures be the word of God, or whether they be the invention of men; and whether the story concerning Jesus Christ be anything but a fable." He continues: "Sometimes when they hear arguments for [Scripture], they assent that it is true; but upon every little objection or temptation arising, they call it in question, and are always wavering and are never settled about it." [30] Therefore, it would be wrong to assume that Edwards's audience automatically attributed authority to Scripture. This makes his positing of its authority without proof all the more telling.

Edwards does offer two caveats regarding Scripture's self-authentication, however. First, as McClymond points out, "This self-authenticating power of Scripture is not recognized by all readers, because one must have a receptive frame of mind to perceive it."[31] In other words, not perceiving the truth of God's Word reflects on the spiritual condition of the one doing the perceiving, but not on the truth of the Word itself. Thus, as argued in chapters 2 and 3 above, regeneration and the new sense are necessary if one is to perceive Scripture for what it is.

Second, the fact that the Bible is self-authenticating does not mean that there are no external evidences that support its claims. Scripture's self-authentication and evidences are not mutually exclusive. Rather, they can coexist in a proper relationship. Consequently, Edwards defends the rationality of both Scripture and Christianity as subordinate, yet beneficial, in demonstrating the

30. *The Works of Jonathan Edwards*, 2 vols., ed. Edward Hickman (1834; reprint, Edinburgh: Banner of Truth, 1974), 2:58.
31. McClymond, *Encounters with God*, 97.

authority and divine origin of Scripture. One of the things that Edwards appeals to is the failed attempts of those who have tried to prove it is false. He writes, "'Tis a convincing argument for the truth of [the Christian] religion and that it stands upon a most sure bottom, that none have ever yet been able to prove it false; though there have been many of all sorts and many [of] fine wits and great learning, that have spent themselves, and ransacked the world for arguments against it."[32] He also appeals to the fitness of redemptive history as recorded in Scripture. In the "Miscellanies," no. 333, he writes, "There is that wondrous universal harmony and consent and concurrence in the aim and drift, such an universal appearance of a wonderful glorious design, such stamps everywhere of exalted and divine wisdom, majesty and holiness in matter, manner, contexture, and aim."[33]

Edwards also responds to higher criticism. Stephen Stein draws attention to this aspect of Edwards's exegetical preparations and ruminations, as recorded in his "Notes on Scripture." Stein observes that Edwards lived at the time, according to Hans Frie, when the precritical period of interpretation was breaking down.[34] Stein continues: "The rising resistance to traditional orthodoxies, religious and cultural, launched by the Renaissance and carried to new heights by the Enlightenment, had immense implications for the study of the Bible." Stein then describes some of these implications: "New knowledge about the nature of the universe, the geography of the earth, and the possibilities of scientific inquiry was combined with a commitment to the supremacy of reason to produce a series of questions that undermined standard assumptions based on the biblical cosmogony."[35]

32. The "Miscellanies," Entry Nos. a–z, aa–zz, 1–500, 332.
33. Ibid., 410.
34. Hans W. Frei, The Eclipse of Biblical Narrative: A Study in Eighteenth and Nineteenth Century Hermeneutics (New Haven: Yale University Press, 1974).
35. Editor's introduction to The Works of Jonathan Edwards, vol. 15, Notes on Scripture, ed. Stephen J. Stein (New Haven: Yale University Press, 1998), 12.

These advances were not lost on the colonies. Stein notes, "Even the remote regions of the English colonies felt the effects of the rise of rationalism because of the increasing availability of European publications."[36] Higher criticism and rationalism, in symbiotic relationship, fueled challenges to the authorship of Scripture, and, hence, to its legitimacy, and replaced revelation with reason as the supreme authority.

Three major figures of modern philosophy, Spinoza, Hobbes, and Locke, each in his own way, undermined the authority of Scripture. First, Spinoza, in his *Tractatus Theologico-Politicus,* writes, "If we would separate ourselves from the crowd and escape from theological prejudices, instead of rashly accepting human commentaries for Divine documents, we must consider the true method of interpreting Scripture."[37] He insists that Scripture must be interpreted naturally, that is, just as any other book, or as nature itself, is interpreted. Roy Harrisville and Walter Sundberg argue that biblical higher criticism germinated in this work by Spinoza, observing that its influence was far-reaching and deeply felt.[38]

Hobbes's perspective on Scripture is quite complex. On the one hand, he reflects a high view of Scripture. On the other hand, he rejects Mosaic authorship of the Pentateuch. He writes, "It is therefore sufficiently evident that the five Books of *Moses* were written after his time."[39] Hobbes also adds a new twist to the nature and role of Scripture's authority. In an attempt to curtail, if not to remove, the authority claimed by the papacy through apostolic succession, Hobbes's work, according to Richard Tuck, resulted in "Christianity [becoming] merely another socially sanctioned way of expressing the feelings of natural religion."[40] Hobbes views revela-

36. Ibid., 13.

37. Benedict de Spinoza, *Tractatus Theologico-Politicus,* 7.8, as reprinted in *The Philosophy of Spinoza,* ed. Joseph Ratner (New York: The World's Popular Classics, 1920), 251.

38. Roy A. Harrisville and Walter Sundberg, *The Bible in Modern Culture: Theology and Historical-Critical Method from Spinoza to Käsemann* (Grand Rapids: Eerdmans, 1995), 32–48.

39. Thomas Hobbes, *Leviathan,* ed. Richard Tuck (Cambridge: Cambridge University Press, 1991), 262.

40. Tuck, introduction to *Leviathan,* by Hobbes, xxiii.

tion as one of three sources of knowledge of God's law: (1) natural reason, or what Hobbes refers to as "the Right of Nature" or "the Natural Kingdom," (2) revelation, and (3) prophecy. He concludes that the latter two are not universal, given that only "those to whom God Himself hath revealed it supernaturally" can, in fact, know revelation and prophecy to be God's word.[41] By default, then, reason is the more desirable and preferred authority. Hobbes's redefinitions of, and restrictions on, biblical authority in *Leviathan* should be read in the context of the British civil wars and the ecclesiastical struggles of the time; however, the ideas he put forth in *Leviathan* contributed to the new way of handling Scripture and the new sense of its authority.

Finally, Locke contributes to the undermining of the authority of revelation by making reason the arbiter of revelation: *"Reason* must be our last Judge and Guide in every Thing." Even revealed propositions from God must be submitted to reason: "If *Reason* finds it [revelation] to be revealed from GOD, *Reason* then declares for it, as much as for any other Truth, and makes it one of her Dictates."[42]

Edwards, in "Notes on Scripture," responds both to specific challenges to the traditional authorship of the Pentateuch and the Gospels, and to general challenges to the primacy of revelation as presented by these three philosophers. Edwards was quite conversant with both the philosophical currents and the biblical scholarship of his day, and he brought the biblical text itself to bear upon these discussions. As Stein observes, Edwards devotes a great deal of attention to questions about the Pentateuch, adding, "As the series [of entries in the notebook] progresses, Edwards' exegetical agenda increasingly reflects the critical issues raised by Enlightenment thinkers." Stein notes that "Edwards' defense of Mosaic authorship included an argument based on the internal witness of Scripture."[43] Edwards also argues that Mosaic authorship is con-

41. Hobbes, *Leviathan*, ed. Tuck, 246.

42. John Locke, *An Essay Concerning Human Understanding,* ed. Peter H. Nidditch (Oxford: Oxford University Press, 1975), 704 (4.19.14) (emphasis original).

43. Stein, editor's introduction to *Notes on Scripture*, 14.

sistent with reason. He shows that writing and record-keeping was practiced during the time of Moses, contrary to the claim that writing developed later. He also defends the consistency of the Pentateuch with later biblical teachings and the plausibility of the historical accounts as recorded in the Pentateuch.

Edwards's use of rational arguments in the sermon "A Divine and Supernatural Light" offers a salient example of his logic. He essentially makes three particular arguments. First, given that the light is divine, it necessarily follows that it is different from human things. As Edwards observes, "We can't rationally doubt that things that are divine, that appertain to the supreme Being, are vastly different from things that are human." There is something vastly different in the Word of God than in the writings of men, and something different in the appearance of divine glory. His second point is that sin blinds one to the divine light; one who sees only naturally is not able to see supernaturally. Finally, "'tis rational to suppose that this knowledge should be given immediately by God, and not be obtained by natural means."[44] To be sure, he argues here within a set of given presuppositions—chiefly the presupposition of the reality of the divine light. What he demonstrates, however, given these presuppositions, is the rational consistency of his thought.

He is restricted from doing more by rational arguments, however, because "it is out of reason's province to perceive the beauty or loveliness of anything: such a perception do[es]n't belong to that faculty." Such a perception is possible because "it depends on the new sense of the heart."[45] This shows that Edwards was not a rationalist and did not rely on evidences to prove Christianity. In his view, rational arguments are insufficient to enable one to perceive the truth of Christianity. He does not discount rational argumentation, although he excludes rationalism. He employs reasons, rational arguments, and evidences to demonstrate the coherence of Christianity as a system. This enables one who possesses the new sense

44. *Sermons and Discourses, 1730–1733*, 420–21.
45. Ibid., 422–23.

to have confidence in the truth of Christianity. It also enables one to proclaim Christianity as a rational and coherent system of thought.

Paul Helm illustrates the apologetic import of Edwards's view of the connection between Scripture's self-authentication and its reasonableness. Similarly to McClymond, he places Edwards's views in a larger stream of thought that he labels the Augustinian-Anselmian approach of "faith seeking understanding." Edwards never writes explicitly of faith seeking understanding, but he belongs in this tradition due to his "providing [of] philosophical elaborations of positions derived from faith."[46] These elaborations provide a cogent defense of revelation. He articulates particular points as primarily scriptural and also rational. Helm accurately places Edwards in this tradition, and by doing so sheds some light on his apologetic.

According to Helm, there are two motives for the faith-seeking-understanding approach: "to aid the believer's own understanding, of God and his ways . . . and to rebut objections and challenges to his faith." This program comes in many varieties, but understanding Augustine's thought in its fullness is crucial to capturing its crucial contours. One of Augustine's key ideas is "that faith involves some understanding, for understanding is a necessary condition of faith, and that the understanding which faith then seeks is further understanding."[47] Further, faith seeking understanding, properly understood, entails the reversal of natural theology, for this approach does not submit faith to rational criteria outside of revelation.

This may be illustrated by the use of philosophical arguments to prove the existence of God. According to Helm, in this approach reason attests to the credibility of revelation. Instead of that, Helm advocates a positing of the existence of God, as declared in revelation, as the basic axiom from which all propositions and knowledge flow.[48] This is an important methodological point for the practice of apolo-

---

46. Paul Helm, *Faith and Understanding* (Grand Rapids: Eerdmans, 1997), 153.

47. Ibid., vii, 28.

48. Ibid., 30–34. Helm advocates ideas that are central to Cornelius Van Til's approach. Note especially p. 35: "Reason is not a neutral tool; its very pretended neutrality is a challenge to the authenticity of the word of God."

getics. Finally, Helm notes that the faith-seeking-understanding program involves "cognitive enquiries address[ing] aspects of the one real world which is God's creation." This entails the idea that the "metaphysical account Augustine and the others give of the relation between God and the world is a unified realist conception. Such an account of God and the world, if it is true, would be true even if religious belief ceased."[49] Helm's point, which accords well with the view of Edwards, is that the truth of the proposition believed is not contingent upon the exercise of faith.

Helm further explains Edwards's contribution to this program: "In the example of faith seeking understanding that we are taking from Jonathan Edwards there is a strong apologetic thrust, but one that arises out of what Edwards regarded as a developed understanding of the faith, and particularly the metaphysics that underlies that faith." That is to say, Edwards's apologetic arises from a given context, or a set of presuppositions. In Helm's words, "He seeks a general philosophical understanding, one rooted in the nature of things as he understood them." Helm observes that Edwards has confidence in the philosophical cogency of the propositions of Christian belief: "It was thus Edwards' conviction that the faith, if properly understood, has the intellectual resources to meet the objections that were being made to it."[50] Helm's understanding of the faith-seeking-understanding program and of Edwards's contribution to it helps to explain Edwards's apologetic method of appealing to Scripture as self-authenticating and to the reasonableness of Christian doctrines.

He takes Edwards's argument in *Original Sin* as a case study that supports his thesis. In this treatise, Edwards uses both scriptural arguments and "evidences of original sin from facts and events, as found by observation and experience."[51] Robert C. Whittemore also places Edwards in Anselm's line, while noting Edwards's distinct contribu-

49. Ibid., 76.
50. Ibid., 152–53.
51. *The Works of Jonathan Edwards,* vol. 3, *Original Sin,* ed. Clyde A. Holbrook (New Haven: Yale University Press, 1970), 105.

tion. He observes, "'I believe in order to understand.' As it is with Anselm, so it is with Edwards, except that the object of the latter's belief is more particularly the witness of scripture and the assurance of a regeneration effected by God's efficacious grace."[52] Whittemore amplifies the role of the Spirit's work in Edwards's understanding of the relationship between faith and reason and its importance for Edwards's apologetic.

In this section, we have seen that the essential theoretical point in Edwards's apologetic methodology is the idea of the primacy of Scripture or revelation, which attests to itself as true knowledge and also demonstrates rational coherence. According to Edwards, the Christian religion is first scriptural and second rational. Hence, a robust faith that accurately portrays God and his world emerges. We will next see how the doctrine of assurance, as well as the related doctrines examined in earlier chapters, makes this possible.

ASSURANCE AND APOLOGETICS

To better appreciate Edwards's use of assurance as an apologetic, it will be helpful to review the role of the Holy Spirit in his apologetics. First, the problem of sin involves the whole person, *totius animae;* in regeneration, the Spirit transforms the whole person. Second, *spiritual* knowledge, which belongs to the regenerate only, and *notional* knowledge, which belongs to the unregenerate, do not represent a bifurcation of knowledge. Rather, these designations reflect one's relationship to knowledge. The difference consists in the covenantal relationship that one has to knowledge—either of rebellion or of reconciliation. Third, given that that is true, one may make rational arguments in apologetics without denying that the work of the Spirit is necessary and without presupposing the autonomy or supremacy of reason. Fourth, however, revelation is primary in apologetic argumentation and is the source of knowledge. Fifth, the

52. Robert C. Whittemore, *The Transformation of the New England Theology* (New York: Peter Lang, 1987), 80.

Holy Spirit's unique function in the *opera ad intra* of communion within the Godhead models his unique function in the *opera ad extra* of revealing, as evidenced in his work of inspiration and illumination. Sixth, Scripture, being inspired by the Holy Spirit, is self-authenticating, and the testimony of the Spirit to the veracity of Scripture is analogous to, and the basis of, the *internum testimonium Spiritus Sancti*. Seventh, the *internum testimonium Spiritus Sancti* is not mystical; although it is internal and personal to the regenerate, it provides an objective, absolute certainty. Eighth, the doctrine of assurance provides an adequate apologetic. Finally, the gospel preached, or the apologetic sermon, serves as an essential vehicle for the threefold work of the Spirit: convicting humanity of sin, of righteousness, and of judgment.

Edwards could thus be called the apologist of the Spirit, playing off of Warfield's designation of Calvin as "pre-eminently *the theologian of the Spirit.*"[53] Warfield argues that the doctrine of the work of the Holy Spirit is Calvin's gift to the church. Edwards's legacy is his application of the various aspects of the doctrine of the Spirit—which he learned from Calvin—to the pressing philosophical issues of his day.

The last point above will be explored in chapter 6 below. The first seven points summarize the arguments of chapters 2 through 4. Let us expand upon these points briefly. Edwards views human nature as reflective of the divine nature. The *imago Dei* in man gives him understanding and a will. Because of the Fall, however, the understanding is incapable of apprehending spiritual knowledge, and the will is disinclined to receive spiritual knowledge—until the regenerating work of the Holy Spirit produces the new sense of the heart. Some misread this as an attempt to subjectify knowledge and mystify Christianity.[54] Spiritual knowledge accurately reflects meta-

53. B. B. Warfield, *Calvin and Augustine,* ed. Samuel J. Craig (Philadelphia: Presbyterian and Reformed, 1956), 484 (emphasis original).

54. This would include such diverse interpreters as Harold Simonson, *Jonathan Edwards: Theologian of the Heart* (Grand Rapids: Eerdmans, 1974), and William James, *The Varieties of Religious Experience: A Study in Human Nature* (1902; reprint, New York: The Modern Library, 1994).

physical realities; it is knowledge of things as they truly are. The belief, or even the experience of believing, does not constitute knowledge, for the perception of knowledge is not knowledge itself. Belief is one's relationship to knowledge, or one's perception of knowledge. Edwards argues, however, that one is naturally prejudiced against spiritual knowledge and quite unable to see it, apart from the work of regeneration. Once that knowledge is seen, or, as Edwards may prefer, sensed, one may have absolute certainty regarding it because of the Spirit's testimony. Additionally, this knowledge is true because it is scriptural; that is, it is from God and is verified as such through its own self-attestation. Also, its truthfulness is evidenced by the fact that it coheres as a system of thought; that is, it is reasonable.

The eighth point is the subject of the present chapter. It may be recalled that earlier in the chapter assurance was described as testimony, and a brief discussion of contemporary epistemological thought regarding testimony as knowledge ensued. Returning to that discussion, it may be observed that Coady's work also entails an examination of testimony in relation to religious knowledge. First, while acknowledging that testimony in religious contexts is a "more heightened, dramatic, and mysterious form," Coady argues that it nonetheless functions as evidence that warrants knowledge. He considers various types of religious testimony, such as the testimony of a martyr or the testimony of what God has done in one's life. And he argues that in these cases, though to varying degrees, the testimony is to the " 'realities' they believe in"; the one testifying is not only reporting his subjective experiences, but "reporting on divine actions."[55]

Coady then qualifies his comments by noting that it is one thing to grant that religious testimony is a reliable witness to reality, but "it is another to hold that these intentions are successful, and another again to accept any of these testimonies as true." He then sets out the criteria by which these things may be judged, observing,

---

55. Coady, *Testimony*, 52.

"Whether this way of talking is ultimately intelligible will depend very much on the special competence and authority that it presumes the witness to have and, granting intelligibility, there is then the question of how one is to weigh the evidence presented."[56]

Two things are worth noting about Coady's observations. First, in spite of his Kantian sensibilities, he argues that there is no *prima facie* reason to distinguish testimony in religious contexts from testimony in general. If one grants that testimony is a source of knowledge in the sciences, for example, then there is no pressing reason to reject testimony as a source of knowledge when it comes to matters of religion. Second, Coady offers criteria to judge testimony. With regard to the present discussion, there are two elements to apply such criteria to, namely, the testimony itself and the one testifying, meaning God as the one testifying. Both of these elements receive Edwards's attention, as discussed previously in this chapter, but more needs to be said.

First, it would be a mistake to take Edwards's doctrine of assurance as teaching that the testimony is the perception that one has of God. In chapter 3 this was dealt with briefly in relation to Edwards's use of the new sense in apologetics. Some attention was also given to the work of William P. Alston in this connection. In *Perceiving God*, he writes: "The central thesis of this book is that experiential awareness of God, or as I shall be saying, the *perception* of God, makes an important contribution to the grounds of religious belief."[57] He refers to the beliefs that arise from such perception as manifestation beliefs ("M-beliefs"). This idea, which he develops in his book, is his contribution to religious epistemology.[58]

In fairness to Alston, he does not claim that this approach is the only one; neither does he claim that it is the best one.[59] Nonethe-

56. Ibid., 53.

57. William P. Alston, *Perceiving God* (Ithaca, N.Y.: Cornell University Press, 1991), 1.

58. See William P. Alston, *Reliability of Sense Perception* (Ithaca, N.Y.: Cornell University Press, 1993), 29, where he argues that a cumulative case consisting of various experiences can be made to justify theistic belief. See also his earlier essay, "Christian Experience and Christian Belief," in *Faith and Rationality,* ed. Alvin Plantinga and Nicholas Wolterstorff (Notre Dame, Ind.: University of Notre Dame Press, 1983), 103–34.

59. Alston, *Perceiving God*, 2.

less, he places quite an emphasis on it. Elsewhere he explains how M-beliefs are justified: "An M-belief is *prima facie* justified if *it arises from an experience that seems to the subject to be an experience of what is believed.*"[60] Alston may be arguing in a circle here, because he sees beliefs arising from the believer's experience. Thus, Alston's approach may not be very helpful in providing justification for religious belief. Plantinga points to this problem in Alston, observing that his own approach is different in that he does not "argue that Christian beliefs have or can have warrant by way of *perception* or experiential awareness of God or his properties, but by way of faith." He further argues, "It isn't by way of perception of God that Christians come to hold their characteristic beliefs, and the warrant those beliefs have for them is not perceptual warrant; it comes rather by way of the Bible, the internal instigation of the Holy Spirit, and faith."[61]

Edwards would likely concur with Plantinga. Although Edwards allows one's perception of God to contribute to one's knowledge of God, he does not let perception constitute the warrant for belief. Hence, it would be a mistake to interpret Edwards as treating testimony of one's experience as the sort of testimony that is involved in assurance. The testimony in view is not the subject's experience, but the testimony of the Spirit. To be sure, the subject does experience this testimony, but the experience is not the testimony. K. Scott Oliphint, summarizing Paul Helm, puts the matter this way: "Thus, self-authentication relates not to the subjective situation *per se,* but rather to the nature of Scripture *as* Scripture."[62] The point here is

60. William P. Alston, "Religious Experience as a Ground of Belief," in *Religious Experience and Religious Belief: Essays in the Epistemology of Religion,* ed. Joseph Runzo and Craig K. Ihara (Lanham, Md.: University Press of America, 1986), 34 (emphasis original).

61. Alvin Plantinga, *Warranted Christian Belief* (Oxford: Oxford University Press, 2000), 287–89. Here Plantinga uses "faith" as a shorthand designation for all three belief-producing mechanisms: Scripture, the internal instigation of the Holy Spirit (Aquinas's *internum testimonium Spiritus Sancti*), and faith.

62. K. Scott Oliphint, "The Apologetical Implications of Alvin Plantinga's Epistemology" (Ph.D. diss., Westminster Theological Seminary, 1994), 350; cf. Paul Helm, *The Varieties of Belief* (London: George Allen and Unwin, 1973), 104–5.

not merely semantic. The testimony is by the Spirit to the truthfulness of the Word, especially to the propositions of the gospel.

The testimony that assurance presents is that of the Spirit to the Word; hence, it is beyond the individual—"out there" in an objective sense. This is, of course, due to Scripture's self-attestation as divinely given and therefore authoritative. Paul Helm explains the matter by observing, "What is said to be self-authenticating is identifiable independently of the experience of self-authentication. 'Self-authentic' is a property not of an experience but of a proposition or a set of propositions."[63] In other words, Scripture's self-attestation as divine provides an unalterable basis for the *internum testimonium Spiritus Sancti*. Within the Reformed tradition, the effort to prove this self-attestation relies secondarily on historical corroboration and the like and primarily on the divine testimony within Scripture. For example, John Murray writes: "In the realm of confrontation or encounter with God there could not be anything of higher evidential quality than God's Word to us." He continues: "The evidence validating the faith of Scripture as the Word of God is the Scripture itself."[64]

The second observation to be made about the testimony in view is that it is presented by the Spirit. That is to say, God is a witness to himself. Again, Paul Helm proves helpful on this point. He argues that certainty is provided concerning the propositions of Scripture because the Scriptures are from God. He observes, "It is God's saying that p that makes p certain." He makes this statement on the basis of God's character: "If complete truthfulness is an essential attribute of God, then it is logically impossible for God to assert what is false, or what could turn out to be false."[65]

This reasoning strikes one as circular, and so it is. The question, however, is not so much whether the argument is circular, but rather what the nature of the circularity is. Consider, for instance, the charge that Alston's position is circular. It is circular in that it is

---

63. Helm, *Varieties of Belief*, 105.

64. John Murray, "Faith," in *The Collected Writings of John Murray*, vol. 2, *Select Lectures on Systematic Theology* (Edinburgh: Banner of Truth, 1977), 241–42.

65. Helm, *Varieties of Belief*, 112–13.

bound to the individual and her experiences. The position here is also circular, but the circle consists of God and his declarations as given in revelation—both supernatural and natural. This ameliorates the charge of circularity.[66]

Edwards's thought on both the testimony itself and the one presenting it needs unpacking, and help is provided by his "Miscellanies," no. 1340. There Edwards criticizes Tindal's *Christianity as Old as the Creation*—often dubbed "the Deist's Bible"—by drawing attention to the limitations of reason.[67] Edwards notes that Tindal makes reason the judge of revelation.[68] Edwards then demonstrates that Tindal's argument is replete with *a priori* propositions, that reason depends on sense experience, and that reason cannot reconcile paradoxes.

In the process, Edwards gives a great deal of attention to testimony. He considers various types of testimony upon which people are dependent, including the testimony of the senses, history and tradition, scientific experimentation, and authority. With respect to testimony of the senses, Edwards notes, "The truth of numberless particular propositions, cannot be known by reason, considered independently of the testimony of our senses, and without an implicit faith in that testimony." And with respect to testimony about the past, he asks, "How numberless are the particular truths concerning what has been before the present age, that cannot be known by reason, considered in themselves, and separately from this testimony,

---

66. This line of thinking is indebted to Cornelius Van Til. See his *A Survey of Christian Epistemology* (Nutley, N.J.: Presbyterian and Reformed, 1969), 200–209. Greg Bahnsen summarizes this perspective when he writes, "Inevitably, arguments over objectivity become 'circular,' for the way in which one views it stems from one's controlling presuppositions. There are really no two ways about it, nor is there any middle ground" (*Van Til's Apologetic: Readings and Analysis* [Phillipsburg, N.J.: P&R Publishing, 1998], 284–85).

67. Matthew Tindal, *Christianity as Old as Creation* (London, 1730).

68. At the end of this entry, Edwards notes that "Tindal's main argument against the need of any revelation, is, that the *law of nature is absolutely perfect*" ("The Insufficiency of Reason as a Substitute for Revelation," in *Works of Jonathan Edwards*, ed. Hickman, 2:484 [emphasis original]). Edwards considers this view "weak and impertinent," stressing instead that the law of nature, in and of itself, is imperfect in that it is in need of Scripture.

which yet are truths, on which all mankind do, ever did, and ever will rely?"[69]

Similarly, we rely upon testimony in the form of experiments that one conducts and witnesses, as well as the testimony given by others regarding their experiments. Edwards writes, "Thus there are many things that I am told concerning the effects of electricity, magnetism, &c. and many things that are recorded in the philosophical transactions of the Royal Society, which I have never seen and are very mysterious; but being well attested, their mysteriousness is no manner of objection against my belief of the accounts." In this manner, Edwards demonstrates the widespread and pervasive dependence upon testimony to arrive at knowledge. He shows how testimony provides warrant for belief in general. He further notes that "any general proposition is recommended to us as true, by any testimony or evidence, that considered by itself seems sufficient." He entertains the possibility of difficulties attending to such propositions. However, "if these difficulties are no greater, and of no other sort, than what might be reasonably expected to attend true propositions of that kind, then these difficulties are not only no valid or sufficient objection against that proposition, but they are no objection at all."[70]

Edwards then turns his attention to revelation as testimony. First, he notes that the testimony is

> a revelation made to mankind by God . . . of what God knows to be the very truth of concerning his own nature; of the acts and operations of his mind with respect to his creatures; of the grand scheme of infinite wisdom in his works, especially with respect to the intelligent and moral world; a revelation of the spiritual and invisible world; a revelation of that invisible world which men shall belong to after this life; a revelation of the greatest works of God, the manner of his creating the world, and of his government of it, especially with regard to the higher and more important parts of it; a revelation delivered in ancient languages.[71]

69. Ibid., 2:480.
70. Ibid., 2:481.
71. Ibid., 2:481–82.

To summarize the salient points, this testimony is first of all a revelation from God about himself. Second, it encompasses both his work of creation and providence and his work of redemption and re-creation. Finally, it is a revelation that is given in human language; that is to say, it is intelligible. Edwards then makes a number of observations about this testimony. It "should be expected in a declaration from God," he says, that there are "difficulties and incomprehensible mysteries."[72] Indeed, if a supposed revelation from God did not contain a level of mystery, then one should question its origin.

Having established these points, Edwards next shows how dependent one who lacks the sense of sight is upon the testimony of others for knowledge: "I suppose a person born blind in the manner described, would nevertheless give full credit to the united testimony of the seeing world, in things which they said about light and colours, and would entirely rest on their testimony."[73] Some of that knowledge could be corroborated by the other senses. For the most part, however, that knowledge is gained through testimony. The person receiving the testimony, then, is dependent for knowledge upon those offering it. This illustration applies on a number of levels. First, all reception of knowledge is informed by it, since all people are dependent upon the testimony of others. It also points to the limitations of human knowledge, even with respect to the sentient world. Finally, in connection with the present discussion, it vividly portrays our dependence on God's testimony for knowledge.

Edwards then returns to the idea of the mysterious nature of Christian revelation. The mysteries of Scripture, he says, "are analogous to the mysteries that are observable in the system of the natural world, and the frame of man's own nature."[74] That is, while some aspects of revelation—general or special—are intelligible, other aspects are not. These things are taken as true, because they are revealed by God. Just as the one who lacks sight gains knowledge from

72. Ibid., 2:482.
73. Ibid., 2:482.
74. Ibid., 2:483.

the testimony of others, so our knowledge derives from God's testimony. Further, belief in his testimony is justified on the basis of his testimony.

In *The Distinguishing Marks of a Work of the Spirit of God,* the necessity of the Spirit's work in this process comes to the fore. Here Edwards distinguishes his view from that of the enthusiasts (as discussed in chapter 4), noting that "they depreciate this written rule [Scripture], and set up the light within, or some other rule above it." Then, referring to the rule of discerning the spirits, he notes that the Holy Spirit leads "persons to truth, convincing them of those things that are true," adding, "the spirit that works thus, operates as a spirit of truth: he represents things as they are indeed."[75] The testimony is known as truth because it is the testimony of the Spirit of truth. In other words, the testimony that God offers of himself, in terms of both the self-attesting Word itself and the *internum testimonium Spiritus Sancti,* is as reliable as his own character. The evidence of this is seen in the reasonableness, or fitness, of God's revelation, his creation, and his work of redemption. Of course, this will only be appreciated by the one who is enlightened to see the revelation.

Edwards's own conversion illustrates this well. In his "Personal Narrative," he notes that following his conversion "the appearance of everything was altered." He could see the "divine glory, in almost everything. God's excellency, his wisdom, his purity and love, seemed to appear in everything."[76] Diana Butler observes that here Edwards follows Calvin with regard to God's revelation in nature. She concludes that for both Calvin and Edwards, "for redeemed men and women, nature is a revelation of God's glory which brings the believer in closer union with him."[77] Applying this to Edwards's doctrine of fitness, the experience of the beauty, harmony, and excel-

75. *The Works of Jonathan Edwards,* vol. 4, *The Great Awakening,* ed. C. C. Goen (New Haven: Yale University Press, 1972), 254–55.

76. *The Works of Jonathan Edwards,* vol. 16, *Letters and Personal Writings,* ed. George S. Claghorn (New Haven: Yale University Press, 1998), 793–94.

77. Diana Butler, "God's Visible Glory: The Beauty of Nature in the Thought of John Calvin and Jonathan Edwards," *Westminster Theological Journal* 52 (1990): 26.

lence of God's general revelation and the reasonableness of his special revelation corroborate his testimony to himself, verifying for the regenerate that divine knowledge is certain and absolute.

In asserting the necessity of assurance, or the *internum testimonium Spiritus Sancti,* Edwards follows his Reformed and Puritan heritage. As Calvin argues, "The certainty [that Scripture] deserves with us, it attains by the testimony of the Spirit."[78] Owen adds:

> That work of the Spirit which may be called an *internal real testimony* is to be granted as that which belongs unto the stability and assurance of faith; for if he did not otherwise work in us or upon us but by the communication of spiritual light unto our minds, enabling us to discern the evidences that are in the Scripture of its own divine original, we should often be shaken in our assent and moved from our stability.[79]

Edwards not only continues in this tradition, but also contributes much to it by stressing that assurance enables one to know the truth and also to proclaim the truth.

CONCLUSION

Whitefield was wrong to think that Edwards denied the witness of the Spirit. Even with Hopkins's help, he failed both to grasp Edwards's teaching on the witness of the Spirit and to see its prominence in Edwards's thought. Given the spiritual nature of knowledge, it follows that the Spirit plays a crucial role at every stage in the acquiring of knowledge—from its being given in revelation, to its being perceived through regeneration, to its certainty being confirmed and made evident through assurance, to its being proclaimed to others. This is set forth in Edwards's major treatises, a number of entries in his "Miscellanies" and his "Notes on Scripture," and many

78. John Calvin, *Institutes of the Christian Religion,* 2 vols., trans. Ford Lewis Battles, ed. John T. McNeill (Philadelphia: Westminster Press, 1960), 1.8.5.

79. John Owen, *The Works of John Owen,* 16 vols., ed. William H. Goold (1850–53; reprint, Edinburgh: Banner of Truth, 1965–68), 4:64.

of his sermons. Because of the nature of reality, the Christian religion and its propositions concerning that reality are philosophically cogent. Or, to put the matter in Edwards's words, "All God's methods are most reasonable."

Edwards's view of this matter is delicate and complex, and consequently it is liable to misinterpretation. Perhaps Paul Helm navigates this area of Edwards's thought best by locating Edwards in the Augustinian-Anselmian tradition of faith seeking understanding. This ascribes priority to revelation's self-authentication. Further, it allows a subordinate role for rational argumentation or reasonableness. Edwards summarized his strategy as arguing that particular points of doctrine are first scriptural, and therefore true, and secondly reasonable, and therefore demonstrative of their truthfulness.

In a series of theological questions that Edwards wrote down and pursued in various places in his writings, he asks, "How do you prove that the Scriptures are a revelation from God? And what are the evidences internal and external?"[80] His answer, as explored above, begins with Scripture's self-attestation, which is its internal evidence. This finds support in the external evidences, which do not establish Scripture's divine origin, but do support it. Edwards was well aware of the need to keep these two elements in their proper relationship, which reflects the proper relationship between faith and reason. Edwards, in short, was well aware of both the usefulness and the limitations of rational argumentation.

This chapter has presented Edwards as the apologist of the Spirit. This is especially the case with regard to assurance, which provides him with the testimony that is necessary to offer as an apologetic for the truthfulness of Christianity. This testimony is given by the Spirit to the truthfulness of the gospel, which is an accurate representation of how things really are. From this stance, one can proclaim the truth of the gospel to others. In this way, Edwards utilizes assurance as an apologetic.

80. Jonathan Edwards, "Theological Questions," in *Works of Jonathan Edwards,* ed. Hickman, 1:690.

Understanding how this testimony of assurance *proves* Christianity is crucial to understanding Edwards's apologetic. First, it proves Christianity in terms of confirming belief already present, thus justifying the belief as knowledge. Second, it proves Christianity in terms of enabling one to present the Christian view as true and non-Christian views as false. Third, it does *not* prove Christianity in terms of convicting one of the truth of Christianity (which Edwards defines as seeing its excellence or beauty), as this is exclusively the Spirit's work. Nonetheless, the Spirit works with the Word proclaimed and works through the proclamation to convict. Edwards would thus agree with Calvin's statement contrasting Christian philosophy with pagan philosophy. Calvin writes that Paul's understanding of truth is lost on philosophers who do not see truth in Scripture, observing that "they set up reason alone as the ruling principle in man, and think that it alone should be listened to; to it alone, in short, they entrust the conduct of life. But the Christian philosophy bids reason give way to, submit and subject itself to, the Holy Spirit."[81]

The next chapter explores Edwards's use of the sermon as a vehicle for apologetics. We will see that the apologetic task was central to his preaching. The three sermons that are analyzed reiterate and further illustrate the themes presented here and weave them together into a unified whole.

---

81. Calvin, *Institutes*, 3.7.1.

6

PERSUASION: EDWARDS AND THE APOLOGETIC SERMON

If it be so that 'tis the work of the Holy Ghost thus to convince men of sin,
of righteousness, and of judgment, then we learn where ministers should have
their dependence in their endeavors, even upon the Holy Ghost.

Jonathan Edwards, "The Threefold Work of the Holy Ghost"

Edwards's primary vehicle for apologetics is the sermon. In fact, as Wilson Kimnach argues, the sermon functions as the primary literary genre for all of his thought. Indeed, "The one literary genre he mastered was the sermon."[1] With few exceptions, his ideas first found public expression in his sermons. Since he was a pastor, this should not be surprising. Consequently, his sermons yield much material for the analysis of his apologetic.

Many of Edwards's well-known sermons, such as "A Divine and Supernatural Light" and "The Threefold Work of the Holy Ghost,"

---

1. Wilson H. Kimnach, "General Introduction to the Sermons: Jonathan Edwards' Art of Prophesying," in *The Works of Jonathan Edwards*, vol. 10, *Sermons and Discourses, 1720–1723*, ed. Wilson H. Kimnach (New Haven: Yale University Press, 1992), xiii.

have been examined above. This chapter explores two additional sermons: "Seeing the Glory of Christ," a sermon on 2 Peter 1:16, preached sometime at Northampton; and "The Work of the Spirit of Christ," on 2 Corinthians 3:18, delivered at Northampton in 1728. Before examining these sermons, however, we will look at his sermon style in its Puritan context. Much has been written on the Puritan sermon and preaching. We will focus on the apologetic nature of the Puritan sermon, especially in Edwards's hands.

THE ART OF PROPHESYING—AND PERSUADING: APOLOGETICS AND THE SERMON

Samuel Eliot Morison observes that the "Puritans cultivated pulpit oratory as a fine art."[2] Preaching was not only an art, but also a science. Numerous preaching manuals show that the evolution of the Puritan sermon was indeed no accident. The first of these manuals, William Perkins's *The Art of Prophesying*, establishes not only the high calling of prophesying, or preaching, but also presents, as many have pointed out, a proposal for sermon delivery based upon the principles of Ramist logic.[3] This proposal essentially recommends dividing the subject at hand into two divisions, and then dividing each division further into two divisions, and so on. Edwards's "'tis scriptural" and "'tis reasonable" paradigm exemplifies this approach. Perkins's manual, and the ones that followed, also entrenched the sermon in the "plain style," which follows a simple pattern of presenting the text with a brief exposition, stating the doctrine(s), and then giving the application. This structure of text, doctrine, and application serves as the hallmark of the Puritan sermon and is readily identifiable in the preaching of Jonathan Edwards.

2. Samuel Eliot Morison, *The Intellectual Life of New England* (Ithaca, N.Y.: Cornell University Press, 1956), 157.

3. William Perkins, *The Art of Prophesying* (reprint, Edinburgh: Banner of Truth, 1996). For a discussion of the various preaching styles in Colonial New England, see David D. Hall, *The Faithful Shepherd: A History of the New England Ministry in the Seventeenth Century* (Chapel Hill: University of North Carolina Press, 1972).

The Puritan sermon, however, was hardly a static phenomenon. Wilson Kimnach draws attention to the innovations within the plain style introduced in Edwards's immediate context—what Kimnach refers to as the "Connecticut Valley school of preaching"—which included Edwards's father, Timothy Edwards, and his Northampton predecessor and grandfather, Solomon Stoddard. The essence of this innovation was a move away from the detached, logical structure to a more affecting style: "Stoddard discovered hidden rhetorical resources in the 'plain style' by insisting upon the evaluation of rhetoric in psychological terms that were more comprehensive and subtle than either the old Ramean logic or the new Reason." After noting the influence of Stoddard on Jonathan Edwards, he says, "Certainly, Edwards grappled for most of his life with rhetorical and artistic issues—not to mention the ecclesiastical ones—that were prompted by Stoddard."[4] Kimnach finds similar emphases in Timothy Edwards. Kimnach's point has also been made by Alan Heimert, who speaks of the tendency of later Calvinistic or Puritan sermons to employ Scripture, "not as an authoritative source of doctrine but as a storehouse of metaphor for making 'lively impressions on the human mind.'"[5] Heimert adds, "It is not surprising that the mark of an excellent preacher was not his careful collation of scriptural proofs but his 'choice of the most rousing and awakening texts'—to be, not expounded, but used for the conviction and awakening on an audience."[6]

Kimnach interprets this innovation as much more than a development of the plain style. He sees it rather as an entirely new approach. In addition to the influence of Stoddard and Timothy Edwards, Kimnach argues for the influence of the British John Edwards

4. *Sermons and Discourses, 1720–1723,* 15. For more on Stoddard's influence in this area, as well as in other areas, see Paul R. Lucas, "'The Death of the Prophet Lamented': The Legacy of Solomon Stoddard," in *Jonathan Edwards's Writings: Text, Context, Interpretation,* ed. Stephen J. Stein (Bloomington: Indiana University Press, 1996), 69–84.

5. Alan Heimert, *Religion and the American Mind: From the Great Awakening to the Revolution* (Cambridge, Mass.: Harvard University Press, 1966), 225.

6. Ibid., quoting John Rowland, "Narrative of the Revival."

and fellow Colonial Cotton Mather.[7] He then observes, "In the place of logic, Stoddard, John Edwards, and Mather put a rationally disciplined but forthright appeal to the emotions."[8] Kimnach interprets Jonathan Edwards as deeply conflicted by this innovation, concluding that he "apparently did everything he could do without actually abandoning the old form entirely, and the only possible conclusion one can draw from the manuscript evidence of his experiments is that he was searching, consciously or unconsciously, for a formal alternative to the sermon model itself."[9] While there is much to be said for Kimnach's appraisal, he perhaps overstates the matter.

Samuel Logan offers a healthy corrective to Kimnach's interpretation. Logan observes the influence of Locke's linguistic theory on Edwards and its tempering effect on the Ramist style. Logan even observes, "Edwards reacted strongly against the Plain Style and against prevailing rationalistic, over-intellectualized faith which it tended to engender."[10] Nevertheless, the affecting element that Edwards added was not an overturning of the plain style *per se,* as much as it was an elaboration of the style to include material aimed at the heart, not just at the head. Logan recognizes Edwards's innovations in the plain style, while avoiding Kimnach's overstatement of them.[11]

Whether engaging the whole person—rationally, emotionally, and spiritually—is an Edwardsean innovation or not, Edwards's sermons nevertheless belong within the stream of Puritan preaching that extends back to Perkins. Two points in particular bear this out. First,

7. In his "Catalogue" of books, Edwards refers to both John Edwards's *The Preacher* (London, 1705) and Cotton Mather's *Manuductio ad ministerium* (Boston, 1726). Kimnach shows numerous examples of dependence on these two books in Edwards's sermons (*Sermons and Discourses, 1720–1723,* 16).

8. Ibid., 20.

9. Ibid., 41. At one point, Kimnach goes so far as to say that Edwards's treatment of the sermon resulted ultimately in the deterioration of the sermon form (p. 36).

10. Samuel T. Logan Jr., "The Hermeneutics of Jonathan Edwards," *Westminster Theological Journal* 43 (1980): 79–86.

11. For a recent, insightful study of Edwards's preaching, see Richard A. Bailey, "Driven by Passion: Jonathan Edwards and the Art of Preaching," in *The Legacy of Jonathan Edwards: American Religion and the Evangelical Tradition,* ed. D. G. Hart, Sean Michael Lucas, and Stephen J. Nichols (Grand Rapids: Baker, 2003), 64–78.

as has been mentioned, he employed the basic Puritan sermon structure. This structure was more than a mere tool of convenience; it reflected his philosophy of preaching—a point, incidentally, not lost on Kimnach.[12] First, the sermon begins with the text. As Kimnach, Minkema, and Sweeney observe, "In Edwards' sermon, the initial biblical text with its explication asserts the priority of the Bible as the source of understanding and all ultimate truth; Edwards asserts nothing in the sermon without the claim of scriptural sanction, and the initial text symbolizes this posture."[13] Sinclair Ferguson finds the same emphasis in Perkins's manual, which requires of the sermon "a clear understanding of the message of Scripture and an ability to explain and apply it to the people."[14] Perkins explains that this priority is due to the nature of Scripture: it alone should be the focus, because "the Word of God is God's wisdom revealing from heaven the truth which is according to godliness." Perkins then points to the apologetic implications of preaching, noting that "the exceptional character of the influence of Scripture consists in two things: 1. Its power to penetrate into the spirit of man. . . . 2. Its ability to bind the conscience, that is, to constrain it before God either to excuse or accuse of sin."[15]

Following the text and a brief exposition of it comes the major portion of the sermon, the "doctrine." For Edwards, this typically consists of a single declarative sentence followed by a number of propositions amplifying the main idea and subpoints. The theory behind this section of the sermon also has apologetic implications. In this section, Edwards marshals his reasons, scriptural and rational, in an ordered and structured way, so as to impress upon his auditors the truthfulness of the doctrine. This section may be reduced to a number of propositions proved through observations, arguments, and scriptural statements.

12. *Sermons and Discourses, 1720–1723*, 32.

13. Wilson Kimnach, Kenneth P. Minkema, and Douglas A. Sweeney, *The Sermons of Jonathan Edwards: A Reader* (New Haven: Yale University Press, 1999), xiii.

14. Sinclair Ferguson, foreword to Perkins, *Art of Prophesying*, xi.

15. Perkins, *Art of Prophesying*, 9–10.

Finally, the sermon concludes with the "application," or the improvement section. Kimnach observes that in this section, the points of application parallel the propositions in the doctrine section.[16] Perkins argues that such a connection should not come as a surprise, given Paul's statement that all Scripture is useful. Perkins, in Ramist fashion, divides the application section into mental and practical applications. The mental application is concerned with "inform[ing] the mind to enable it to come to a right judgment."[17] The practical application deals with lifestyle and behavior. The apologetic implications of this section are transparent.

In addition to the structure of the sermon lending itself to apologetical use, there is the matter of the content of the sermon. According to Perkins, preaching must entail "(i) the hiding of human wisdom, and (ii) the demonstration or manifestation of the Spirit." He continues: "The preaching of the Word is the testimony of God, and the profession of the knowledge of Christ."[18] Therefore, when the preacher speaks, Perkins argues, the goal should be to demonstrate the Spirit, as Paul teaches in 1 Corinthians 2:13. Edwards agrees with this in his sermon on this text for the ordination of his friend Edward Billing. He also articulates these ideas in his sermon "The True Excellency of a Gospel Minister." There Edwards argues that Christ appointed ministers in order that they "may be lights to the souls of men."[19]

Drawing upon one of his favorite metaphors of light, Edwards likens the minister to a star, reflecting the light of Christ, the sun, as contained in Scripture. The first use of this light is to discover or to make manifest. Edwards continues: "Ministers are set to be lights to the souls of men in this respect, as they are to be the means of imparting divine truth to them, and bringing into their view the most glorious and excellent objects, and of leading them to and as-

16. *Sermons and Discourses, 1720–1723*, 39.
17. Perkins, *Art of Prophesying*, 64.
18. Ibid., 71, 73.
19. *The Works of Jonathan Edwards*, 2 vols., ed. Edward Hickman (1834; reprint, Edinburgh: Banner of Truth, 1974), 2:956.

sisting them in the contemplation of these things."[20] Additionally, in "The Threefold Work of the Holy Ghost," Edwards urges ministers to be dependent upon the Spirit in their endeavors. The Word of God is sharp, he adds, "but it is so only through the cooperation of that Spirit that gave the word."[21]

As Ralph Turnbull writes, "Perkins' advice is reflected in Edwards' practice."[22] Harry Stout also observes this emphasis in Edwards's preaching: "Careful preparation and study were important, but the Holy Spirit was most active through the sermon, and the minister had to prepare himself for maximum concentration in that time."[23] Following Perkins, Edwards viewed the sermon as a vehicle for the demonstration of the Spirit. Further, Edwards utilized the sermon as an apologetic tool, finding that its structure of text, doctrine, and application provided a helpful instrument in presenting an argument for the truth of Christianity in general, or the truth of particular doctrines. These observations are more noteworthy, given the prominence of the sermon in Edwards's corpus: his extant sermon manuscripts number over 1,200. We will now examine two sermons that illustrate the centrality of apologetics in his preaching.

"SEEING THE GLORY OF CHRIST"

Very little is known of the sermon "Seeing the Glory of Christ," which has been only recently transcribed. This sermon on 2 Peter 1:16 was probably preached at Northampton, but its date is uncertain. However, it contributes to understanding the role of apologetics in Edwards's thought. It focuses on Peter's experience of being

20. Ibid.

21. *The Works of Jonathan Edwards*, vol. 14, *Sermons and Discourses, 1723–1729*, ed. Kenneth P. Minkema (New Haven: Yale University Press, 1997), 433.

22. Ralph G. Turnbull, *Jonathan Edwards: The Preacher* (Grand Rapids: Baker, 1958), 103. Turnbull also draws attention to a note in Edwards's "Commonplace Book" concerning Perkins's comment on the Holy Spirit in preaching.

23. Harry S. Stout, *The New England Soul: Preaching and Religious Culture in Colonial New England* (Oxford: Oxford University Press, 1986), 228. Stout shows how Edwards accomplished this task by using sermon outlines and vivid metaphors.

an eyewitness to the glory of Christ, which convinced him of both the perfection of Christ and the truth of the gospel. Thus, Edwards derives the doctrine "that seeing the glory of Christ is what tends to assure the heart of the truth of the gospel."[24]

Before Edwards gives the doctrine, however, he offers an exposition of the text. He notes, from the context of 2 Peter 2–3, that the original audience of the book faced the challenge of false teachers who denied the apostle's teaching, treating it as "fables cunningly devised by Jesus their master to set up himself as the head of a sect and to obtain a name in the world. And that his disciples were such fools as to believe him and follow the fables that he had craftily invented" (3–4). Consequently, Peter assures his audience that Christianity is not a matter of fables, but of realities, and he bases this on the fact that he has seen Christ's glory. Edwards observes:

> What [Peter] then saw of Christ's glory and majesty fully convinced him and assured him that Christ was the son of God. It was such [that it] removed all doubt. He saw such divine glory [that] was so admirably excellent and had such a bright and evident appearance of divinity that it perfectly assured him that [Christ] was what he professed to be. [Peter] was satisfied and sufficiently convinced that his gospel was no cunningly devised fable. (5)

This then leads to the doctrine already stated above. Edwards offers a quick elaboration of the doctrine before he offers a systematic treatment of it. In this brief section, he speaks of seeing Christ's glory in terms of the new sense. This "lively sense" provided Peter with a "good ground of conviction that Christ is the son of God and that

---

24. Jonathan Edwards, "Seeing the Glory of Christ Tends to Assure the Heart," Jonathan Edwards Sermon Manuscript Collection, Beinecke Rare Manuscript and Book Library, Yale University, 5. The sermon was transcribed under the supervision of Kenneth P. Minkema. This sermon was not revised or edited by Edwards, and there is no evidence that he preached it again. All references, given hereafter in the body of the text, are to the transcribed manuscript. I have standardized the spelling, capitalization, and punctuation. Other minor emendations have been placed in brackets. Where further editing was necessary, my version appears in the text, and the original is in a note.

162

the gospel is divine and true" (8). It similarly provides anyone with "a certain evidence . . . of the divine authority and [the] truth of it" (8). Edwards goes on to note that one has such a certainty "without sitting down to reason about it" (8). He then develops the doctrine by addressing three inquiries: "1. Enquire what [the] glory of Christ is that is seen. 2. [Enquire] what is meant by seeing that glory? 3. [Enquire] how the seeing of it tends to convince and assure" (9).

Edwards answers the first inquiry in two parts. First, the glory that is seen is the deity of Christ, or the glory of his person, or the divine perfections. When one sees the glory of Christ, one is seeing the glory of God himself. Second, seeing the glory of Christ involves seeing his glory as Savior, that is, seeing the glory of the gospel. Edwards here introduces the idea of fitness, or the harmony and excellence of the gospel, a theme that is common in his other writings and one that he explores later in this sermon. Next he answers the second inquiry by arguing that what is meant by seeing the glory of Christ is *not* "having strong impressions made upon the imagination" (11–12). In other words, a mystical experience is not here in view. Rather, what is meant is to have a new sense of the heart, a sense that involves both the understanding and the will. But this is not rational or, as he refers to it elsewhere, notional knowledge. "They may have a rational knowledge," he observes, "of Christ's being holy and being gracious. But they [do not have] a sense of the excellency and loveliness of his holiness and grace" (13).

This is in accordance with Edwards's distinction between notional and spiritual knowledge, as argued in chapter 2 above.[25] He also speaks of this seeing as a "clear and lively idea" (15), evidencing again his debt to Locke. The soul that is "truly enlightened has a more lively sense of the holiness of God and of the greatness of God and of the wonderful mercy of Jesus and the love of Christ in redeeming" (15). He notes that a natural person is incapable of such

---

25. Cf. his sermon on Hebrews 5:12, "Christian Knowledge: or, The Importance and Advantage of a Thorough Knowledge of Divine Truth," in *Works of Jonathan Edwards*, ed. Hickman, 2:157–63.

sight, thus emphasizing the role of the Spirit in enabling one to be aware of the divine excellence.

Edwards then offers three answers to the third inquiry, namely, how this seeing of Christ's glory leads to assurance and certainty. First, he notes that "a sight of the glory of Christ removes the prejudices of the soul against the gosp[el]" (16). This is due to the natural prejudices of the heart: "The heart is so corrupt and has such an enmity against everything that is holy and divine that the truths of the gospel don't suit it" (16). The glory of Christ makes the heart "willing now to believe the truth of the gospel," and "the heart now lies open to the force of the arguments" (18).

This point is worth emphasizing. Although Edwards stresses the experience of seeing Christ's glory, he does not shy away from arguments. The problem is not that the arguments are weak, but rather that the human mind is too weak to comprehend their force. He writes, "Many wicked men hear arguments enough from time to time to convince 'em if they were not prejudiced. Because of those prejudices remaining, despite your arguing ever so wisely, they will never be fully convinced" (18).[26] This is so because of the effects of sin upon one's reasoning processes. This changes at conversion, however: "But when they come to see the excellency of Christ and the gospel, that sanctifies the reason of a man. The [faculty of] reason which before was carnal is now spiritual. Now the soul is ready to give arguments for the truth of the gospel their due and just weight" (19). Once again, Edwards places his thought squarely within the faith-seeking-understanding approach articulated by Paul Helm.[27] In so doing, Edwards expresses his perspective on the role of arguments in apologetics.

The second answer to the third inquiry pertains to the self-authentication of the divine glory. "The self-evidencing glory of the word," he also notes, "evidences itself to be divine glory itself"

26. The original reads: "Many wicked men hear Arguments Enough from time to time to Convince em. if they were not Prejudiced but that Prejudices Remaining bring what arguments you will argue never so wisely they will never be fully Convinced."

27. Paul Helm, *Faith and Understanding* (Grand Rapids: Eerdmans, 1997).

(20). Edwards here moves from seeing the glory of God to seeing the glory of God in the gospel or in Scripture. The gospel, he observes, "shows itself to be a divine emanation, that it is God's word and that God's mind is revealed in it and God's works are declared in it" (21).[28] He then employs his typical strategy of arguing that because his idea is from Scripture, which is self-authenticating, it is true. He writes of the stamps of divine glory upon Scripture, of its divine character, and of its fitness and harmony. He adds, however, that only the one who is spiritual and views it accordingly "can be certain that it is no human work," but a divine revelation (23).[29] He concludes, "A person spiritually enlightened may upon as good grounds be satisfied that they are God's work [and] that it is [God's] contrivance and that 'tis God that speaks in the gospel" (24).[30] As he observes later in the sermon, "The gospel carries its own evidence along with it wherever it goes" (27).

As his third answer to the third inquiry, Edwards states that the gospel declares the glory of Christ. Because the glory of Christ is the gospel, the gospel declared "would persuade us to believe that Christ is an excellent savior [and] that the way of his salvation is glorious" (24–25). He then offers his conclusion:

Therefore when this glory is seen persons are eyewitnesses of the truth of the gospel for they see the sufficiency of [Christ's] righteousness, the excellency and suitableness of his way of salvation, the glory of the ends proposed, and the adaptedness of the means to obtain that end so as to answer all purposes. [These are] the things which the gospel would persuade us of. (25–26)

28. The original reads: ". . . shows it self to be a divine emanation that it is Gods word and then it is Gods mind that is there revealed & Gods work that is there declared."

29. The original reads: "He that spiritually understands the Gosp may only by viewing of it be as certain that it is no human work."

30. Compare Edwards's thought here with that of "The Threefold Work of the Spirit." There he writes that the Ascension renders Christ "a complete object of the faith of believers, the last thing needed in order to there being sufficient grounds for the world's being convinced of the sufficiency of his righteousness" (in *Sermons and Discourses, 1723–1729*, 392–93).

Edwards presents here the argument that Scripture is self-authenticating, that the only way that one is able to see this evidence is through the work of the Holy Spirit, and that the only way to be certain of this knowledge is through the Spirit's witness to the gospel. Additionally, he models an apologetic based on this theoretical foundation by proclaiming the gospel as truth.

Edwards develops these themes further in the application section of his sermon, emphasizing the role of the Spirit more explicitly. He states, "The truth of the gospel is a thing of God's revealing. He reveals it by his Spirit and he reveals it to whom he pleases" (30). The gospel is the power of God, which is "given by the demonstration of the Spirit" (30). He further observes that only the illumination of the Spirit is "sufficient . . . to convince of the truth of the gospel" (35). The Spirit's work is necessary, given the limitations of reason. Since apprehending the gospel is not a matter of intellectual sophistication, "men of all sorts are capable of believing the gospel . . . [and] should not [lack] evidence of the truth of the gospel" (26). If Edwards has the deists, or even the Arminians, in view here, then his words are intended as a polemic against such rationalist positions. This stresses revelation over reason as the means by which one comes to know truth with certainty. Later in the sermon, Edwards notes that arguments for Scripture's truthfulness may be "very plausible," yet they are incapable of leading anyone to true faith (39). Hence, Edwards subordinates rational argumentation to revelation.

Following his typical pattern in the application section, Edwards calls upon his auditors to use this teaching as a way to examine themselves.[31] True faith is distinguished from common assent to religion in this, that "the seeing of the excellency of the things of the gosp[el] convinces the heart that they are divine and that they are real things" (36).[32] He notes that "all [believers have] this that they are convinced then it is a real thing and all agree in this again that they have

31. See Kimnach, editor's introduction to *Sermons and Discourses, 1720–1723,* 39.

32. Compare this to the following from "A Divine and Supernatural Light": "This spiritual and divine light . . . may be thus described: a true sense of the divine excellency of the things revealed in the Word of God, and a conviction of the truth and reality of them, thence

such a conviction arising from the excellency of spiritual things" (40). The certainty that one has is the distinguishing factor of true faith. And, as he argues here and elsewhere, such certainty derives from the witness of the Spirit. According to Edwards, then, one's assurance involves not only an internal conviction, but also knowledge of true reality. One can be certain because this is the way things really are.

He concludes his sermon by noting five reasons why such assurance is the "best evidence that you can obtain of the truth of the [gospel]" (45). First, it is the most direct and immediate.[33] There are other ways to argue for the truth of the gospel, Edwards concedes, but they are indirect and mediated. This manner of argument is similar to his strategy of arguing first that an idea is scriptural, and then that it is also reasonable, as seen in chapter 5 above. In other words, Edwards does grant a place to argumentation or reasons. However, the force of such reasons depends on that which establishes their truthfulness, which is to say that because a given idea is scriptural, it will also be reasonable. This order of argument must be kept intact, in order to understand Edwards's use of evidences.

The indirect evidence that Edwards mentions here consists of fulfilled prophecies and confirmation through archaeology or historical records. It is impossible that the biblical records of the events of Christ's life were forged, for the events were public and the gospel faced Jewish opposition. If Christianity had been a fraud, it would have been exposed (47).

The second reason why assurance is the best evidence is that "the soul wants no other evidence" (48). This is so because it is direct and therefore better than any other evidence. Third, and again because it is the best evidence, assurance is unalterable—"the most abiding[, the] least liable to be shaken" (50). This coalesces with the

---

arising" (*The Works of Jonathan Edwards*, vol. 17, *Sermons and Discourses, 1730–1733*, ed. Mark Valeri [New Haven: Yale University Press, 1999], 413).

33. He places similar stress on the immediate nature of the Spirit's work in "A Divine and Supernatural Light," observing that this light is "immediately imparted to the soul by God" (*Sermons and Discourses, 1730–1733*, 410).

fourth reason, namely, that this evidence of assurance alone "will bring the heart to rest in Christ for salvation. 'Tis only this that so fully convinces that Christ is indeed the Savior of the world and that he is sufficient to save" (52). Lastly, assurance is the best evidence because it not only fully convinces, but also "effectively dispose[s] and incline[s] the heart unto a holy life" (53). Edwards here follows his line of reasoning in *Religious Affections.*

In summary, assurance is the basis for the certainty of one's knowledge of the gospel and the certainty of one's apprehension of it. Such assurance comes from the Spirit in regeneration or the imparting of the new sense, in the giving of revelation, and in testifying to the truth of revelation. This work of the Spirit provides, as it were, an absolute sort of certainty. Seeing the glory of Christ, which is tantamount to having a sense of the excellence and harmony of the gospel, authenticates its own truth and its correspondence to reality. In keeping with the distinction between notional and spiritual knowledge, it is difficult for people to see the truth of Christianity, not because of any weakness in the arguments for it *per se,* but rather because of people's sinful prejudices against that truth. In this sense, both revelation and the new sense transcend rational argumentation, although, in Edwards's view, they are not contrary to it. Further, by insisting that the Spirit's work of revealing, illuminating, and assuring is the best evidence for the truth of Christianity, he demonstrates the centrality of the Spirit to his apologetic.

"THE WORK OF THE SPIRIT OF CHRIST"

Edwards's thought concerning the work of the Holy Spirit, evident in his more well known sermons, such as "A Divine and Supernatural Light" and "The Threefold Work of the Holy Ghost," is matched in "The Work of the Spirit of Christ," preached early in his ministry at Northampton during the year 1728. This time period in his life was marked by many milestones.[34] He was married in 1927,

34. Kenneth P. Minkema, "Preface to the Period," in *Sermons and Discourses, 1723–1729,* 49.

and was ordained as the assistant to Solomon Stoddard, the "Pope" of the Connecticut River Valley, in the influential Northampton Church. Then in 1729 Stoddard died, and young Edwards became the minister of "one of New England's most prestigious parishes."[35] Stoddard's death meant increased pastoral duties for Edwards, not to mention the revivals during the next two decades.

The two-year period from 1727 to 1728, then, was a special time in Edwards's pastoral career. Having completed his master's degree at Yale, followed by brief pastorates in New York and Bolton, Edwards became a tutor at Yale before going to Northampton. This provided him with much intellectual stimulation and enabled him to engage in various philosophical and theological controversies. He also had the advantage of already having a few sermons meticulously prepared. Additionally, he shared preaching duties with Stoddard, which reduced the number of sermons he was expected to deliver. Consequently, Edwards's intellectual activity was quite prominent during this period, and his sermons reflected it.

Minkema refers to a number of concerns that worked their way into Edwards's sermons during this period. He gave attention to Arminianism, his interest in which extended back to his master's *Quaestio* and to his sermons on the divine light and spiritual knowledge, which depicted salvation as solely a work of God. Another matter of concern to him was the doctrine of the Trinity, as Arianism and Socinianism were spreading across Europe and beginning to make their presence felt in the colonies. Finally, during this period he focused on the spiritual light or the new sense. As Minkema observes, "The characterization of the saints as endowed with a heightened 'sense' or awareness of divine things was to become a hallmark of Edwards' preaching." He adds, "This sense that resulted in knowledge of divine things was communicated by God in the form of spiritual light, which in fact was the Holy Spirit dwelling in the human soul."[36] These three areas of emphasis are all present in "The Work of the Spirit of Christ."

35. Ibid., 11.
36. Ibid., 18.

Edwards extracts two doctrines from the following words of Paul in 2 Corinthians 3:18: "But we all, with open face beholding as in a glass the glory of the Lord, are changed into the same image from glory to glory, even as by the Spirit of the Lord." The first doctrine is: "That believers have such a sight of the glory of Christ as revealed in the gospel as changes 'em into a likeness of the same glory."[37] The second doctrine (on which he preached first) is: "That 'tis the work of the Spirit of Christ only to give a true sight of Christ" (3).

In this first doctrine, Edwards reiterates a number of his emphases in "Seeing the Glory of Christ." He comments, "Natural men [who] live under the gospel hear as much about the excellency of Christ as others. They . . . hear the same reasons that evidence his excellency . . . they read in the same Scripture, they have the same ministers to show 'em Christ's excellency, but yet they see no glory in Christ" (43–44). Believers have this sight of glory only because of the work of the Spirit. Here he again repudiates the notion that the sight of Christ's glory is an impression upon the imagination or some type of mystical experience. Rather, he says, "it consists in the inward sense of the heart," thus emphasizing his doctrine of the new sense (45). He also notes, as he did in his sermon on 2 Peter 1:16, that seeing the glory of Christ consists in seeing "the holiness of his person and the holiness of his design as mediator" (47). In other words, it consists in seeing the perfection or excellence of the person and work of Christ. The glory of Christ is "declared in that we are informed of the wonderful works of Christ whereby he has manifested his glory" (55). And Edwards makes it clear in the context that this declaration is in Scripture. He further refers to Scripture as "the instrument which God makes use [of] to reveal the beauty of Christ unto the soul" (65). Edwards here echoes Calvin's notion

37. Jonathan Edwards, sermon manuscript on 2 Corinthians 3:18, Jonathan Edwards Sermon Manuscript Collection, Beinecke Rare Manuscript and Book Library, Yale University, 3. For convenience, this sermon will be referred to as "The Work of the Spirit of Christ," a title derived from the second doctrine. The sermon was transcribed under the supervision of Kenneth P. Minkema and has never been published. I have standardized the spelling, capitalization, and punctuation. Other minor emendations have been placed in brackets.

of the Spirit working with the Word in the process of revealing the gospel.[38]

In the application of this doctrine, Edwards calls upon his auditors to examine themselves as to "whether or not you have ever seen the divine glory" (61).[39] He then offers three criteria by which to judge this. First, a genuine sense of divine glory "will convince you of the truth of the gospel" (67).[40] Second, "if you have had a true sight of Christ it will make your hearts rest in him as a Savior" (69). Finally, a true sight of divine glory will result in Christian practice or a desire "to live more worthy of him" (70).[41] These themes reflect his thought in "Seeing the Glory of Christ." Consequently, this sermon furnishes more material that illustrates his use of these doctrines of the Holy Spirit in an apologetic fashion.

With respect to the second doctrine, Edwards stresses not only the necessity of the Spirit's work in bearing witness to Scripture and in assurance, but also the Spirit's work in inspiration, illumination, and regeneration. The doctrine, as previously stated, is "That 'tis the Spirit of Christ only to give a true sight of Christ," and it gets developed in three propositions (3). The first implication of this doctrine is that the Spirit is "the immediate teacher and instructor [who] gives a true sight of Christ" (3). The Spirit is the immediate teacher in two ways. First, through inspiration, the Spirit gave the apostles and the prophets the word of God. Second, through illumination, the Spirit enables one to see Scripture as it really is. Edwards describes this latter work in terms of the new sense or regeneration. This leads to his second proposition: "'Tis like opening the eyes of the blind," thus enabling a new way of seeing (6). He then connects his ideas explicitly to the work of the Spirit: "'Tis the Spirit of Christ

---

38. See John Calvin, *Institutes of the Christian Religion*, 2 vols., trans. Ford Lewis Battles, ed. John T. McNeill (Philadelphia: Westminster Press, 1960), 3.2.33.

39. Edwards wrote this line with a different ink, which may indicate that he added it to the manuscript after he preached the sermon.

40. This line was also written with a different ink.

41. As in "Seeing the Glory of Christ," Edwards's words here correspond to the twelfth sign in *Religious Affections*, 383–461.

that makes this great change in the soul that gives a new nature" (7). Edwards likens this work of the Spirit to the Spirit's original work of creation and specifically to the Spirit's involvement in the creation of humanity.[42] Edwards also cites the *locus classicus* for the doctrine of regeneration, namely, John 3. He ties these three doctrines together into a unified understanding of the work of the Spirit in enabling one to come to a saving knowledge of the gospel.

His third proposition opens the door for a thorough discussion of intra-Trinitarian relations. He begins this discussion by noting that only the Spirit is capable of "giving spiritual understanding, opening the eyes of the mind, and giving a new heart," and consequently this work is done by the Spirit alone (10). While ministers are "to endeavor to persuade men to be reconciled to God, all that they can do is to speak to men externally, they cannot change and renew the heart. They can tell of the glories of Christ, but cannot give eyes to see it" (11). This expresses both the task and the limits of the sermon. Edwards views the sermon as the vehicle through which God's glory or the truth of the gospel may be seen—which again expresses the idea of the Spirit working with the Word.

This text, with Paul's curious reference to "the Spirit of the Lord," causes Edwards to ask "why the Spirit of God is called the Spirit of Christ" (17).[43] He offers two answers. The first has to do with the procession of the Spirit from the Father and the Son. Edwards finds support for this notion in Revelation 22, which speaks of the river of the water of life that proceeds from the throne of God and from the throne of the lamb. He notes, "This river of living water is doubtless the Spirit of God, as it is interpreted by the Holy Ghost himself

42. He writes, "The work of assimilating unto Christ or making like unto him is begun by the Spirit of Christ in regeneration in the new creation. As we read, the Spirit of God moved upon the face of the dark, unformed world in the first creation and brought it into a beautiful order, so the Spirit of Christ moves upon the hearts of men that are naturally as dark and unformed to work in [them] divine beauty and excellency" ("The Work of the Spirit of Christ," 8).

43. For a discussion of the exegetical issues related to this phrase in 2 Cor. 3:18, see Paul Barnett, *The Second Epistle to the Corinthians*, New International Commentary on the New Testament (Grand Rapids: Eerdmans, 1997), 202. Barnett follows Edwards's interpretation.

in John 7:38–39" (17).[44] Second, Edwards argues that the Spirit is called the Spirit of Christ because it is the Spirit's unique task to testify of Christ, as Christ teaches in John 16:7.

The Spirit, in his work of enlightening, regenerating, and assuring, is "a messenger of Christ" (18). Christ's unique role within the Godhead consists in providing salvation, while "the Holy Spirit carr[ies] on his work and appl[ies] his redemption" (19). Additionally, as argued in chapter 2, Edwards refers to the Spirit's unique role of communicating within the Godhead and communicating outside the Trinity in revelation, so that the Spirit's *opera ad intra* mirrors his *opera ad extra*. The Spirit "communicates" grace, or the work of God, as well as God himself to humanity (14). These ideas reflect the thought of Edwards in both his "Essay on the Trinity" and his sermon on "The Threefold Work of the Holy Ghost," both of which were examined in chapter 2.[45]

In fact, this sermon presents the early version of Edwards's thought on these subjects, which he later amplifies and refines in those other two writings. However, the germ of his thought is present here, namely, that the Spirit, through the work of inspiration and illumination, has the unique task of giving revelation to humanity. This is central to Edwards's apologetic, for it is the minister's task to demonstrate the divine glory by proclaiming the Word. Thus, Edwards exhorts his auditors in the application to acknowledge that the Spirit "comes to enlighten your eyes, he comes to give you a sight of the glory of Jesus Christ" (25).

Conclusion

The sermon provided Edwards with a powerful apologetic tool. He honed and meticulously crafted that tool in order to demonstrate

44. This follows his reasoning in "Essay on the Trinity," in Paul Helm, *Treatise on Grace and Other Posthumously Published Writings by Jonathan Edwards* (London: James Clarke, 1971), 99–131. Edwards also puts forward this understanding of both John 7:38–39 and Rev. 22:1 in his note on the former text in *The Works of Jonathan Edwards*, vol. 15, *Notes on Scripture*, ed. Stephen J. Stein (New Haven: Yale University Press, 1998), 209–10.

45. *Sermons and Discourses, 1723–1729*, 375–436.

the certainty of the truths of Christianity, which, he said, were slighted to one's peril and, after regeneration by the Spirit, were received to one's delight. The sermon was Edwards's primary literary form. His sermons are the gateway into his thoughts, his theology, and his philosophy, which come together in his apologetics. This is especially true today, now that his previously unknown and unstudied manuscripts have been published. The two sermons examined in this chapter are no exception; they illustrate the themes that have been presented in this study.

174

CONCLUSION

This work began with the idea that reading Edwards as an apologist might well lead to the center of his thought. This strategy, it was argued, would not only account for, but also bring together, the divergent aspects of his writings. In particular, Edwards's epistemology serves as a good test case for this thesis. By first identifying the different strands of his thought on such doctrines as revelation, inspiration, illumination, and regeneration and his reflection on knowledge, perception, and testimony, and then examining them together, a unified portrait of Edwards emerged, which enhances our understanding of his work.

Central to Edwards's epistemology is God and, particularly, the third person of the Trinity. The Holy Spirit is absolutely essential to, and permeates, Edwards's apologetics. This is so, first, because of humanity's problem of sin infecting the whole person, *totius animae*. As the doctrine of regeneration teaches, the Spirit must transform the whole person. Consequently, Edwards stresses the new sense not only as an entirely new way of seeing the world and God's purposes for it, but also as an entirely new way of relating to God and the world.

Second, Edwards distinguishes between spiritual knowledge and notional knowledge, not to posit two types of knowledge, but rather to stress the relationship that one has to knowledge. Without the Spirit, one has only speculative or notional knowledge, but with the

Spirit one has spiritual knowledge. Our knowledge is covenantal, for it finds us in either a relationship of rebellion against God or in a relationship of reconciliation, communion, and union with him.

Edwards also stresses the necessity of Scripture, which is given through the Spirit's work of inspiration and then is illumined at conversion. This stresses the Holy Spirit's unique function in the *opera ad intra* of communion within the Godhead, which leads to his unique function in the *opera ad extra* of inspiration and illumination. Revelation is then confirmed to be divinely given by the Sprit's work of assurance, or the *internum testimonium Spiritus Sancti*. This witness is not mystical, although it is internal and personal to the regenerate. Nevertheless, it is an objective, absolute sort of certainty.

Further, given the necessity of revelation, reason is insufficient to prove the truthfulness of Scripture. Nevertheless, reason does play a subordinate role in supporting one's faith. Edwards works this out methodologically by first stressing the self-authentication of Scripture. The Spirit's internal witness enables one to see the divine nature and authority of Scripture. Then, Edwards demonstrates the reasonableness of Christianity in terms of its fitness or harmony. Christianity is cogent, although our ability to acknowledge that cogency is predicated upon our relationship to the Holy Spirit. As Edwards puts it, in order to know the sweetness of honey, one must taste it.

Finally, in its finest form within the Puritan tradition, the sermon is a demonstration of the Spirit. For Edwards, the sermon serves as an essential vehicle for the threefold work of the Spirit, convicting humanity of sin, of righteousness, and of judgment. Edwards utilizes the sermon as an apologetic tool, adding the notion of persuasion to the Puritan "art of prophesying." His sermons contain his mature reflections and refined thoughts on the controversies around him, his Northampton and Stockbridge congregations, the colonies, and also the European world of the eighteenth century. His extant, yet unstudied, sermons provide a repository of his thought that will likely lead to continued interest in, and continued learning about, this celebrated figure.

It is difficult to write about Edwards because so much has already been written about him. This study is indebted to that material. At the same time, it is hoped that this study has a meaningful contribution to make. As we have seen, the doctrines of the Holy Spirit permeate Edwards's writings. As an apologist, Edwards weaves together the doctrines of inspiration, illumination, regeneration, and assurance with the epistemological issues of perception and testimony, in order to present a unified understanding of the way in which we come to know and hold knowledge with certainty—an absolute sort of certainty.

Edwards emerges from this study as a skillful apologist, crafting an apologetic for his time that also has implications for ours. This way of reading Edwards as an apologist also contributes to grasping the elusive center in interpreting him. In short, understanding Edwards as an apologist serves well in interpreting Edwards and his writings *in toto*.

BIBLIOGRAPHY

WRITINGS OF JONATHAN EDWARDS

Images or Shadows of Divine Things. Edited by Perry Miller. New Haven: Yale University Press, 1948.

A Jonathan Edwards Reader. Edited by John E. Smith, Harry S. Stout, and Kenneth P. Minkema. New Haven: Yale University Press, 1995.

Jonathan Edwards Sermon Manuscript Collection, Beinecke Rare Book and Manuscript Library, Yale University.

The Philosophy of Jonathan Edwards from His Private Notebooks. Edited by Harvey G. Townsend. Eugene: University of Oregon Monographs, 1955.

Selections from the Unpublished Writings of Jonathan Edwards. Edited by Alexander B. Grosart. 1865. Reprint, Ligonier, Pa.: Soli Deo Gloria, 1992.

The Sermons of Jonathan Edwards, A Reader. Edited by Wilson H. Kimnach, Kenneth P. Minkema, and Douglas A. Sweeney. New Haven: Yale University Press, 1999.

Treatise on Grace and Other Posthumously Published Writings. Edited by Paul Helm. Cambridge: James Clarke, 1971.

The Works of Jonathan Edwards. 2 vols. Edited by Edward Hickman. 1834. Reprint, Edinburgh: Banner of Truth, 1974.

The Works of Jonathan Edwards. Edited by Perry Miller, John E. Smith, and Harry S. Stout. New Haven: Yale University Press, 1957–.

Vol. 1, *Freedom of the Will*. Edited by Paul Ramsey, 1957.

Vol. 2, *Religious Affections*. Edited by John E. Smith, 1959.

Vol. 3, *Original Sin*. Edited by Clyde A. Holbrook, 1970.

Vol. 4, *The Great Awakening*. Edited by C. C. Goen, 1972.

179

Vol. 5, *Apocalyptic Writings*. Edited by Stephen J. Stein, 1977.

Vol. 6, *Scientific and Philosophical Writings*. Edited by Wallace E. Anderson, 1980.

Vol. 7, *The Life of David Brainerd*. Edited by Norman Pettit, 1985.

Vol. 8, *Ethical Writings*. Edited by Paul Ramsey, 1989.

Vol. 9, *A History of the Work of Redemption*. Edited by John F. Wilson, 1989.

Vol. 10, *Sermons and Discourses, 1720–1723*. Edited by Wilson H. Kimnach, 1992.

Vol. 11, *Typological Writings*. Edited by Wallace E. Anderson and Mason I. Lowance Jr., with David Watters. 1993.

Vol. 12, *Ecclesiastical Writings*. Edited by David D. Hall, 1994.

Vol. 13, *The "Miscellanies," Entry nos. a-z, aa-zz, 1–500*. Edited by Thomas A. Schafer, 1994.

Vol. 14, *Sermons and Discourses, 1723–1729*. Edited by Kenneth P. Minkema, 1997.

Vol. 15, *Notes on Scripture*. Edited by Stephen J. Stein, 1998.

Vol. 16, *Letters and Personal Writings*. Edited by George S. Claghorn, 1998.

Vol. 17, *Sermons and Discourses, 1730–1733*. Edited by Mark Valeri, 1999.

Vol. 18, *The "Miscellanies," Entry nos. 501–832*. Edited by Ava Chamberlain, 2000.

Vol. 19, *Sermons and Discourses, 1734–1738*. Edited by M. X. Lesser, 2001.

Vol. 20, *The "Miscellanies," Entry nos. 833–1152*. Edited by Amy Plantinga Pauw, 2002.

OTHER SOURCES

Ahlstrom, Sidney. *Religious History of the American People*. New Haven: Yale University Press, 1972.

Aldrich, A. O. "Edwards and Hutcheson." *Harvard Theological Review* 44 (1951): 45–53.

Alston, William P. "Christian Experience and Christian Belief." In *Faith and Rationality*, edited by Alvin Plantinga and Nicholas Wolterstorff, 103–34. Notre Dame, Ind.: University of Notre Dame Press, 1983.

———. *Perceiving God: The Epistemology of Religious Experience*. Ithaca, N.Y.: Cornell University Press, 1991.

———. *The Reliability of Sense Perception*. Ithaca, N.Y.: Cornell University Press, 1993.

———. "Religious Experience as a Ground of Belief." In *Religious Experience and Religious Belief: Essays in the Epistemology of Religion,* edited by Joseph Runzo and Craig K. Ihara, 31–51. Lanham, Md.: University Press of America, 1986.

Ames, William. *The Marrow of Divinity*. Reprint, Boston: Pilgrim Press, 1968.

Anderson, Paul Russell, and Max Harold Fisch. *Philosophy in America: From the Puritans to James*. New York: Octagon Books, 1969.

Anderson, Wallace E. Editor's introduction to *Scientific and Philosophical Writings*. Vol. 6 of *The Works of Jonathan Edwards*. New Haven: Yale University Press, 1980.

Augustine. *City of God*. Translated by Marcus Dods. Reprint, New York: The Modern Library, 1993.

Ayers, Michael. *Locke*. Vol. 1, *Epistemology*. London: Routledge, 1991.

Bahnsen, Greg. *Van Til's Apologetic: Readings and Analysis*. Phillipsburg, N.J.: P&R Publishing, 1998.

Bailey, Richard A. "Driven by Passion: Jonathan Edwards and the Art of Preaching." In *The Legacy of Jonathan Edwards: American Religion and the Evangelical Tradition,* edited by D. G. Hart, Sean Michael Lucas, and Stephen J. Nichols, 64–78. Grand Rapids: Baker, 2003.

Barth, Karl. *Church Dogmatics*, I, 2. Edinburgh: T. & T. Clark, 1956.

Beeke, Joel R. *Assurance of Faith: Calvin, English Puritanism, and the Dutch Second Reformation*. New York: Peter Lang, 1991.

———. "Personal Assurance of Faith: The Puritans and Chapter 18.2 of the *Westminster Confession*." *Westminster Theological Journal* 55 (1993): 1–30.

———. *The Quest for Full Assurance: The Legacy of Calvin and His Successors*. Edinburgh: Banner of Truth, 1999.

Bercovitch, Sacvan. *The Puritan Origins of the American Self*. New Haven: Yale University Press, 1975.

Berkeley, George. *The Works of George Berkeley, Bishop of Cloyne*. 9 vols. Edited by A. A. Luce and T. E. Jessup. London: Thomas Nelson, 1948–57.

Billing, Edward, to Jonathan Edwards, June 11, 1750, Beinecke Rare Book and Manuscript Library, Yale University.

Bogue, Carl. *Jonathan Edwards and the Covenant of Grace*. Cherry Hill, N.J.: Mack Publishing, 1975.

Bouwsma, William J. "Calvin and the Renaissance Crisis of Knowing." *Calvin Theological Journal* 17 (1982): 190–211.

———. *John Calvin: A Sixteenth-Century Portrait*. New York: Oxford University Press, 1988.

Brand, David C. *Profile of the Last Puritan: Jonathan Edwards, Self-Love, and the Dawn of the Beatific*. Atlanta: Scholars Press, 1991.

Brauer, Jerald C. "Types of Puritan Piety." *Church History* 56 (1987): 39–58.

Breitenbach, William. "Piety and Moralism: Edwards and the New Divinity." In *Jonathan Edwards and the American Experience,* edited by Nathan O. Hatch and Harry S. Stout, 177–204. Oxford: Oxford University Press, 1988.

Brown, Robert E. *Jonathan Edwards and the Bible*. Bloomington: Indiana University Press, 2002.

Bushman, Richard L., ed. *The Great Awakening: Documents on the Revival of Religion, 1740–1745*. Chapel Hill: University of North Carolina Press, 1989.

Butler, Diana H. "God's Visible Glory: The Beauty of Nature in the Thought of John Calvin and Jonathan Edwards." *Westminster Theological Journal* 52 (1990): 13–26.

Calvin, John. *Calvin's Commentaries*. Vol. 20, *Commentary on the Epistles of Paul the Apostle to the Corinthians*. Translated and edited by John Pringle. Reprint, Grand Rapids: Baker, 1996.

———. *The Institutes of the Christian Religion*. 2 vols. Translated by Ford Lewis Battles. Edited by John T. McNeill. Philadelphia: Westminster Press, 1960.

Carse, James P. *Jonathan Edwards and the Visibility of God*. New York: Charles Scribner's Sons, 1967.

Carson, D. A. "Reflections on Christian Assurance." *Westminster Theological Journal* 54 (1992): 1–29.

Chai, Leon. *Jonathan Edwards and the Limits of Enlightenment Philosophy*. Oxford: Oxford University Press, 1998.

Chamberlain, Ava. "Self-Deception as a Theological Problem in Jonathan Edwards's 'Treatise Concerning Religious Affections.'" *Church History* 63 (1994): 541–46.

Cherry, Conrad. *Nature and Religious Imagination: From Edwards to Bushnell*. Philadelphia: Fortress Press, 1980.

———. "The Puritan Notion of the Covenant in Jonathan Edwards' Doctrine of Faith." *Church History* 34 (1965): 328–41.

————. *The Theology of Jonathan Edwards: A Reappraisal.* Bloomington: Indiana University Press, 1990.

Claghorn, George S. Editor's introduction to *Letters and Personal Writings.* Vol. 16 of *The Works of Jonathan Edwards.* New Haven: Yale University Press, 1998.

Clark, Stephen M. "Jonathan Edwards: The History of the Work of Redemption." *Westminster Theological Journal* 56 (1994): 45–58.

Clarke, Samuel. *A Discourse Concerning the Being and Attributes of God, the Obligations of Natural Religion, and the Truth and Certainty of the Christian Revelation.* London, 1711.

Coady, C. A. J. *Testimony: A Philosophical Study.* Oxford: Oxford University Press, 1992.

Conforti, Joseph A. *Jonathan Edwards, Religious Tradition, and American Culture.* Chapel Hill: University of North Carolina Press, 1995.

————. "Jonathan Edwards's Most Popular Work: 'The Life of David Brainerd' and Nineteenth-Century Evangelical Culture." *Church History* 54 (1985): 188–201.

Cudworth, Ralph. *The True Intellectual System of the Universe.* London, 1678. Reprint, Stuttgart-Bad: Cannstatt, 1964.

Daniel, Stephen H. *The Philosophy of Jonathan Edwards: A Study in Divine Semiotics.* Bloomington: Indiana University Press, 1994.

Davidson, Edward H. "From Locke to Edwards." *Journal of the History of Ideas* 24 (1963): 355–72.

Delattre, Roland Andre. *Beauty and Sensibility in the Thought of Jonathan Edwards.* New Haven: Yale University Press, 1968.

DeProspo, R. C. *Theism in the Discourse of Jonathan Edwards.* Newark: University of Delaware Press, 1985.

Dowey, Edward A., Jr. *The Knowledge of God in Calvin's Theology.* Grand Rapids: Eerdmans, 1974.

Erdt, Terence. *Jonathan Edwards, Art and the Sense of the Heart.* Amherst: University of Massachusetts Press, 1980.

Faust, Clarence H., and Thomas H. Johnson, eds. Introduction to *Jonathan Edwards: Representative Selections.* New York: Hill and Wang, 1962.

Fiering, Norman. *Jonathan Edwards's Moral Thought and Its British Context.* Chapel Hill: University of North Carolina Press, 1981.

————. "Will and Intellect in the New England Mind." *William and Mary Quarterly* 29 (1972): 512–58.

Flower, Elizabeth, and Murray G. Murphey. *A History of Philosophy in America.* 2 vols. New York: Capricorn Books, 1977.

Frei, Hans W. *The Eclipse of Biblical Narrative: A Study in Eighteenth and Nineteenth Century Hermeneutics.* New Haven: Yale University Press, 1974.

Gaustad, Edwin. *The Great Awakening in New England.* Gloucester, Mass.: Peter Smith, 1965.

Gay, Peter. *A Loss of Mastery: Historians in Colonial America.* Berkeley: University of California Press, 1966.

Geivett, R. Douglas, and Brendan Sweetman, eds. *Contemporary Perspectives on Religious Epistemology.* Oxford: Oxford University Press, 1992.

Gerstner, John H. "Jonathan Edwards and the Bible." *Tenth* 9 (1979): 1–90.

———. "An Outline of the Apologetics of Jonathan Edwards." *Bibliotheca Sacra* 133 (1976): 3–10, 99–107, 195–201, 291–98.

———. *The Rational Biblical Theology of Jonathan Edwards.* 3 vols. Powhatan, Va.: Berea Publications, 1991–93.

Goen, C. C. Editor's introduction to *The Great Awakening.* Vol. 4 of *The Works of Jonathan Edwards.* New Haven: Yale University Press, 1972.

———. *Revivalism and Separatism in New England, 1740–1800.* New Haven: Yale University Press, 1962.

Guelzo, Allen C. *Edwards on the Will: A Century of American Theological Debate.* Middletown, Conn.: Wesleyan University Press, 1989.

Hall, David D., ed. *The Antinomian Controversy, 1636–1638: A Documentary History.* 2d ed. Durham: Duke University Press, 1990.

———. Editor's introduction to *Ecclesiastical Writings.* Vol. 12 of *The Works of Jonathan Edwards.* New Haven: Yale University Press, 1994.

———. *The Faithful Shepherd: A History of the New England Ministry in the Seventeenth Century.* Chapel Hill: University of North Carolina Press, 1972.

Harrisville, Roy A., and Walter Sundberg. *The Bible in Modern Culture: Theology and Historical-Critical Method from Spinoza to Käsemann.* Grand Rapids: Eerdmans, 1995.

Hart, D. G. "Revivals, Presbyterians and." In *Dictionary of the Reformed and Presbyterian Tradition in America,* edited by D. G. Hart and Mark A. Noll, 216–18. Downers Grove, Ill.: InterVarsity Press, 1999.

Hart, D. G., Sean Michael Lucas, and Stephen J. Nichols, eds. *The Legacy of Jonathan Edwards: American Religion and the Evangelical Tradition.* Grand Rapids: Baker, 2003.

Hatch, Nathan O., and Harry S. Stout, eds. *Jonathan Edwards and the American Experience.* Oxford: Oxford University Press, 1988.

Heimert, Alan. *Religion in the American Mind: From the Great Awakening to the Revolution.* Cambridge, Mass.: Harvard University Press, 1966.

Helm, Paul. *Faith and Understanding.* Grand Rapids: Eerdmans, 1997.

———. "John Locke and Jonathan Edwards: A Reconsideration." *Journal of the History of Ideas* 7 (1969): 51–61.

———. *The Varieties of Belief.* London: George Allen and Unwin, 1973.

Hesselink, I. John. *Calvin's First Catechism: A Commentary.* Louisville: Westminster John Knox Press, 1997.

Hick, John. *Philosophy of Religion.* 4th ed. Englewood Cliffs, N.J.: Prentice Hall, 1990.

Hobbes, Thomas. *Leviathan.* Edited by Richard Tuck. Reprint, Cambridge: Cambridge University Press, 1991.

Holbrook, Clyde A. Editor's introduction to *Original Sin.* Vol. 3 of *The Works of Jonathan Edwards.* New Haven: Yale University Press, 1970.

———. *The Ethics of Jonathan Edwards: Morality and Aesthetics.* Ann Arbor: University of Michigan Press, 1973.

———. *Jonathan Edwards, The Valley and Nature: An Interpretive Essay.* Lewisburg, Pa.: Bucknell University Press, 1987.

Holmes, Oliver Wendell. "Jonathan Edwards." In *The Works of Oliver Wendell Holmes.* Vol. 8, *Pages from an Old Volume of Life: A Collection of Essays, 1857–1881,* 366–70. Boston: Houghton, Mifflin, 1892.

Holmes, Stephen R. *God of Grace and God of Glory: An Account of the Theology of Jonathan Edwards.* Grand Rapids: Eerdmans, 2000.

Hoopes, James. "Jonathan Edwards's Religious Psychology." *Journal of American History* 69 (1983): 859.

Hopkins, Samuel. *The Works of Samuel Hopkins, D.D.* 3 vols. Reprint, Boston: Doctrinal Book and Tract Society, 1854.

Hume, David. *Enquiries Concerning the Human Understanding and Concerning the Principles of Morals.* 3d ed. Edited by P. H. Nidditch. Oxford: Oxford University Press, 1975.

———. *An Enquiry Concerning the Principles of Morals.* Edited by Tom L. Beauchamp. Oxford: Oxford University Press, 1998.

———. *A Treatise of Human Nature.* 2d ed. Edited by P. H. Nidditch. Oxford: Oxford University Press, 1978.

Hutcheson, Francis. *Collected Works of Francis Hutcheson.* 7 vols. Edited by Bernhard Fabian. Hildesheim: George Olms, 1969–71.

———. *An Essay on the Nature and Conduct of the Passions and Affections with Illustrations on the Moral Sense.* 3d ed. 1742. Reprint, Gainesville, Fla.: Scholar's Facsimiles & Reprints, 1969.

James, William. *The Varieties of Religious Experience: A Study in Human Nature.* New York: The Modern Library, 1994.

Jamieson, John F. "Jonathan Edwards's Change of Position on Stoddardeanism." *Harvard Theological Review* 74 (1981): 79–99.

Jenson, Robert W. *America's Theologian: A Recommendation of Jonathan Edwards.* Oxford: Oxford University Press, 1988.

———. Review of *Jonathan Edwards, The Valley and Nature,* by Clyde Holbrook; *Jonathan Edwards,* by Iain Murray; and *The Philosophical Theology of Jonathan Edwards,* by Sang Hyun Lee. *Christian Century* 106 (1989): 660–65.

Kant, Immanuel. *Critique of Practical Reason.* Translated and edited by Mary Gregor. Reprint, Cambridge: Cambridge University Press, 1997.

———. *Critique of Pure Reason.* Translated by Norman Kemp Smith. Reprint, New York: St. Martin's Press, 1968.

Kimnach, Wilson H. Editor's introduction to *Sermons and Discourses, 1720–1723.* Vol. 10 of *The Works of Jonathan Edwards.* New Haven: Yale University Press, 1992.

Knight, Janice. *Orthodoxies in Massachusetts: Rereading American Puritanism.* Cambridge: Harvard University Press, 1994.

Kuklick, Bruce. *Churchmen and Philosophers: From Jonathan Edwards to John Dewey.* New Haven: Yale University Press, 1985.

———. "Jonathan Edwards and American Philosophy." In *Jonathan Edwards and the American Experience,* edited by Nathan O. Hatch and Harry S. Stout, 246–59. Oxford: Oxford University Press, 1988.

Lambert, Frank. *Inventing the "Great Awakening."* Princeton: Princeton University Press, 1999.

Lang, Amy Schrager. " 'A Flood of Errors': Chauncey and Edwards in the Great Awakening." In *Jonathan Edwards and the American Experience,* edited by Nathan O. Hatch and Harry S. Stout, 160–73. Oxford: Oxford University Press, 1988.

Laurence, David. "Jonathan Edwards, John Locke, and the Canon of Experience." *Early American Literature* 15 (1980): 107–23.

Lee, Sang Hyun. *The Philosophical Theology of Jonathan Edwards.* Princeton: Princeton University Press, 1988.

Lee, Sang Hyun, and Allen C. Guelzo, eds. *Edwards in Our Time: Jonathan Edwards and the Shaping of American Religion.* Grand Rapids: Eerdmans, 1999.

Lehrer, Keith. *Thomas Reid.* London: Routledge, 1989.

Lesser, M. X. *Jonathan Edwards.* Boston: Twayne Publishers, 1988.

————. *Jonathan Edwards: A Reference Guide.* Boston: G. K. Hall, 1981.

————. *Jonathan Edwards: An Annotated Bibliography, 1979–1993.* Westport, Conn.: Greenwood Press, 1994.

Locke, John. *An Essay Concerning Human Understanding.* Edited by Peter Nidditch. Oxford: Oxford University Press, 1975.

————. *The Reasonableness of Christianity.* Edited by I. T. Ramsey. Stanford: Stanford University Press, 1958.

Logan, Samuel T. "Antinomian Controversy." In *Dictionary of Christianity in America,* edited by Daniel G. Reid, Robert D. Linder, Bruce L. Shelley, and Harry S. Stout, 69. Downers Grove, Ill.: InterVarsity Press, 1990.

————. "The Doctrine of Justification in the Theology of Jonathan Edwards." *Westminster Theological Journal* 46 (1984): 26–52.

————. "The Hermeneutics of Jonathan Edwards." *Westminster Theological Journal* 43 (1980): 79–96.

Lowe, E. J. *Locke on Human Understanding.* London: Routledge, 1995.

Lucas, Paul R. " 'The Death of the Prophet Lamented': The Legacy of Solomon Stoddard." In *Jonathan Edwards's Writings: Text, Context, Interpretation,* edited by Stephen J. Stein, 69–84. Bloomington: Indiana University Press, 1996.

Lucas, Sean Michael. "Jonathan Edwards Between Church and Academy: A Bibliographic Essay." In *The Legacy of Jonathan Edwards: American Religion and the Evangelical Tradition,* edited by D. G. Hart, Sean Michael Lucas, and Stephen J. Nichols, 228–47. Grand Rapids: Baker, 2003.

Luther, Martin. *The Bondage of the Will.* Translated by J. I. Packer and O. R. Johnston. Westwood, N.J.: Revell, 1957.

Manspeaker, Nancy. *Jonathan Edwards: Bibliographical Synopses.* New York: Edwin Mellon, 1981.

Marsden, George M. *Jonathan Edwards: A Life.* New Haven: Yale University Press, 2003.

————. "Jonathan Edwards Speaks to Our Technological Age." *Christian History* 4 (1985): 26–28.

May, Henry F. *The Enlightenment in America.* Oxford: Oxford University Press, 1976.

————. "Jonathan Edwards and America." In *Jonathan Edwards and the American Experience,* edited by Nathan O. Hatch and Harry S. Stout, 19–33. Oxford: Oxford University Press, 1988.

McClymond, Michael J. *Encounters with God: An Approach to the Theology of Jonathan Edwards*. Oxford: Oxford University Press, 1998.

———. "God the Measure: Toward a Theocentric Understanding of Jonathan Edwards's Metaphysics." *Scottish Journal of Theology* 47 (1994): 43–59.

———. "Spiritual Perception in Jonathan Edwards." *Journal of Religion* 77 (1997): 195–216.

McDermott, Gerald R. "The Deist Connection: Jonathan Edwards and Islam." In *Jonathan Edwards's Writings: Text, Context, Interpretation*, edited by Stephen J. Stein, 39–51. Bloomington: Indiana University Press, 1996.

———. *Jonathan Edwards Confronts the Gods: Christian Theology, Enlightenment Religion, and Non-Christian Faiths*. Oxford: Oxford University Press, 2000.

———. *One Holy and Happy Society: The Public Theology of Jonathan Edwards*. University Park: Pennsylvania State University Press, 1992.

———. "A Possibility of Reconciliation: Jonathan Edwards and the Salvation of Non-Christians." In *Edwards in Our Time: Jonathan Edwards and the Shaping of American Religion*, edited by Sang Hyun Lee and Allen C. Guelzo, 173–202. Grand Rapids: Eerdmans, 1999.

Miller, Perry. *Errand into the Wilderness*. Cambridge, Mass.: Harvard University Press, 1956.

———. *Jonathan Edwards*. New York: William Sloane, 1949.

———. "Jonathan Edwards on the Sense of the Heart." *Harvard Theological Review* 41 (1948): 123–45.

———. *The New England Mind: From Colony to Province*. Reprint, Cambridge, Mass.: Harvard University Press, 1981.

———. *The New England Mind: The Seventeenth Century*. Reprint, Cambridge, Mass.: Harvard University Press, 1981.

Minkema, Kenneth P. "Preface to the Period." In *Sermons and Discourses, 1723–1729*, edited by Kenneth P. Minkema, 3–46. Vol. 14 of *The Works of Jonathan Edwards*. New Haven: Yale University Press, 1997.

Minkema, Kenneth P., and Richard A. Bailey. "Reason, Revelation, and Preaching: An Unpublished Ordination Sermon by Jonathan Edwards." *Southern Baptist Journal of Theology* 3 (1999): 16–33.

Mitchell, Louis Joseph. "The Experience of Beauty in the Thought of Jonathan Edwards." Ph.D. diss., Harvard University, 1995.

Morgan, Edmund S. *Visible Saints: The History of a Puritan Idea*. Ithaca, N.Y.: Cornell University Press, 1963.

Morimoto, Anri. *Jonathan Edwards and the Catholic Vision of Salvation.* University Park: Pennsylvania State University Press, 1995.

Morison, Samuel Eliot. *The Intellectual Life of New England.* Ithaca, N.Y.: Cornell University Press, 1956.

———. *The Oxford History of the American People.* Oxford: Oxford University Press, 1965.

Murray, Iain H. *Jonathan Edwards: A New Biography.* Edinburgh: Banner of Truth, 1987.

Murray, John. *The Collected Writings of John Murray.* Vol. 2, *Select Lectures in Systematic Theology.* Edinburgh: Banner of Truth, 1977.

Newton, Isaac. *Optics or a Treatise of the Reflections, Refractions, Inflections and Colours of Light.* Reprint, New York: Dover Publications, 1954.

———. *Philosophiae Naturalis Principia Mathematica.* Translated by Andrew Motte. New York: Prometheus Books, 1995.

Nichols, Stephen J. *Jonathan Edwards: A Guided Tour of His Life and Thought.* Phillipsburg, N.J.: P&R Publishing, 2003.

———. "Jonathan Edwards' Contribution to Moral Philosophy: *True Virtue.*" *Philosophia Christi* 20 (1997): 43–56.

———. "Last of the Mohican Missionaries: Jonathan Edwards at Stockbridge." In *The Legacy of Jonathan Edwards: American Religion and the Evangelical Tradition,* edited by D. G. Hart, Sean Michael Lucas, and Stephen J. Nichols, 47–63. Grand Rapids: Baker, 2003.

Niebuhr, H. Richard. *The Kingdom of God in America.* New York: Harper and Row, 1937.

Noll, Mark A. *A History of Christianity in the United States and Canada.* Grand Rapids: Eerdmans, 1992.

Nuttall, Geoffrey F. *The Holy Spirit in Puritan Faith and Experience.* Oxford: Basil Blackwell, 1947.

Oberg, Barbara B., and Harry S. Stout, eds. *Benjamin Franklin, Jonathan Edwards, and the Representation of American Culture.* Oxford: Oxford University Press, 1993.

Oliphint, K. Scott. "Jonathan Edwards: Reformed Apologist." *Westminster Theological Journal* 57 (1995): 165–86.

———. "Plantinga on Warrant." *Westminster Theological Journal* 57 (1995): 415–35.

Opie, John, ed. *Jonathan Edwards and the Enlightenment.* Lexington, Mass.: D. C. Heath, 1969.

Owen, John. *The Works of John Owen.* 16 vols. Edited by William H. Goold. Edinburgh: Banner of Truth, 1965–68.

Pahl, Jon. "Jonathan Edwards and the Aristocracy of Grace." *Fides et Historia* 25 (1993): 62–72.

Parker, T. H. L. *Calvin: An Introduction to His Thought.* Louisville: Westminster John Knox Press, 1995.

Pauw, Amy Plantinga. "Heaven Is a World of Love: Edwards on Heaven and the Trinity." *Calvin Theological Journal* 30 (1995): 393–400.

———. *The Supreme Harmony of All: The Trinitarian Theology of Jonathan Edwards.* Grand Rapids: Eerdmans, 2002.

Pelikan, Jaroslav. *The Christian Tradition.* Vol. 4, *Reformation of Church and Dogma (1300–1700).* Chicago: University of Chicago Press, 1983.

Perkins, William. *The Art of Prophesying.* Edinburgh: Banner of Truth, 1996.

Pettit, Norman. Editor's introduction to *The Life of David Brainerd.* Vol. 7 of *The Works of Jonathan Edwards.* New Haven: Yale University Press, 1985.

Phillips, D. Z. *Faith and Philosophical Enquiry.* London: Routledge, 1970.

Plantinga, Alvin. "Reason and Belief in God." In *Faith and Rationality: Reason and Belief in God,* edited by Alvin Plantinga and Nicholas Wolterstorff, 16–93. Notre Dame, Ind.: Notre Dame University Press, 1983.

———. *Warrant and Proper Function.* Oxford: Oxford University Press, 1993.

———. *Warranted Christian Belief.* Oxford: Oxford University Press, 2000.

Platner, John Winthrop, ed. *Exercises Commemorating the Two-Hundredth Anniversary of the Birth of Jonathan Edwards.* Andover, Mass.: Andover Press, 1904.

Post, Stephen. "Disinterested Benevolence: An American Debate over the Nature of Christian Love." *Journal of Religious Ethics* 14 (1986): 356–68.

Proudfoot, Wayne. "Perception and Love in *Religious Affections.*" In *Jonathan Edwards's Writings: Text, Context, Interpretation,* edited by Stephen J. Stein, 122–36. Bloomington: Indiana University Press, 1996.

Ramsey, Paul. Editor's introduction to *Ethical Writings.* Vol. 8 of *The Works of Jonathan Edwards.* New Haven: Yale University Press, 1989.

———. Editor's introduction to *Freedom of the Will.* Vol. 1 of *The Works of Jonathan Edwards.* New Haven: Yale University Press, 1957.

Redwood, John. *Reason, Ridicule, and Religion: The Age of Enlightenment in England, 1660–1750.* Cambridge, Mass.: Harvard University Press, 1976.

Reid, Thomas. *Thomas Reid's Inquiry and Essays.* Edited by Ronald Beanblossom and Keith Lehrer. Indianapolis: Hackett, 1983.

Ricketts, Allyn Lee. "The Primacy of Revelation in the Philosophical Theology of Jonathan Edwards." Ph.D. diss., Westminster Theological Seminary, 1995.

Rorty, Richard. *Objectivity, Relativism, and Truth.* Cambridge: Cambridge University Press, 1991.

———. *Philosophy and the Mirror of Nature.* Princeton: Princeton University Press, 1979.

Rupp, George. "The 'Idealism' of Jonathan Edwards." *Harvard Theological Review* 62 (1969): 209–26.

Schafer, Thomas A. Editor's introduction to *The " Miscellanies," Entry Nos. a-z, aa-zz, 1–500.* Vol. 13 of *The Works of Jonathan Edwards.* New Haven: Yale University Press, 1994.

Shea, Daniel B., Jr. "Jonathan Edwards: The First Two Hundred Years." *Journal of American Studies* 14 (1980): 181–97.

Smith, Claude A. "Jonathan Edwards and the 'Way of Ideas.'" *Harvard Theological Review* 59 (1966): 153–73.

Smith, John E. Editor's introduction to *Religious Affections.* Vol. 2 of *The Works of Jonathan Edwards.* New Haven: Yale University Press, 1959.

———. *Jonathan Edwards: Puritan, Preacher, Philosopher.* Notre Dame, Ind.: University of Notre Dame Press, 1992.

Spinoza, Benedict de. *The Philosophy of Spinoza.* Edited by Joseph Ratner. New York: The World's Popular Classics, 1920.

Spohn, William C. "Sovereign Beauty: Jonathan Edwards and *The Nature of True Virtue.*" *Theological Studies* 42 (1981): 394–421.

Sproul, R. C., John H. Gerstner, and Arthur Lindsley. *Classical Apologetics: A Rational Defense of the Christian Faith and a Critique of Presuppositional Apologetics.* Grand Rapids: Zondervan, 1984.

Stein, Stephen J. Editor's introduction to *Apocalyptic Writings.* Vol. 5 of *The Works of Jonathan Edwards.* New Haven: Yale University Press, 1977.

———. Editor's introduction to *Notes on Scripture.* Vol. 15 of *The Works of Jonathan Edwards.* New Haven: Yale University Press, 1998.

———, ed. *Jonathan Edwards's Writings: Text, Context, Interpretation.* Bloomington: Indiana University Press, 1996.

Steinmetz, David. *Calvin in Context.* Oxford: Oxford University Press, 1995.

Stephens, Bruce M. "Changing Conceptions of the Holy Spirit in American Protestant Theology from Jonathan Edwards to Charles G. Finney." *Saint Luke's Journal of Theology* 33 (1990): 209–23.

Stewart, M. A., ed. *Studies in the Philosophy of the Scottish Enlightenment.* Oxford: Oxford University Press, 1990.

Stout, Harry S. "Edwards and Puritanism." In *Jonathan Edwards and the American Experience*, edited by Nathan O. Hatch and Harry S. Stout, 142–59. Oxford: Oxford University Press, 1988.

———. The *New England Soul: Preaching and Religious Culture in Colonial New England.* Oxford: Oxford University Press, 1986.

Sweeney, Douglas A. "Edwards, Jonathan." In *Historical Handbook of Major Biblical Interpreters,* edited by Donald McKim, 309–12. Downers Grove, Ill.: InterVarsity Press, 1998.

Tindal, Matthew. *Christianity as Old as Creation.* London, 1730.

Tracy, Patricia J. *Jonathan Edwards, Pastor: Religion and Society in Eighteenth-Century Northampton.* New York: Hill and Wang, 1980.

Turnbull, Ralph G. *Jonathan Edwards the Preacher.* Grand Rapids: Baker, 1958.

Turner, James. *Without God, Without Creed: The Origins of Unbelief in America.* Baltimore: Johns Hopkins University Press, 1985.

Valeri, Mark. "Preface to the Period." In *Sermons and Discourses, 1730–1733,* 3–44. Vol. 17 of *The Works of Jonathan Edwards.* New Haven: Yale University Press, 1999.

Van Til, Cornelius. *Christian Apologetics.* Nutley, N.J.: Presbyterian and Reformed, 1976.

———. *A Survey of Christian Epistemology.* Nutley, N.J.: Presbyterian and Reformed, 1969.

Veto, Miklos. "Spiritual Knowledge According to Jonathan Edwards." Translated by Michael McClymond. *Calvin Theological Journal* 31 (1966): 161–81.

Wainwright, William. "Jonathan Edwards and the Language of God." *Journal of the American Academy of Religion* 48 (1980): 519–30.

———. "Jonathan Edwards and the Sense of the Heart." *Faith and Philosophy* 7 (1990): 43–62.

Walker, Williston. *The Creeds and Platforms of Congregationalism.* New York: Pilgrim Press, 1991.

———. *Great Men of the Christian Church.* Chicago: University of Chicago Press, 1908.

Wallace, Ronald S. *Calvin's Doctrine of the Word and Sacrament.* Edinburgh: Oliver and Boyd, 1953.

Warfield, Benjamin B. *Calvin and Augustine.* Edited by Samuel Craig. Philadelphia: Presbyterian and Reformed, 1956.

————. "Edwards and the New England Theology." In *Encyclopedia of Religion and Ethics,* edited by James Hastings, 5:220–35. New York: Charles Scribner's Sons, 1955.

Weber, Donald. "The Recovery of Jonathan Edwards." In *Jonathan Edwards and the American Experience,* edited by Nathan O. Hatch and Harry S. Stout, 50–72. Oxford: Oxford University Press, 1988.

Weddle, David L. "The Melancholy Saint: Jonathan Edwards's Interpretation of David Brainerd as a Model of Evangelical Spirituality." *Harvard Theological Review* 81 (1988): 297–318.

Westra, Helen Petter. "Divinity's Design: Edwards and the History of the Work of Revival." In *Edwards in Our Time: Jonathan Edwards and the Shaping of American Religion,* edited by Sang Hyun Lee and Allen C. Guelzo, 131–57. Grand Rapids: Eerdmans, 1999.

————. "Jonathan Edwards and 'What Reason Teaches.'" *Journal of the Evangelical Theological Society* 34 (1991): 495–503.

————. *The Minister's Task and Calling in the Sermons of Jonathan Edwards.* Lewiston, Maine: Edwin Mellen Press, 1986.

White, Eugene E. *Puritan Rhetoric: The Issue of Emotion in Religion.* Carbondale: Southern Illinois University Press, 1972.

Whittemore, Robert C. *The Transformation of the New England Theology.* New York: Peter Lang, 1987.

Wilson, John F. Editor's introduction to *A History of the Work of Redemption.* Vol. 9 of *The Works of Jonathan Edwards.* New Haven: Yale University Press, 1989.

Winslow, Ola Elizabeth. *Jonathan Edwards, 1703–1758.* New York: Collier Books, 1961.

Wittgenstein, Ludwig. *On Certainty.* Edited by G. E. M. Anscombe and G. H. Von Wright. Oxford: Blackwell, 1969.

Wolterstorff, Nicholas. *John Locke and the Ethics of Belief.* Cambridge: Cambridge University Press, 1996.

Yarbrough, Steven R., and John C. Adams. *Great American Orators.* Vol. 20, *Delightful Conviction: Jonathan Edwards and the Rhetoric of Conversion.* Westport, Conn.: Greenwood Press, 1993.

Zwingli, Ulrich. "On the Clarity and Certainty of the Word of God." In *Zwingli and Bullinger,* edited by G. W. Bromiley, 59–95. Philadelphia: Westminster Press, 1953.

INDEX OF SUBJECTS AND NAMES

Stephen J. Nichols (M.A.R. and Ph.D., Westminster Theological Seminary; M.A., West Chester University) is an associate professor at Lancaster Bible College and Graduate School. A member of the Evangelical Theological Society, he chairs the society's Jonathan Edwards Study Group. He is also author of *Jonathan Edwards: A Guided Tour of His Life and Thought,* and *Martin Luther: A Guided Tour of His Life and Thought.*